Cracking Windows Phone and BlackBerry Native Development

Cross-Platform Mobile Apps Without the Kludge

Matthew Baxter-Reynolds

Apress®

Cracking Windows Phone and BlackBerry Native Development: Cross-Platform Mobile Apps Without the Kludge

ISBN-13 (pbk): 978-1-4302- 3374-9

ISBN-13 (electronic): 978-1-4302- 3375-6

President and Publisher: Paul Manning
Lead Editor: Jonathan Hassell
Technical Reviewer: Matthew Fitchett
Editorial Board: Steve Anglin, Mark Beckner, Ewan Buckingham, Gary Cornell, Jonathan Gennick, Jonathan Hassell, Michelle Lowman, James Markham, Matthew Moodie, Jeff Olson, Jeffrey Pepper, Frank Pohlmann, Douglas Pundick, Ben Renow-Clarke, Dominic Shakeshaft, Matt Wade, Tom Welsh
Coordinating Editor: Anita Castro
Copy Editor: Mary Ann Fugate
Compositor: Bytheway Publishing Services
Indexer: BIM Indexing & Proofreading Services
Artist: April Milne
Cover Designer: Anna Ishchenko

Distributed to the book trade worldwide by Springer Science+Business Media, LLC., 233 Spring Street, 6th Floor, New York, NY 10013. Phone 1-800-SPRINGER, fax (201) 348-4505, e-mail orders-ny@springer-sbm.com, or visit www.springeronline.com.

For information on translations, please e-mail rights@apress.com, or visit www.apress.com.

Apress and friends of ED books may be purchased in bulk for academic, corporate, or promotional use. eBook versions and licenses are also available for most titles. For more information, reference our Special Bulk Sales–eBook Licensing web page at www.apress.com/bulk-sales.

The source code for this book is available to readers at www.multimobiledevelopment.com.

For Martha and Elliott

Contents at a Glance

iv

Contents

About the Author

■ **Matthew Baxter-Reynolds** is an independent software development consultant, trainer, and author based in the UK, specializing in mobile technology solutions. He can be contacted via LinkedIn at www.linkedin.com/in/mbrit.

About the Technical Reviewer

In 2004, **Matthew Fitchett**, with experience in VB.Net, joined a small e-commerce team to trial C# within a (then) small DVD- and CD–focused e-commerce company.

Play.com went on to become one of Europe's largest e-commerce companies, with Matthew playing a major role as one of a handful of senior software developers. After six and a half enjoyable years, Matthew decided to move on to specialize in mobile technology, which he sees as a significant growth area for software developers and enterprises.

Working alongside Matthew Baxter-Reynolds, Matthew produced prototypes on a variety of technology platforms (Android, iPhone, Windows Phone 7, to name three) for a leading company in the mobile survey software market.

Matthew and his beautiful wife, Sarah, have two young boys, Isaac and Harry, and live in the beautiful town of Bury St. Edmunds. He enjoys films, games, music, and eating good food while drinking good beer, and he regularly practices Muay Thai.

His blog at www.mattfitchett.com covers all of the above, along with more mobile technology discussion.

Acknowledgments

With much thanks and appreciation to my wife, Andy, for the patience and support she has shown during writing and development of this book, Matt Fitchett for his excellent suggestions and review work, and Jonathan Hassell, Anita Castro, and the others at the Apress team for their sterling work in turning this book into reality.

CHAPTER 1

■■■

Introduction

For me, this book has become all about change. In the time that I have been watching the mobile computing marketplace and developing software solutions for it, there has never been a time when there has been a more rapid series of shifts and changes. A good friend of mine tells me that this is because of market consolidation. As of the time of writing (March 2011), we're looking at the time when the people who will be leaders in this space for the next 20 years jostle for position. There is a ton of money out there being spent, which is fantastic news for the typical reader of this book. Position yourself correctly, and you could earn a seriously good living out of it all.

To illustrate this point about change, I proposed this book to Apress in February 2010, and in the time between then and March 2011, a massive amount of changes have happened.

In a normal year, in a normal market, just a few of these things would be big news.

- Microsoft was still developing and building Windows Mobile 6.5. Windows Phone 7 had not been announced. No one really knows what sort of impact Windows Phone 7 will have.

- The iPad had not been announced, let alone sold the millions and millions of units that it has, and, of course, this has now been followed up with iPad 2. (For me, this is perhaps the biggest change of all—the world will never be the same now that this class of device has been introduced.)

- There was no sign of Android running on tablets. Now we're looking forward to Gingerbread making for a fabulous tablet experience.

- The Pre/webOS was included in the original proposal. HP has now bought Pre, and in the last week or so HP has announced that it intends to include webOS on all of its shipped PCs.

- Android has been growing, and growing, and growing. IDC has this week announced it is the fastest growing OS of all time.

- Canalys has also recently announced that 50 percent of BlackBerry users are looking to defect to iOS or Android.

- The image of Flash hadn't been damaged by Apple's insistence that it had no place on its platform. Although there was a short resurgence, Mozilla has come out saying that it sees little future in it as a platform.

- iPhone 4 had not been announced or released, and "Antennagate" had not happened. Now the rumor mill is talking about iPhone 5.

- You couldn't multitask on an iPhone.

- iOS was still a trademark owned by Cisco.

- Gartner had not come out and likened Symbian to "re-arranging the deck chairs on the Titanic" in the face of the Android threat. Symbian then seemed to spend the next few months dying, not with a bang, but with a whimper. Now, Microsoft and Nokia are moving to become strange bedfellows, effectively moving to Windows Phone 7 as its primary platform.

- No one knew anything about QNX and the BlackBerry PlayBook. It looks like now the PlayBook will even run Android apps.

- Steve Ballmer hadn't said that Apple had sold more iPads than he would have liked and that "Microsoft-powered tablets are 'job one' urgency." Microsoft still won't look at rolling out the Windows Phone 7 platform onto tablet devices, insisting that Windows 8 is the platform of choice.

- There was no Amazon Appstore, and no one was doing anything as cool as firing up a Dalvik VM in the cloud to try the app before you buy. (How cool!)

- We didn't know that Google could remote uninstall applications from any Android phone using a "kill switch." It has recently used this to kill off a score of applications that were causing problems with users.

- Amazon hadn't announced its Android app store, although even today the details of it are sketchy.

- The United Arab Emirates had not turned off BlackBerry Enterprise Services within the country.

- Motorola was looking very sick indeed, but it is now looking much healthier thanks to the Droid, Droid X, and Xoom.

- MeeGo had not been announced (and as of the time of writing is not substantial enough to include in this book). My prediction, for what it's worth, is that this will get traction in spaces like automotive as opposed to slate or phone factors.

- Microsoft announced, launched, and killed a device called "Kin." To give you some idea of how much money is being thrown around, Microsoft attributes US$240 million of written-off monies to Kin. That's not small change.

In fact, this book has been difficult to write because of the velocity of all of this change. I'll be forever grateful to the team at Apress for managing to corral it into the place where, I hope, it's helpful and relevant to you, in spite of this almost constant upheaval in the market.

What's the Purpose of This Book?

In 2001, I set up a web site called .NET 247 (www.dotnet247.com/) that at the time achieved some success in the community that had sprung up around Microsoft's new software development toolset. The premise of the site was to help me as a developer migrate my knowledge from pre-.NET technologies (Win32, MFC, classic ASP, etc.) over to .NET. I found it frustrating that spinning up a thread or opening a file would be a few seconds' work prior to .NET, but in .NET it took hours of research.

With this book, I've looked to do a similar thing—answer the common questions and give you a leg up into understanding the platform so that you can get on and do the clever thing that only you've thought of. The idea of this book is not to go into masses of detail on every little thing; however, if you work through all of the different platforms in this book and its companion, you'll know enough to be proficient on any platform that you turn your hand to.

Specifically, what I've tried to concentrate on is the following:

- Getting to a point where you can compile and run an application on the emulator or device

- Showing how to build a user interface—specifically move between forms, handle events, get data on the screen, and capture input

- Showing how to connect to HTTP-based resources so that you can talk to services in the cloud

- Showing how to store and cache data locally for performance and for offline support

- Showing how to build a simple but real application that works end to end

How Is This Book Structured?

This book is split into three sections. There's an introduction section, which takes you through the background of the two applications that we're going to build. There is then a section on Windows Phone 7 and another section on BlackBerry. There is also a bonus chapter on Windows Mobile.

In addition, this book has a sister book, which is structured similarly and takes you through building the same application that we're going to build in this book. The book's title—*Multimobile Development: Building Applications for Android and iPhone*—should tell you what you need to know.

Each section starts with instructions on how to install the toolset that you are supposed to use with the platform. Some toolsets are very easy to install, while some have gotchas; thus the aim of the toolset installation chapter is mainly to cover the gotchas.

The next three chapters in each section take you through building what's called the "Six Bookmarks" application. This is a very simple application that is designed to show six buttons on the screen, and each button can be configured with a URL that invokes the device's default browser. The purpose of the application is not to be a fantastic piece of UI—it's designed to be a "carrier" to help you understand how to build all of the back-end bits and pieces that you need to make an application functional. Figure 1-1 shows an example.

Figure 1-1. *The Six Bookmarks application running on an iPhone*

Each volume contains two chapters that are *essential* to following the work in the book, and I strongly recommend that you read them first.

To reduce the amount of work required to build the application, Six Bookmarks works on the assumption that there is a cloud-based service that holds the user's bookmarks. In order to use the software on a device, the user needs an account on this service. (This model will seem familiar to all readers of this book, I hope.) Chapter 2 discusses the structure of this service and familiarizes you with the service calls that make the application work.

The second important chapter is Chapter 3, which discusses the functional specification of the Six Bookmarks application and the technical architecture. Again, it's important that you read this in order to understand what it is that you are trying to build.

Where Can You Get Help and Support?

This book has a companion web site, located at www.multimobiledevelopment.com/, which hosts important resources that will support you in getting the most out of this book. Specifically, you will find the following:

- Downloads of all of the code for all of the platforms

- The Six Bookmarks cloud service implementation that you need to use to make the applications work

- A hosted version of the Six Bookmark HTML application (discussed in detail in Volume 2)

- Support forums (I'll be monitoring and contributing to these, so if you have a question or a problem, this is the best place to try.)

Finally, going back to my earlier point about the amount of flux in the market at the moment, I'll be updating the web site to keep it up-to-date with changes in the toolsets and other movements within the industry.

Conclusion

Thanks for purchasing this book. Remember that if you do need help or support, then please visit the web site's discussion forums; but if you would like to contact me personally, you can find me at www.linkedin.com/in/mbrit/.

Matthew Baxter-Reynolds, April 2011

■ ■ ■

CHAPTER 2

The Six Bookmarks Server Service

We're going to talk more about the architecture and specification of the Six Bookmarks application in Chapter 3. In this chapter, we're going to look at the Six Bookmarks service. To support this book, I have set up a server with REST-based (a.k.a. "RESTful") services that allow the application to log on, retrieve bookmarks over the OData protocol, and post updates back, again using the OData protocol. (We'll talk more about OData later on.)

As discussed previously, Six Bookmarks is a commercial product provided in two ways—once as a commercial product and once as an open source product. In this book, we're going to be accessing a service based on the open source version of the code. Both applications communicate with a publically accessible server. The open source server operates a sandbox, and in order to complete the work in this book, you'll need your own account.

■ **Note** It's currently very popular to talk about the "cloud" and storing things "in the cloud." The Six Bookmarks server service is one of these "cloud" services—I've provided a server hosted on the public Internet that allows you to store bookmarks "in the cloud" and retrieve bookmarks "from the cloud."

We will not be covering how to build this service in the book; however, the source code for the service can be downloaded from the source repository at http://code.multimobiledevelopment.com/. This code and all of the other code downloads are distributed under the Mozilla Public License 1.1. More information on this can be found here: www.mozilla.org/MPL/MPL-1.1-annotated.html.

Creating an API Account

To create an API account, visit the services web site at http://services.multimobiledevelopment.com/. You will find a link on that page entitled "Register a new API account". Click this to access a standard registration form, as shown in Figure 2-1.

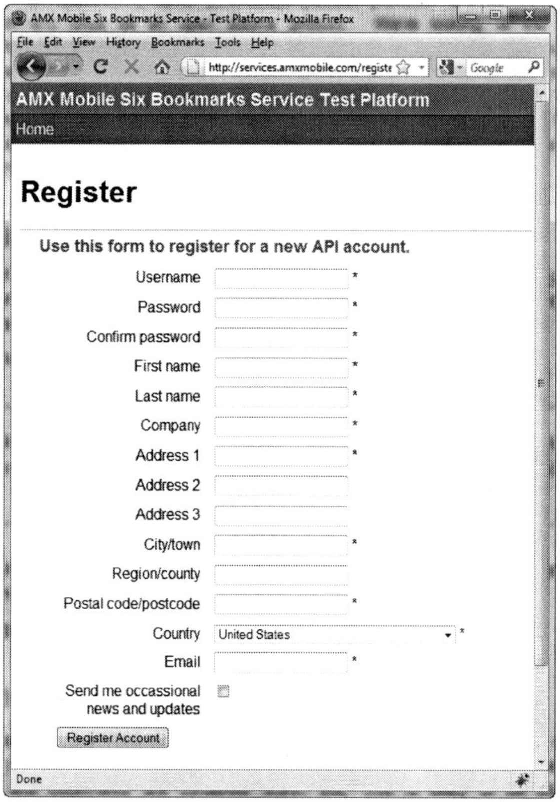

Figure 2-1. The service registration form

▨ **Note** The site at http://services.multimobiledevelopment.com is a live work in progress. Some of the screenshots presented here may differ from the current reality of the site as you see it today. Also, the site you are using is not secured when accessed over HTTPS, as this is a test site not intended for production use. Were you to build a similar thing for production applications, it would be essential that you secure the site using HTTPS.

Go ahead and create your account. Please provide a valid e-mail address, as you will need this should you need to reset your password in the future. (You will not get spammed.)

Registering your account will automatically log you on.

Creating a User

The purpose of registering for an account is to partition off a private section of the database for you to keep your own data in. A single SQL Server database exists on the server, and everyone's users and bookmarks are contained within this. This is likely to be slightly different for your own applications. For this book, we need to provide you with a sandbox service that makes it easier for you to work with the chapters on the actual application creation on the devices; however, in production applications, you typically do not need this. I have to hive off individual readers' data into separate "virtual databases" to prevent corruption of data and weird behavior, and with potentially tens of thousands of you out there doing this, it's impractical to create physically separate databases.

Under the covers, you're going to be working with three tables: ApiKeys, Users, and Bookmarks. The entity-relationship diagram (ERD) shown in Figure 2-2 illustrates.

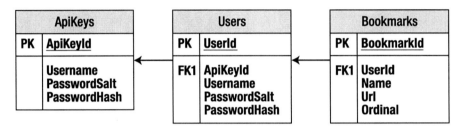

Figure 2-2. ERD showing relationship between the ApiKeys, Users, and Bookmarks tables

When you register for an API account, you do not get any users created for you. A user in this context relates to someone who would use an instance of the various mobile Six Bookmarks applications targeted for separate device platforms. To create a user, click the Manage Users link. You will be presented with a message that indicates no users are available, as per Figure 2-3.

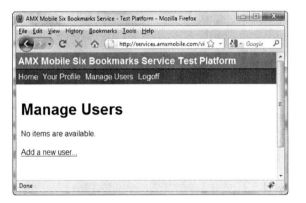

Figure 2-3. The Manage Users page showing no available users

Click the "Add a new user" link to enter a new user. Figure 2-4 illustrates.

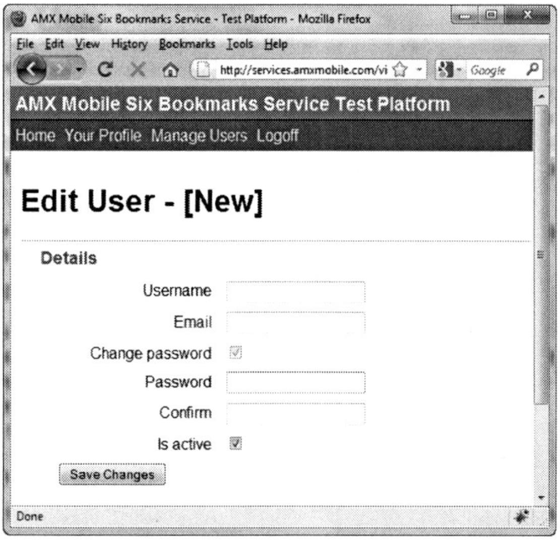

Figure 2-4. *The Edit User page*

You'll need to create at least one user in order to proceed to the next section.

The Users Service

The "Users" service is a RESTful web service that provides a capability to log on a user. (This book deals only with logging users on; however, the service is capable of other functions, including registering users.) It's important to familiarize yourself with how the service works, as it will aid in understanding the flow of the applications that we will build in later sections.

RESTful Web Services

A "RESTful" web service is a service that is based on the principle of REST, which stands for "Representational State Transfer." It is not a formal, standardized protocol, but rather a set of principles or constraints that describes the shape and operational usage of a service that you can get data from or provide data to. It is a very natural way of working with remote services, which is why they are so popular and prevalent. That naturalness translates into being very easy to build, and equally very easy to consume.

One common and straightforward way of structuring a RESTful web service is to request data using an HTTP GET request and retrieving results back as XML. The HTTP request can be a GET request, including parameters specified in the query string. Alternatively, the parameters can be made via a POST request that works by passing up XML.

Let's continue this by looking in more detail at the logon operation on the Users service.

Testing the Calls

The API relies on sending up custom HTTP headers, and as such we can't test it using a regular web browser. Rather than asking you to build some custom code to call the service, you can download a test harness for trying the service. You can download this from the source repository at `http://code.multimobiledevelopment.com/`. Look for a file in the Downloads section of the form `Amx.Services-<Version>-TestClient.zip`. This is a .NET application, and hence you'll need the .NET runtime installed on the machine you're looking to use.

If you download the utility and run it, you'll see you have an area to enter a URL and an area to enter two values: the `API username` header and the `Token` header. We'll talk about these values later, but essentially they provide additional information to the service to help guide the response.

Examining Logon Operations

The first thing we can try to do with our Users service is log on a user. Ultimately, a successful logon will return a token that we can use in subsequent requests.

If you open the test harness, the URL will be given as follows:

```
http://services.multimobiledevelopment.com/services/apirest.aspx?operation=logon&password=AP
IPASSWORD
```

Click the Send Request button, and you'll see a result like Figure 2-5.

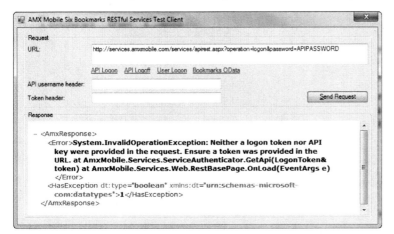

Figure 2-5. *An example of a failed request to the API service*

You can see in the response that an error has been returned.

The protocol for the REST services exposed by the service is that exceptions are returned back in the `Error` element, and the `HasException` element is set to `true` if an error has been returned. (The value shown in the XML is `1`, but the `datatypes` schema is used to indicate that this is a Boolean value.)

■ **Note** This error notification and transmission are just how I have designed the service—it doesn't follow that all RESTful web services will use this approach. It's down to the owner of the service to design a protocol that is sensible and logical to use within the loose construct of what a RESTful service typically looks like.

Referring back to Figure 2-5, we see the error indicates that "Neither a logon token nor API key were provided in this request." What this is telling us is that the headers have not been provided to the server.

To call the operations on the server, we need a token. In order to get a token, we need to call the server, so we have a chicken and egg situation! However, one operation on the server does not need a token—this is the Logon operation on the API service, which is used solely to obtain a token for use with the other methods.

Obtaining a Token

By default, when you start the harness, it will be set to connect to the API service and to call the Logon method. Firstly, into the API username header text box, enter the username of the account you created in the first part of the chapter. Secondly, modify the password value in the URL to be the username on your account.

If you click Send Request now and the details are correct, you'll see something similar to the image shown in Figure 2-6.

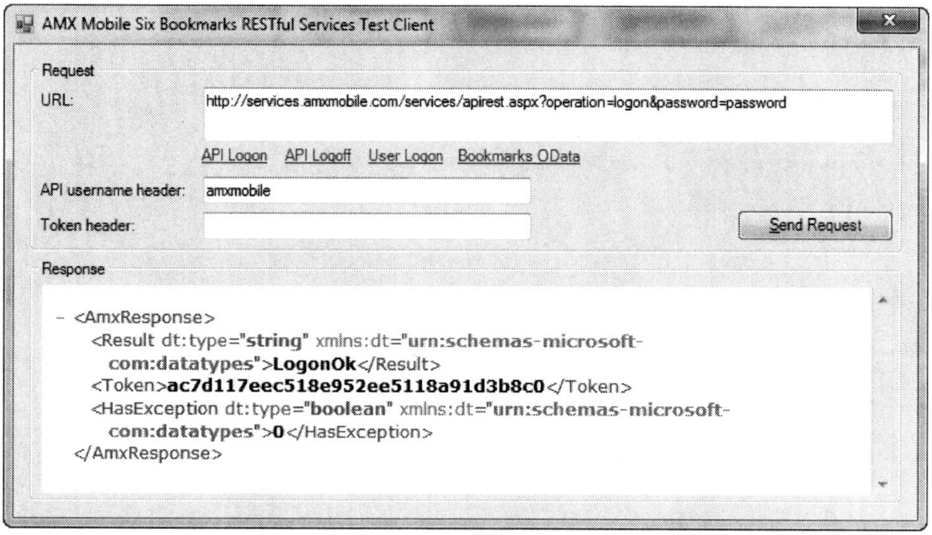

Figure 2-6. *An example of the result of a successful request to the API service*

You'll see in this case an error has not been returned. The Result element will be set to LogonOk or InvalidPassword. (Any other errors will result in an exception being returned.)

The most important element here is the Token value. This is the token that we'll use in all other requests. Copy the token into the clipboard, and then paste it into the Token header field. We'll use this later.

Logging On the User

Now that we have obtained a token to use and authenticated the API, we can actually log on the user. We've used the API service so far—we're now going to use the Users service.

If you click the User Logon link on the test harness, the URL will be rewritten to the following:

```
http://services.multimobiledevelopment.com/services/usersrest.aspx?operation=logon&username=
USERNAME&password=PASSWORD
```

This URL is configured to call the Users REST service. If you replace the USERNAME and PASSWORD placeholders in that string, and assuming you have copied the token into the Token header field, and click Send Request, you'll get a response like Figure 2-7, which, apart from the URL, looks identical to Figure 2-6.

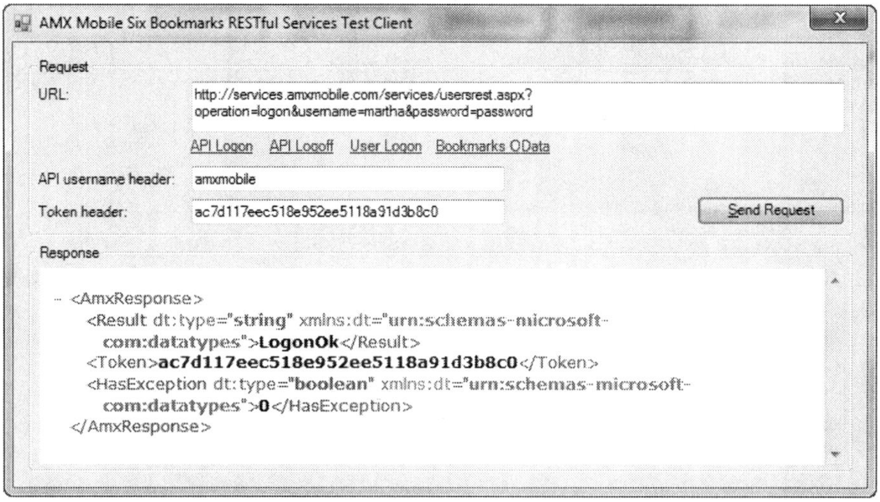

Figure 2-7. An example of a response from a successful request to the Users service

Assuming this works, you'll see another LogonOk response. What a LogonOk tells you here is that the token is now bound to the user you authenticated. (This is important—this means that you cannot use the same token with different users. This will never be a problem on a mobile device as these are typically solo-user devices and one's global state only ever refers to oneself, but in a web application, it is worth considering.) Other results you can get back from the service are InvalidUsername, InvalidPassword, or AccountInactive.

Cleaning Up

To clean up the service, we have to log off of the API. This is done via the Logoff operation. Click the "API logoff" link on the harness, and the URL will be rewritten once again. Click the Send Request button, and you'll see a response much like in Figure 2-8.

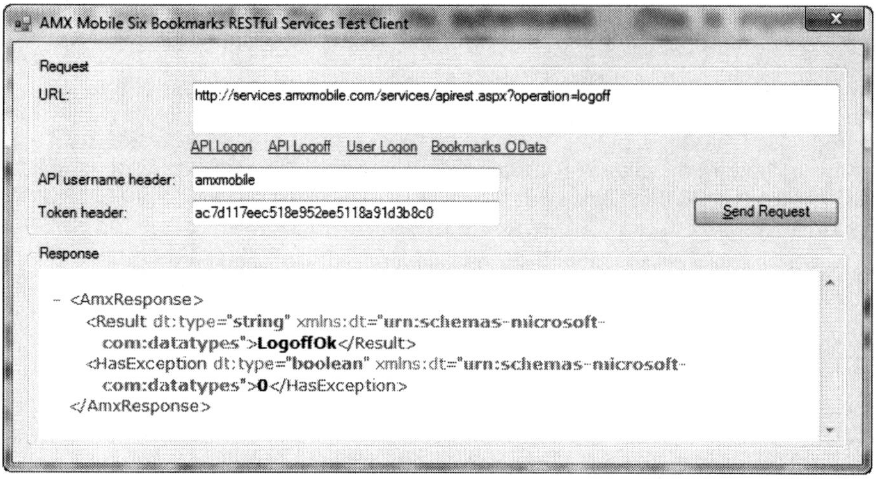

Figure 2-8. An example of a successul Logoff call to the API service

This operation is used to give the server the opportunity to clean up resources related to the token. (Specifically, it deletes a row in the database.) We'll look at token cleanup in more detail when we build the native device applications.

The Bookmarks Service

The final service exposed from the server is the Bookmarks OData service. OData is an up-and-coming data format that is currently being pitched as the proposed *de facto* standard for data interchange in a Web 2.0 world. My opinion is that it is a decent standard with a good, practical working method, and hence I've chosen to use it in this book to bridge the gap between relational data stored in the cloud and data stored on the device.

■ **Tip** You can find out more about OData at the official site: www.odata.org/.

Adding Some Test Data

In order to see how the OData service works, you're going to need some test data. There's an interface on the service that lets you maintain the bookmarks against a user.

Log on to services.multimobiledevelopment.com, and find a user that you want to work with. Click the "Manage this user's bookmarks" link at the bottom of the page. You will see an interface that allows you to define bookmarks. Figure 2-9 illustrates.

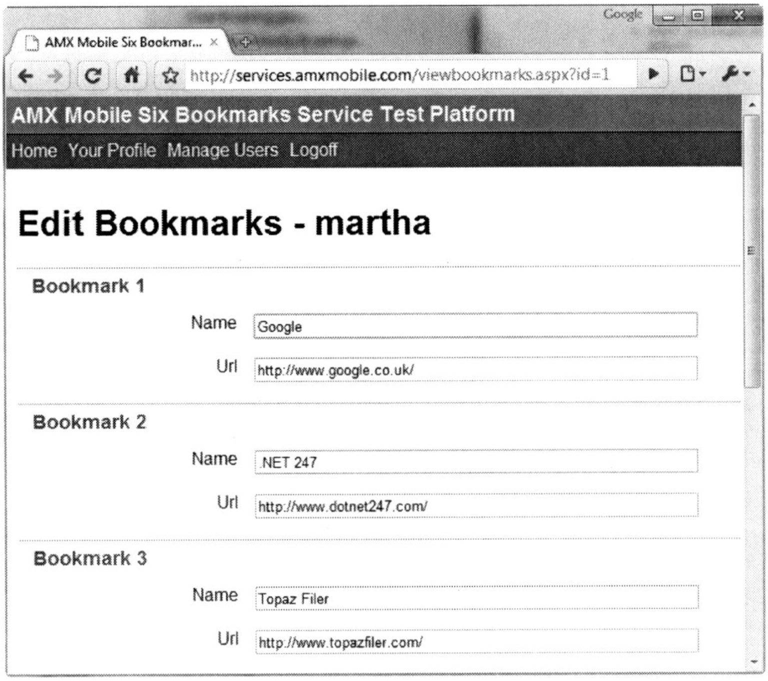

Figure 2-9. The Edit Bookmarks screen showing three bookmarks

Add a number of bookmarks, and click Save Changes.

Working with OData

Now that we have some bookmark data, we can look at using the Bookmarks service. We're going to be using the test harness again, and you will need a token—so if you do not currently have a token, go through the steps described previously to obtain one.

On the harness, if you click the Bookmarks OData link, you'll get a rewritten URL, like this one: http://services.multimobiledevelopment.com/services/bookmarks.svc/.

Click Send Request, and you'll get a response like Figure 2-10. You should note that the test harness continues to send up the special headers. The service call would be rejected should these headers be missing or incorrect.

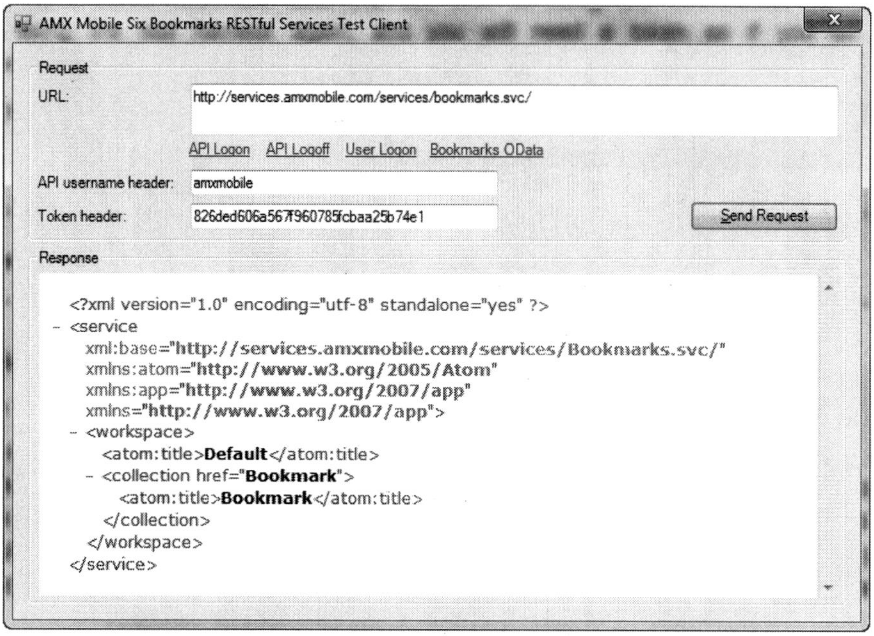

Figure 2-10. An example of a successful call to the Bookmarks OData service

---

■ **Note** The OData standard allows for data to be returned either in Atom or JSON format. Atom format is the most relevant here—JSON is typically used when working with Ajax calls from a web page. The actual format of the data is not important—what is important is that OData is built on open standards. (Notably, Microsoft sees OData as a core data protocol going forward, starting with a full implementation in .NET 3.5 SP1 and support on the Azure platform.)

The preceding output is telling us that the Bookmarks service is about to return data of type Bookmark (look for the //collection/atom:title element in the XML). Thus, if we issue this URL, again using the test harness, we'll get back some bookmarks. Here's the URL:

```
http://services. multimobiledevelopment.com/services/ bookmarks.svc/Bookmark
```

From this point, I'm going to show you the XML output as a listing, rather than screenshots. This will make it easier to follow the discussion.

In the following example, three bookmarks are returned from this call, and these are shown in the following listing. (Your output will vary depending on the bookmarks you've set up against the user that you've logged in as, obviously.) Here's the listing:

```xml
<?xml version="1.0" encoding="iso-8859-1" standalone="yes"?>
<feed xml:base="http://services. multimobiledevelopment.com/services/Bookmarks.svc/"↵
 xmlns:d="http://schemas.microsoft.com/ado/2007/08/dataservices"↵
 xmlns:m="http://schemas.microsoft.com/ado/2007/08/dataservices/metadata"↵
 xmlns="http://www.w3.org/2005/Atom">
 <title type="text">Bookmark</title>
 <id>http://services. multimobiledevelopment.com/services/bookmarks.svc/Bookmark</id>
 <updated>2010-04-18T10:54:32Z</updated>
 <link rel="self" title="Bookmark" href="Bookmark" />
 <entry>
   <id>http://services. multimobiledevelopment.com/services/Bookmarks.svc/Bookmark(1002)</id>
   <title type="text"></title>
   <updated>2010-04-18T10:54:32Z</updated>
   <author>
     <name />
   </author>
   <link rel="edit" title="Bookmark" href="Bookmark(1002)" />
   <category term="AmxMobile.Services.Bookmark"↵
 scheme="http://schemas.microsoft.com/ado/2007/08/dataservices/scheme" />
   <content type="application/xml">
     <m:properties>
       <d:BookmarkId m:type="Edm.Int32">1002</d:BookmarkId>
       <d:UserId m:type="Edm.Int32">1001</d:UserId>
       <d:Name>.NET 247</d:Name>
       <d:Url>http://www.dotnet247.com/</d:Url>
       <d:Ordinal m:type="Edm.Int32">1</d:Ordinal>
     </m:properties>
   </content>
 </entry>
 <entry>
   <id>http://services. multimobiledevelopment.com/services/Bookmarks.svc/Bookmark(1001)</id>
   <title type="text"></title>
   <updated>2010-04-18T10:54:32Z</updated>
   <author>
     <name />
   </author>
   <link rel="edit" title="Bookmark" href="Bookmark(1001)" />
   <category term="AmxMobile.Services.Bookmark"↵
 scheme="http://schemas.microsoft.com/ado/2007/08/dataservices/scheme" />
   <content type="application/xml">
     <m:properties>
       <d:BookmarkId m:type="Edm.Int32">1001</d:BookmarkId>
       <d:UserId m:type="Edm.Int32">1001</d:UserId>
       <d:Name>Google</d:Name>
       <d:Url>http://www.google.co.uk/</d:Url>
       <d:Ordinal m:type="Edm.Int32">0</d:Ordinal>
     </m:properties>
   </content>
 </entry>
 <entry>
   <id>http://services.multimobiledevelopment.com/services/Bookmarks.svc/Bookmark(1003)</id>
```

```
        <title type="text"></title>
        <updated>2010-04-18T10:54:32Z</updated>
        <author>
          <name />
        </author>
        <link rel="edit" title="Bookmark" href="Bookmark(1003)" />
        <category term="AmxMobile.Services.Bookmark"↩
  scheme="http://schemas.microsoft.com/ado/2007/08/dataservices/scheme" />
        <content type="application/xml">
          <m:properties>
            <d:BookmarkId m:type="Edm.Int32">1003</d:BookmarkId>
            <d:UserId m:type="Edm.Int32">1001</d:UserId>
            <d:Name>Topaz Filer</d:Name>
            <d:Url>http://www.topazfiler.com/</d:Url>
            <d:Ordinal m:type="Edm.Int32">2</d:Ordinal>
          </m:properties>
        </content>
      </entry>
  </feed>
```

Thanks to the clarity of the Atom format, it's very easy to understand the format of the data, even though the dataset is an unfamiliar one. Each of the feed/entry elements contains a single data item (which we'll be calling an "entity" throughout to keep in line with nomenclature on the object relational mapping structures that we're going to be using). The m:properties element within them contains the data.

An interesting element here is the ID element against each entry. These provide a URL that can be used to access an individual item. (But remember that you need to pass up the special headers in order for the service to return the data.)

Pick the ID of an item in your set of bookmarks and issue a request for it, passing in the token—for example, the following:

```
http://services.multimobiledevelopment.com/services/bookmarks.svc/Bookmark(1003)
```

This time you will just see that item, as per the following listing:

```
<?xml version="1.0" encoding="iso-8859-1" standalone="yes"?>
<entry xml:base="http://services.multimobiledevelopment.com/services/Bookmarks.svc/"↩
 xmlns:d="http://schemas.microsoft.com/ado/2007/08/dataservices"↩
 xmlns:m="http://schemas.microsoft.com/ado/2007/08/dataservices/metadata"↩
 xmlns="http://www.w3.org/2005/Atom">
  <id>http://services.multimobiledevelopment.com/services/Bookmarks.svc/Bookmark(1003)</id>
  <title type="text"></title>
  <updated>2010-04-18T10:55:13Z</updated>
  <author>
    <name />
  </author>
  <link rel="edit" title="Bookmark" href="Bookmark(1003)" />
  <category term="AmxMobile.Services.Bookmark"↩
 scheme="http://schemas.microsoft.com/ado/2007/08/dataservices/scheme" />
```

```
  <content type="application/xml">
    <m:properties>
      <d:BookmarkId m:type="Edm.Int32">1003</d:BookmarkId>
      <d:UserId m:type="Edm.Int32">1001</d:UserId>
      <d:Name>Topaz Filer</d:Name>
      <d:Url>http://www.topazfiler.com/</d:Url>
      <d:Ordinal m:type="Edm.Int32">2</d:Ordinal>
    </m:properties>
  </content>
</entry>
```

OData Queries

The OData standard provides for a number of operations that should be available on providers. One of these is the $metadata directive. This is a neat way of determining the format of data returned by the service. For example, if you issue the following request, you'll see the structure of the data, as per the following listing.

```
http://services.multimobiledevelopment.com/services/ bookmarks.svc/$metadata
```

```
<edmx:Edmx Version="1.0" xmlns:edmx="http://schemas.microsoft.com/ado/2007/06/edmx">
  <edmx:DataServices xmlns:m="http://schemas.microsoft.com/ado/2007/08/dataservices↵
/metadata" m:DataServiceVersion="1.0">
    <Schema Namespace="AmxMobile.Services"↵
 xmlns:d="http://schemas.microsoft.com/ado/2007/08/dataservices"↵
 xmlns:m="http://schemas.microsoft.com/ado/2007/08/dataservices/metadata"↵
 xmlns="http://schemas.microsoft.com/ado/2007/05/edm">
      <EntityType Name="Bookmark">
        <Key>
          <PropertyRef Name="BookmarkId" />
        </Key>
        <Property Name="BookmarkId" Type="Edm.Int32" Nullable="false" />
        <Property Name="UserId" Type="Edm.Int32" Nullable="false" />
        <Property Name="Name" Type="Edm.String" Nullable="true" />
        <Property Name="Url" Type="Edm.String" Nullable="true" />
        <Property Name="Ordinal" Type="Edm.Int32" Nullable="false" />
      </EntityType>
      <EntityContainer Name="BookmarkCollection" m:IsDefaultEntityContainer="true">
        <EntitySet Name="Bookmark" EntityType="AmxMobile.Services.Bookmark" />
      </EntityContainer>
    </Schema>
  </edmx:DataServices>
</edmx:Edmx>
```

Another useful method is the ability to issue queries to constrain the data. For example, if you wanted to return all of the bookmarks where the name was equal to Google, you can issue the following:

```
http://services.multimobiledevelopment.com/services/ bookmarks.svc/Bookmark?$filter=Name eq
'google'
```

▦ **Note** You should note here is where the additional constraints are being added to the query so that the set of bookmarks the service is working with contains only the bookmarks of the logged-in user. There's more information on the mechanics of this later.

In this book, we're using this service only to retrieve all of the bookmarks for a user and to send back changes, although feel free to experiment with the OData. The web site at www.odata.org/ contains plenty of information on the protocol and also includes references to sample datasets that are more interesting and more fully featured than the Six Bookmarks service. See www.odata.org/producers for some live OData services.

Issuing Updates over OData

As mentioned previously, we are looking to use OData to update our server-side data; however, this is difficult to demonstrate using a web browser, and therefore we'll cover updating the data in later chapters.

Constraining Data to the Logged-On User

Internally to the service, when a request is received by IIS, ASP.NET, ADO.NET, and the Windows Communication Foundation (WCF) work together to process the request. This ultimately results in a SQL statement being formed and passed to SQL Server. Just before this SQL statement is executed, an additional constraint is added so that only bookmarks where the user ID equals the logged-on user are returned. Therefore, if WCF wants to issue the statement select * from bookmarks, an additional constraint is added behind the scenes that makes it read select * from bookmarks where userid=27, or whatever the user ID happens to be. This is done by using URL rewriting to extract the token from the URL, storing the token in the HttpContext.Current.Items collection, and then de-referencing that at the appropriate time and attaching the additional constraint to the SQL query.

You'll see this code if you download the server source code package, but, as I've mentioned before, it would be unusual if your own server needed this functionality.

Conclusion

In this chapter, we've taken our first look at the cloud services that we're going to use to provide data and functionality to our client applications going forward. We have looked at how to call the API and Users RESTful services, and also how to request data over the Bookmarks OData service. In the next section, we'll look at the architecture and specification of the Six Bookmarks application.

CHAPTER 3

■ ■ ■

Application Architecture and Functional Specification

In this book and its sister book, we're going to build the same application natively on five mobile phone platforms—Android, iPhone, Windows Phone, Windows Mobile, and BlackBerry. So that we know what we're going to build, we're going to spend the first half of this chapter defining the functional specification of the Six Bookmarks application. In the second half, we're going to have a quick look at the application architecture as a sort of quasi-technical specification.

As mentioned in the introduction, this book covers Windows Phone, Windows Mobile, and BlackBerry development. This chapter (which incidentally exists in both books) covers all of the platforms to give you a good overview of each platform regardless of whether you have one book, the other book, or both.

A Word About Tablets

The examples used in this book and its sister book are all applications that run on smartphones, such as the iPhone and the crop of Android phones on the market. This is largely due to the time at which this book was proposed and developed—when it was started, the iPad had not been announced and there was little industry interest in iPad-class devices, which over time have adopted the moniker of tablets, erstwhile used for Microsoft's disastrous "tablet PC" initiatives.

At the time of writing (March 2011), there is massive interest in tablets, the iPad 2 recently having been announced and currently under restricted supply. Everyone is waiting for Android slates to come out, complete with the "Gingerbread" build of that OS optimized for the larger device formats, plus the BlackBerry Playbook is waiting in the wings (together with its rumored Android application support). HP is also doing something with webOS, although only time will tell if that's going to be interesting.

Although we won't look specifically at building applications for tablet devices, what you learn in this book will be valuable. The underlying libraries remain the same—all that you need to do to port an application from, for example, iPhone to iPad is to build a new user interface.

Functional Specification

To illustrate the functional specification, I'm going to use the screenshots from the iOS application. To write this book, I've already written the five native applications, and so I can use these as a basis for the functional specification. Obviously, in the real world, this wouldn't happen, although you may have a prototype to work from.

We'll break the functional specification down into screens, and we'll state what the user will be able to do on each of the screens.

Logging On

The logon screen looks like Figure 3-1.

Figure 3-1. The logon screen

The required functions are the following:

- The user must be able to key in his or her username and password.

- If logon is successful, the local database is synchronized (see later) and the navigator screen displayed (also see later).

- The user must be able to indicate that his or her credentials should be remembered for next use.

- Where credentials have been remembered, the application should attempt to use these.

Synchronizing

The synchronize operation does not have a user interface. The required functions are the following:

- If no local database exists, a new one must be created.

- If no bookmarks table exists, a new one must be created.

- If the local database contains changes to send to the server, they must be sent to the server.

- Regardless of whether changes were sent to the server, the up-to-date list of bookmarks from the server must be downloaded, the local bookmarks table created, and the local bookmarks table updated from the server set.

Navigator

The navigator screen, with my sample bookmarks, looks like Figure 3-2.

Figure 3-2. The navigator screen

The required functions are the following:

- If a bookmark exists at a given ordinal, the text of the corresponding button must be set to the name of the bookmark.

- If a bookmark does not exist at a given ordinal, the text of the corresponding button must be set to an ellipsis ("**...**").

- If the user presses a configured button, the device's default browser must be invoked to show the URL related to the bookmark/button.

- If the user presses an unconfigured button, the configuration function (see the following) must be invoked.

- The user must have a way of accessing the configuration function directly.

- The user must be able to invoke a logoff function, which will clear the current user, reset any remembered credentials, and return the user to the logon form.

- The user must be able to invoke an "about" function, which will take the user to the `www.multimobiledevelopment.com/` site.

Configuring Bookmarks

The configuration screen looks like Figure 3-3.

Figure 3-3. The configuration screen

The required functions are the following:

- The user must be presented with a list of the defined bookmarks.

- If the user selects a bookmark, he or she must be taken to the "configure singleton" form (see the following).

- The user must be able to add a bookmark, up to a maximum of six.

- The user must be able to delete existing bookmarks.

Configuring a Single Bookmark ("Configure Singleton")

The singleton configuration screen looks like Figure 3-4.

Figure 3-4. The "configure singleton" screen

The required functions are the following:

- The user must be able to change the bookmark's name.

- The user must be able to change the bookmark's URL.

- If the user tried to save a bookmark without entering both a name and a URL, an error must be displayed.

Missing Functionality

The Six Bookmarks applications are intended to be as close to real-world applications as is possible within the limitations of writing a book. There are some things that I have left out, and in each case when I've left something out, it's with the express intention of making the central thrust of the discussion easier to understand. The areas are the following:

- *New user registration:* Users will not be able to register for an account on the device. This would typically be a requirement if you were rolling an application like this out for real.

- *Offline support:* The applications will all run without having to have an active TCP/IP connection; however, code has been omitted to gracefully handle a lack of such a connection. I made this decision primarily to make the code more straightforward.

- *Defensive coding:* The code listings do not demonstrate a level of defensive coding, again to make the central thrust of things clear. (This is particularly true of the iOS chapters.)

Application Architecture and Technical Specification

Now that we know what we're going to build, let's have a look at how we're going to build it.

The interesting bit of this book is about how you solve the same problem on each of the platforms. Although we're building five applications, since Microsoft has deprecated Windows Mobile, in this section we're going to discuss Android, iOS, Windows Phone, and BlackBerry.

Approach

What I wanted to demonstrate with this book is that there are common things that all of the applications have to be able to do regardless of vendor. Moreover, the application has to assume that the master version of the data is held in the cloud and that each device holds a locally cached copy of the server-side master set. (But, with regards to this last point, a number of device independent software vendors (ISVs) just don't get this, particularly on iOS, and they think the device holds the master data. This is a fundamentally wrong approach.) We saw in Chapter 2 that we have a cloud-based, always-on service that holds our master dataset. What I'm also keen to do as an approach is make this as "real-world" as possible.

Given that, each application has to be able to do the following:

- *Issue an HTTP request to the server to access a proprietary RESTful service:* Although I own/designed the Six Bookmarks service, it is likely that you will need to access cloud-based services that operate on protocols not of user design but based on RESTful principles.

- *Read XML documents:* The RESTful services and OData services return XML, and we need to be able to read it!

- *Read data over the OData protocol:* OData will very probably become the prevalent data transfer mechanism over HTTP. Building our applications on OData a) future-proofs it but b) gives you experience with an alternative and more complex RESTful service protocol.

- *Maintain a local store of its own data:* Ideally this would be as a SQL-compliant relational database management system.

- *Store preference data locally:* The devices each have an API for storing preference data locally, and this should always be used to reduce support problems and prevent problems with being accepted into the vendor's applications store (see the following).

- *Present a user interface using the native device framework:* In the world of mobile software, each user has a phone that he uses, and he wants all of his applications to look and feel the same. You cannot do this with a shared framework; hence each application has to use the native framework directly.

- *Write an XML document:* To push changes over OData, we need to be able to write an XML document.

- *Submit changes over OData:* If we know we can make an HTTP request and build an XML document, we should be able to push changes up.

- *Be acceptable to the vendor's applications store policy:* This varies on a case-by-case basis for each vendor, and we're not specifically going to "disassemble" each vendor's policy in this book. However, by using open standards and using each vendor's recommended tools, frameworks, and standards, the applications should go through into the application stores without a hitch.

One requirement I have not included is a single stack of source code for each of the platforms. My personal view on this is that it is simply not possible, although tools like Mono make the world of cross-compilation and partially equal code stacks easier. Around the time this book was written, the press coverage about Steve Jobs wanting to keep intermediate frameworks (like Java and Flash) off of iOS, I think, is entirely justified—these platforms and tools are just all too different to create a single thing that does not compromise. The answer will probably end up being HTML5, but that's going to take many years (2015 onward) to become viable.

Another important principle is that all of this could be done using the standard downloads for the platform—e.g., if you downloaded the iPhone SDK, you did not then have to download another SDK to get some part of the application built. Everything we do will use the standard toolset.

Let's look now at how we solve these problems on each platform.

Object-Relational Mapping

The key architectural premise that I wanted to discuss in this chapter is the way that we're going to store data locally on the device. This will be done using an approach called "object-relational mapping," or ORM. Since I started my career, I have been a huge fan of ORM, and my keenness on it and familiarly with it have obviously informed my decisions with regards to using it in this book.

For your information, I am the maintainer of an open source project called BootFX (www.bootfx.com/). The project is an application framework for .NET that has been under development since 2002. The ORM design that we're going to use in this book is based on BootFX, although it will be a heavily cut-down version.

Metadata

I want to start by talking about "metadata." In my opinion, the quality of any ORM tool, or any data access layer (DAL), lives or dies by its metadata. I would go so far as to say it's better to have an ORM implementation with excellent metadata that's quite slow than it is to have an ORM implementation with poor metadata that's quite fast.

The reason for this is that my approach is to optimize the development process and minimize the hassle of maintenance as opposed to build an application that's blazingly fast in production. Most people work on small projects with a small set of users that's easily served by run-of-the-mill hardware, but our community tends to encourage people to design applications that are ultra-high-performance and ultra-scalable. Most of the time, "you ain't gonna need it."

What good quality metadata does for you is allow for code that is flexible and adapts to changes within the application. For example, you may have a need to create a database table when an application starts. With good metadata, you can dynamically build the SQL statement to create the table. Thus, if you change that table's structure over time, you can reuse the code that builds the SQL statement to build the new table, all without you having to do too much work.

The metadata system that I'm going to present is modeled on the excellent type metadata system in .NET. In .NET you have a `System.Type` object that represents—for example—a class in your application. That `Type` instance can be used to reflect against the methods, properties, events, fields, etc. of that type.

In our projects, we're going to create a class called `EntityType`, which holds a collection of fields on a table. `EntityType` will map one-to-one with a database table. (In the more fully featured BootFX, `EntityType` holds information on relationships, indexes, constraints, etc.) Thus, `EntityType` will contain a collection of `EntityField` instances.

`EntityType` will extend a class called `EntityItem`. `EntityItem` will do something quite important for us—it will hold two names for each item. The reason for this is that oftentimes in ORM you are inheriting someone else's database schema, and you may want to abstract out naming conventions that are hard to work with (for example, TBL_CUST vs. Customer). Thus `EntityItem` will include a "native name" (via the `NativeName` property) and a "programmatic name" (via the `Name` property).

`EntityField` will also extend `EntityItem`, but will include extra information about the field—specifically the data type, size, and an indication as to whether it's a key field. Figure 3-5 shows a UML static structure sketch that shows these fields in play.

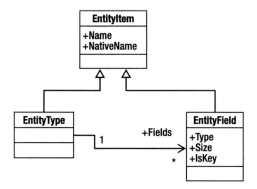

Figure 3-5. UML static structure sketch of the metadata system

Again, to reiterate the point, what this structure lets us do is very easily write code that builds dynamic SQL statements. For example, if we want to build a `SELECT` statement, we know the native name of the table, we know the fields on the table, and we know the name of each field, and from that we can build up our `SELECT`. (We can also add `WHERE` clauses to constrain the `SELECT`, which we'll go into later.)

Now that you have an idea of how the metadata system is put together, let's look at how rows are represented in memory.

Entities

An `EntityType` is a one-to-one mapping with a database table. An `Entity` is a representation of a row on the entity. Each strongly typed entity has fields that map to the columns on the database. This is where the "object-relational mapping" comes in—we have an object, and we're mapping it to a relational database.

For example, we might have a class called Customer that extends Entity. Customer might then have properties CustomerId, FirstName, LastName, and Email that map to the columns on the underlying table. When an entity is hydrated from a row in the database, the various field-mapped properties will be populated. This allows you to do code like this:

```
foreach(Customer customer in Customer.GetAll())
        Console.WriteLine(customer.Email);
```

Internally within the entity, what happens is that each entity discovers its EntityType instance, looks at the number of fields and creates "slots" within it. So, if you have four fields, you will end up with a "slots" array that is four items in size. The properties then—simplistically—get or set values from the slots.

Thus if you hydrate an object from the database, all you have to do is create an entity instance to receive the data, allow it to create the slots and then read the column values from the database and store it in the appropriate slot.

Likewise, if you want to create an entity to store in the database, you can instantiate one in the normal way, use the properties to set the slot values, and then ask the entity to save itself. This issue of "asking the entity to save itself" is something that we'll cover shortly.

Figure 3-6 shows a UML static structure sketch of the entity and our example Customer class.

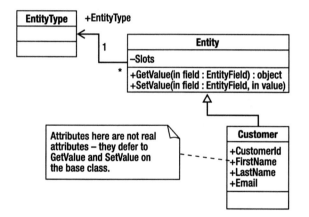

Figure 3-6. *UML static structure sketch of the* Entity *class*

Generating Entities

This sort of system makes sense only if you use a code generator to create the classes, otherwise it is a real pain keeping the entities up-to-date. Although BootFX comes with a fully fledged code generator for just this purpose, the examples in this book do not include one, and we'll roll the entities by hand.

■ **Note** That said, keep an eye out on the web site, as I may well end up writing an entity code generator compatible with the work in this book for Android or iOS, or perhaps an intrepid reader will.

SQL Statements

So we've discussed in theory how we can manage database records in memory, but we haven't mentioned anything about how we instruct the server to that effect.

The approach used in BootFX is to use a class called a SqlStatement. The purpose of the SqlStatement is to wrap up a command string and a collection of parameters.

A common "mistake" when building data access layers is to create methods that require the statement to be passed in as parameters—for example, the following:

```
void Database.ExecuteNonQuery(string commandString, object[] params);
```

The problem with this approach is that it's very brittle. It's much better to wrap up the definition of a statement in a separate class because a) it makes the interface to your DAL more straightforward, but b) it allows you to issue instructions to the database that are not quite fully formed.

Let me explain that last point. If you create an interface called ISqlStatementSource, add a method to this called GetSqlStatement, and make your DAL accept the interface—for example, as follows—it gives you more leeway about what you can pass in.

```
void Database.ExecuteNonQuery(ISqlStatementSource sql);
```

One example of what you could pass in is a SqlFilter instance.

The purpose of a SqlFilter is to allow you to dynamically build a SELECT statement on the principle that you create a filter that will select everything from the table that it's mapped to, but allows you to constrain the results. For example, a filter created without constraints would return all customers. A filter with a constraint with the last name starting with "C" would, obviously, return just those people whose name begins with "C."

If we make SqlFilter implement ISqlStatementSource, we can pass it directly into the DAL and let it de-reference a full statement just before it needs to run it. This makes it very easy to build the filter class, creates a DAL with a very clean and simple interface, and also allows the DAL to be extended with other types of queries going forward (for example, a full-text query).

Figure 3-7 shows a UML static structure sketch of the classes that we just discussed.

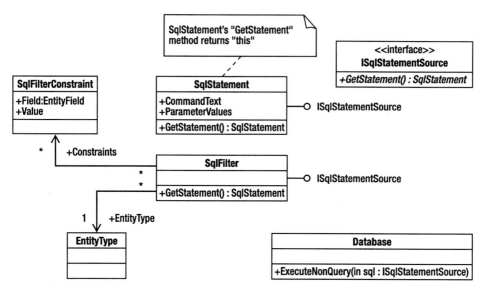

Figure 3-7. *UML static structure sketch of* SqlStatement *and companion classes*

Change Processors

The final part of our ORM tool relates to saving changes back into the database. This is done through the EntityChangeProcessor.

There will be some deeper logic in our entity implementation that relates to keeping track of the internal state of the entity and the slots in order to understand what the state of the entity is. For example, an entity that's been loaded from the database without a field property being set remains in a state of "unchanged." If you set a property, it will become "modified." You may want to call a method that sets it to "deleted." Finally, you may create a new entity, in which case it needs to be flagged as "new."

Depending on the state, the ORM subsystem has to issue an INSERT ("new"), UPDATE ("modified"), or DELETE ("deleted") statement, or indeed do nothing if none of those states is active. Again, thanks to the metadata, this is easy—the ORM subsystem knows the fields that make up the entity, it knows the value in each slot, and it also knows the state. The metadata also mentions which field is the key field, and thus the UPDATE and DELETE statements can include WHERE clauses to touch just the relevant row.

That brings us to the end of our discussion on ORM. We can now look at the other major architecture component—server communication.

Server Communication

■ **Note** This section assumes a familiarity with the discussion in Chapter 2.

In Chapter 2, I discussed how we were going to use a proprietary REST web service for some of the calls and OData for the rest of the calls. I did this primarily because I wanted to create a semi-real-world example of how you would deal with communicating with a server that you did not own.

Readers who have used SOAP web services on the Microsoft stack before will be familiar with how easy it is to code against. If you haven't, what happens is that Visual Studio creates a proxy class that looks like the service you are trying to call. Thus if you have a method exposed by a SOAP web service called HelloWorld that takes a string and returns a string, you can access it like this:

```
HelloWorldWs ws = new HelloWorldWs();
string result = ws.HelloWorld("Bob");
Console.WriteLine(result);
```

The huge "win" with this approach is that it's dead easy. The huge "loss," and why it hasn't really caught on, is that SOAP puts a ton of magic in the way that makes cross-platform communication too difficult. Over the ten or so years since SOAP was released, it's been overtaken by web services that are constructed in a "here's an XML document, can I have an XML document back?" way, with the XML going each way (we hope) in as easy a fashion as possible.

What I've wanted to do with the architecture of the way we deal with these services is try to get to a point where we get some of the wins of SOAP, but still have a really easy web service in the background. Thus, when we want to call the "logon" method on the API service, we'll create an ApiService class and call the Logon method. Packaging up the request and error handling will all be dealt with by base classes.

Specifically, we'll build ServiceProxy, RestServiceProxy, and ODataServiceProxy base classes. RestServiceProxy will specialize calls to the RESTful services. ODataServiceProxy will specialize calls to the OData service. ApiService, UsersService, and BookmarksService will all provide specific implementations. Figure 3-8 illustrates.

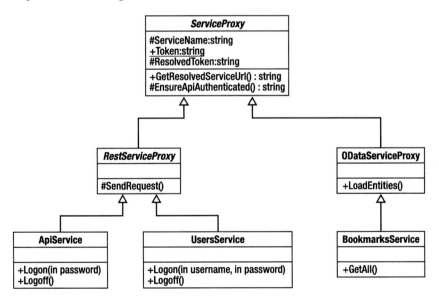

Figure 3-8. *UML static sketch of the service proxy hierarchy*

I'm not going to go into too much more detail here on this—when we build the code in the specific Android and iOS implementations, there's plenty more detail. The important fact from this chapter to take away is that we want to make calling the services as easy and as natural as possible.

Technical Approach Broken Down by Platform

In this section, we'll look at each of the major things that we wish to achieve and state the technology that we're going to use in each case.

With regards to the HTML application, in this book's sister book, where we go through this (remember you can download the code from `http://code.multimobiledevelopment.com/` regardless of whether you own the book), we build an ASP.NET-based web site. Therefore the details in this section related to HTML discuss the .NET classes that you need to use. You can, of course, build mobile web applications using any platform.

Core Toolset

Table 3-1 documents the code toolset used for each platform. "HTML via ASP.NET web site" options have been given for added interest for those familiar with this platform.

Table 3-1. Toolsets by Platform

Platform	Approach
Android	Eclipse, available on Mac, Windows, or Linux with the "Android ADT" plug-in providing extra functionality within Eclipse (`http://developer.android.com/sdk/eclipse-adt.html`)
iOS	Xcode, available only on Mac
Windows Phone	Visual Studio 2010, available only on Windows
Windows Mobile	Visual Studio 2008, available only on Windows
BlackBerry	Eclipse, available on Mac, Windows, or Linux with the "BlackBerry Java Plug-in for Eclipse" providing extra functionality within Eclipse (`http://na.blackberry.com/eng/developers/javaappdev/javaplugin.jsp`)
HTML via ASP.NET web site	ASP.NET via Visual Studio

Issue HTTP Requests

This applies to calling the Six Bookmarks proprietary RESTful services, downloading OData data, and pushing changes over OData. Table 3-2 lists the technology in each case.

Table 3-2. Technologies Used for Issuing HTTP Requests

Platform	Approach
Android	Apache HTTP Client library (`http://hc.apache.org/httpcomponents-client/`) `org.apache.http.*`
iOS	Cocoa Touch `NSConnection` class and related types
Windows Phone	`System.Net.HttpWebRequest` and related classes for ad hoc requests—see the following for OData requests.
Windows Mobile	`System.Net.HttpWebRequest` and related classes
BlackBerry	`javax.microedition.io.Connector` class and related classes
HTML via ASP.NET web site	`System.Net.HttpWebRequest` and related classes

Read XML Document (Including Reading OData Results)

Generally speaking, there are two ways of reading an XML document—loading the entire thing into a document object model (DOM) tree and querying it as an object-hierarchy, or using a parser that is able to start at the top and read through the document, gathering data as it goes. Table 3-3 lists the technology in each case.

Table 3-3. Technologies Used for Reading XML Documents

Platform	Approach
Android	DOM-based approach using standard Java implementation `org.w3c.dom.*`
iOS	Forward-only reader/parser using `NSXMLParser`
Windows Phone	DOM-based approach using `System.X ml.Linq.XDocument` for RESTful services, Visual Studio proxy class for OData
Windows Mobile	DOM-based approach using `System.Xml.XmlDocument`
BlackBerry	DOM-based approach using standard Java implementation `org.w3c.dom.*`
HTML via ASP.NET web site	DOM-based approach using `System.Xml.XmlDocument` or `System.X ml.Linq.XDocument` depending on preference

Write an XML Document

Like reading an XML document, you can write an XML document either by creating a DOM tree or by writing elements in turn programmatically. Table 3-4 lists the technology in each case.

Table 3-4. Technologies Used for Writing XML Documents

Platform	Approach
Android	Writer approach using XMLPull library and `org.xmlpull.v1.XmlSerializer`
iOS	Writer approach using Libxml2 library via native C-style API
Windows Phone	DOM-based approach using `System.X ml.Linq.XDocument` (However, we will not see this in the book, as Windows Phone creates a proxy for talking to OData services that hides this from us.)
Windows Mobile	DOM-based approach using `System.Xml.XmlDocument`
BlackBerry	Writer approach using a custom/proprietary implementation based on the XMLPull library and `org.xmlpull.v1.XmlSerializer`. (See the notes in the related chapter for more on this.)
HTML via ASP.NET web site	DOM-based approach using `System.Xml.XmlDocument` or `System.X ml.Linq.XDocument` depending on preference

Maintain a Local Store

SQLite is available on all of the platforms apart from Windows Phone, which gives us a great opportunity for a common implementation. A relational store makes the most sense for this book on the principle that proper, real-world applications would likely need a relational store. Our actual requirements for Six Bookmarks are that we're going to have only one table with a small number of rows in it, and practically, if that were a real-world requirement, storing the bookmarks in an XML file would likely make more sense. Table 3-5 lists the technology in each case.

Table 3-5. Technologies Used for Maintaining a Local Store

Platform	Approach
Android	Managed API over SQLite via `android.database.sqlite.SQLiteOpenHelper` and related types
iOS	Direct access to SQLite via native C-style API
Windows Phone	No relational database available—will store XML files on disk using isolated storage

Platform	Approach
Windows Mobile	Managed API over SQLCE via `System.Data.SqlServerCe.SqlCeConnection` class and related types
BlackBerry	Managed API over SQLite via `net.rim.device.api.database.Database` and related types
HTML via ASP.NET web site	Not needed (However, if server-side storage is needed, a relational database such as SQL Server or MySQL fits the bill.)

■ **Note** As a short rant, the fact that Windows Phone is coming to market initially without a relational database is shocking, especially as SQL Server Compact has been around for well over a decade. It would be excellent if Microsoft decided to bake SQLite into the platform like the other vendors have done.

Conclusion

In this chapter, we have taken an in-depth look at the application that we intend to build, discussed in some detail the object-relational mapping approach that we're going to take with local data storage, discussed the network communications and approach, and enumerated against each device the technology we intend to use in order to achieve common goals.

CHAPTER 4

■ ■ ■

Windows Phone 7: Installing the Toolset

In this chapter, we're going to look at installing the Windows Phone 7 toolset. Installation is very straightforward—so prepare for a very short chapter!

Silverlight vs. XNA

There are two ways that you can develop applications for Windows Phone 7—Silverlight or XNA.

Silverlight is the method that we are going to look at in this book. Silverlight is Microsoft's product/strategy for building rich experiences on the desktop, now on mobile phones through Windows Phone 7 and for the Web. XNA is purely a game development platform.

Visual Studio 2010

Windows Phone 7 development is done within Visual Studio 2010, and hence this needs to be installed as a prerequisite. I have not included instructions on how to install this, as it's obvious to do.

Installing the Windows Phone Developer Tools

Once VS 2010 has been installed, you can install the Windows Phone Developer Tools. These can be found at `http://developer.windowsphone.com/`. Follow the links through to download the appropriate package.

The installer will take you through getting up and running. Figure 4-1 shows an example screen from the installer.

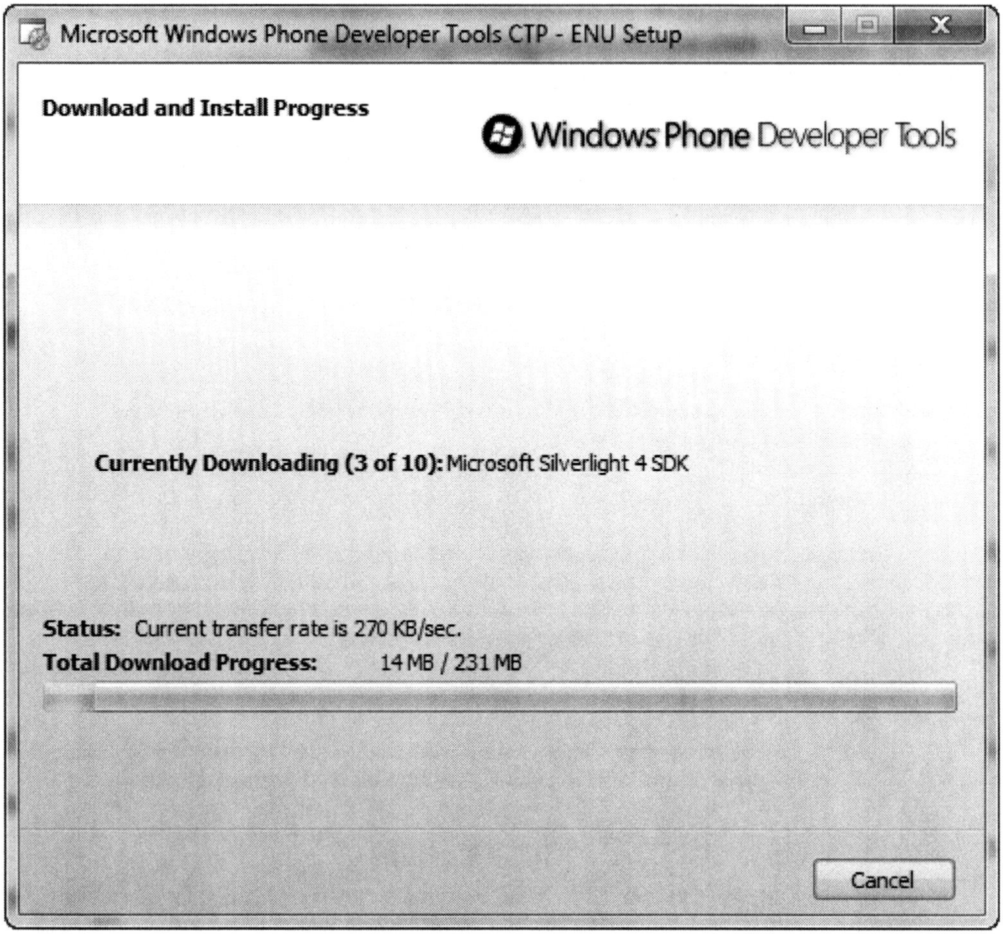

Figure 4-1. *The developer tools setup wizard*

Creating a Test Application

Once the installation is done, we can jump straight into creating our test application. Open VS 2010, and you'll see the New Project link on the start page (Figure 4-2).

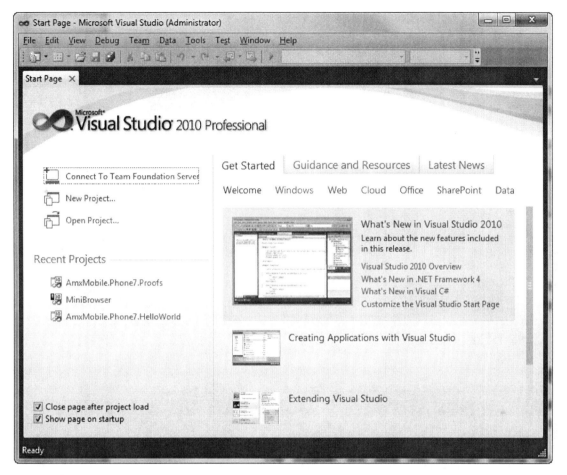

Figure 4-2. Visual Studio 2010

Click New Project, and you'll be presented with options to create projects in the Silverlight for Windows Phone 7 category. We want to create a new Windows Phone application in C#. Give the project any name you like, and click OK. Figure 4-3 illustrates the New Project dialog.

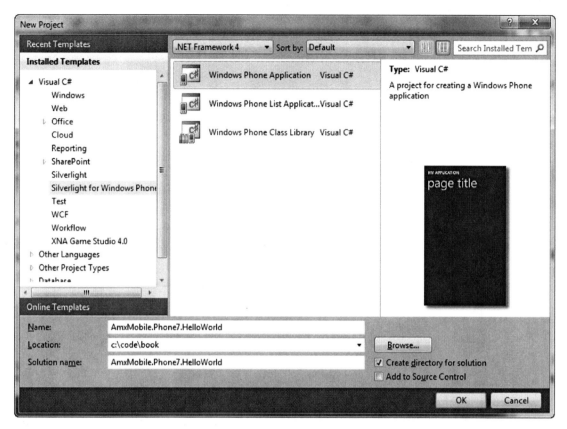

Figure 4-3. *The new Windows Phone 7 project option*

Silverlight is a framework that combines a declarative markup language for the user interface called XAML (pronounced "za-mal") with the .NET Framework. On the phone, we use a subset of the .NET Framework called the .NET Compact Framework. The huge advantage of Windows Mobile and Windows Phone development is that it really is true to say that if you know how to write .NET code for the Web or desktop applications, you already know how to build mobile applications. The only wrinkle now that Windows Mobile has been deprecated is that developers are forced to learn Silverlight—although Silverlight is actually pretty easy.

Figure 4-4 shows the default editor that you get when you create the project. You get a (nicely rendered) phone on the left and a bunch of XAML on the right. (This is where we start to see the major investment that Microsoft has made in this stuff pay off—the developer tools and APIs are unbelievably refined and easy to work with. Personally, I really like Android development, but it does have a hobbyist feel; when you've worked with the other platforms for a while, the Microsoft stuff feels like it's from the future.)

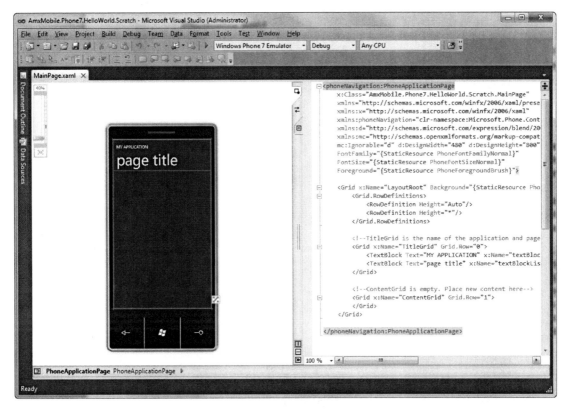

Figure 4-4. The design surface within Visual Studio

What we'll do for our example is create a simple "Hello World" application as we have done for Android and for iPhone. The first thing we'll do is change the text at the top of the page. You can do this using the designer or in the markup—my personal preference is to use the markup. In the XAML, you will find two TextBlock elements. Change their Text attributes to read Six Bookmarks and Hello, World respectively. This listing illustrates:

```
<phone:PhoneApplicationPage
    x:Class="AmxMobile.Phone7.HelloWorld.MainPage"
    xmlns="http://schemas.microsoft.com/winfx/2006/xaml/presentation"
    xmlns:x="http://schemas.microsoft.com/winfx/2006/xaml"
    xmlns:phone="clr-namespace:Microsoft.Phone.Controls;assembly=Microsoft.Phone"
    xmlns:shell="clr-namespace:Microsoft.Phone.Shell;assembly=Microsoft.Phone"
    xmlns:d="http://schemas.microsoft.com/expression/blend/2008"
    xmlns:mc="http://schemas.openxmlformats.org/markup-compatibility/2006"
    FontFamily="{StaticResource PhoneFontFamilyNormal}"
    FontSize="{StaticResource PhoneFontSizeNormal}"
    Foreground="{StaticResource PhoneForegroundBrush}"
    SupportedOrientations="Portrait" Orientation="Portrait"
```

```
    mc:Ignorable="d" d:DesignWidth="480" d:DesignHeight="768"
    shell:SystemTray.IsVisible="True">

    <!--LayoutRoot contains the root grid where all other page content is placed-->
    <Grid x:Name="LayoutRoot" Background="Transparent">
        <Grid.RowDefinitions>
            <RowDefinition Height="Auto"/>
            <RowDefinition Height="*"/>
        </Grid.RowDefinitions>

        <!--TitlePanel contains the name of the application and page title-->
        <StackPanel x:Name="TitlePanel" Grid.Row="0" Margin="24,24,0,12">
            <TextBlock x:Name="ApplicationTitle" Text="Six Bookmarks" Style="{StaticResource
PhoneTextNormalStyle}"/>
            <TextBlock x:Name="PageTitle" Text="Hello, World" Margin="-3,-8,0,0"
Style="{StaticResource PhoneTextTitle1Style}"/>
        </StackPanel>

        <!--ContentPanel - place additional content here-->
        <Grid x:Name="ContentGrid" Grid.Row="1">
        </Grid>
    </Grid>

</phone:PhoneApplicationPage>
```

Figure 4-5 shows what the top of the designer view looks like now.

Figure 4-5. *Detail of modified labels on the design surface*

We now need to add a button. For brevity, the easiest way to do this is to drag and drop a button onto the form. (When building applications properly, it's better to add it directly to the markup, as this provides for more control over the layout, especially when making sure the layout works if you change the device orientation.) Next, drag and drop a new button onto the design surface and you'll see something like Figure 4-6.

Figure 4-6. Positioning a button on the design surface

With the button selected, hit Alt+Enter and the properties window will open. Change the Content property to Say Hello. You also need to change the name of the control to buttonSayHello—this is done using a hidden text box right at the top of the Properties window. Figure 4-7 illustrates the properties. You may also wish to make the button a little wider.

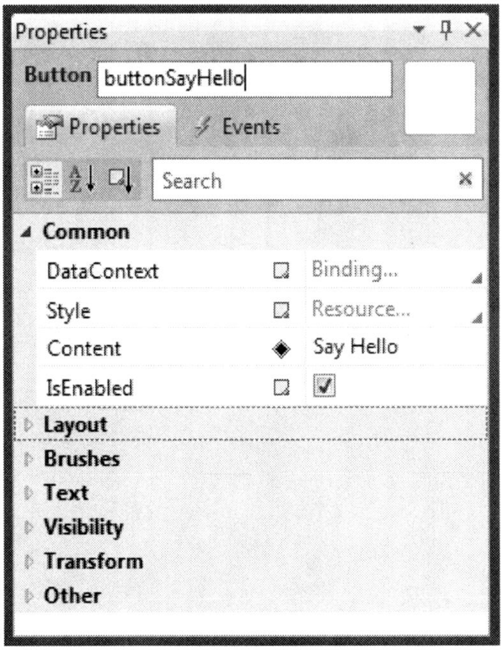

Figure 4-7. The Properties window

To make the button do something, double-click it and it will wire up an event handler into the code-behind class. Here's the listing for the code-behind:

```
private void buttonSayHello_Click(object sender, RoutedEventArgs e)
{
    MessageBox.Show("Hello, world.", "Six Bookmarks", MessageBoxButton.OK);
}
```

To run the project, select Debug – Start Debugging from the menu. This will build the project, start the emulator, and run the project.

Figure 4-8 shows the emulator running. You can click the button, the message box will be shown, and you'll see something like Figure 4-9.

Figure 4-8. The emulator running our application

Figure 4-9. The emulator showing a message box

Conclusion

That's it! Now that we know that we can build and run projects, we can start work on the Six Bookmarks application for Windows Phone 7.

CHAPTER 5

Windows Phone 7: Building the Logon Form and Consuming REST Services

At this point in the book, we've built the Six Bookmarks application to run natively on Android and iPhone and also built the generic web application. We're now going to look at building the Six Bookmarks application for Windows Phone 7. In this chapter, we'll build the logon form and the infrastructure for calling up to the web services. In the next chapter, we'll look at downloading the bookmarks over the OData service and storing them locally. In the third chapter of this section, we'll look at sending the changes back up over OData.

Creating the Project

To start with, we need to create the new project in Visual Studio 2010. We created a new Windows Phone Application project in the last chapter. We need to do this again and create a new project called AmxMobile.Phone7.SixBookmarks. Figure 5-1 illustrates.

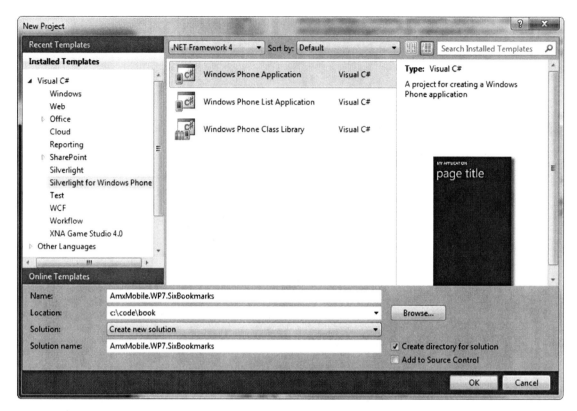

Figure 5-1. Creating the new project

Click OK, and the new project will be created. Solution Explorer will show MainPage.xaml as the main file for the project.

Before you progress, you will need to add a reference to the System.Xml.Linq.dll assembly to your project. In Solution Explorer, right-click References, select Add Reference, and add the assembly.

Building the Logon Form

We'll jump right in and create our new logon form. We want to keep our naming sensible, and "main page" doesn't tell us much about what our page actually does. First of all, delete MainPage.xaml from the solution, right-click the solution, and select Add – New Item. You will be met with a dialog presenting a *lot* of options—in the list on the right, select Silverlight for Windows Phones and then select Windows Phone Portrait Page from the resulting list. Call the new page LogonPage.xaml. Figure 5-2 illustrates.

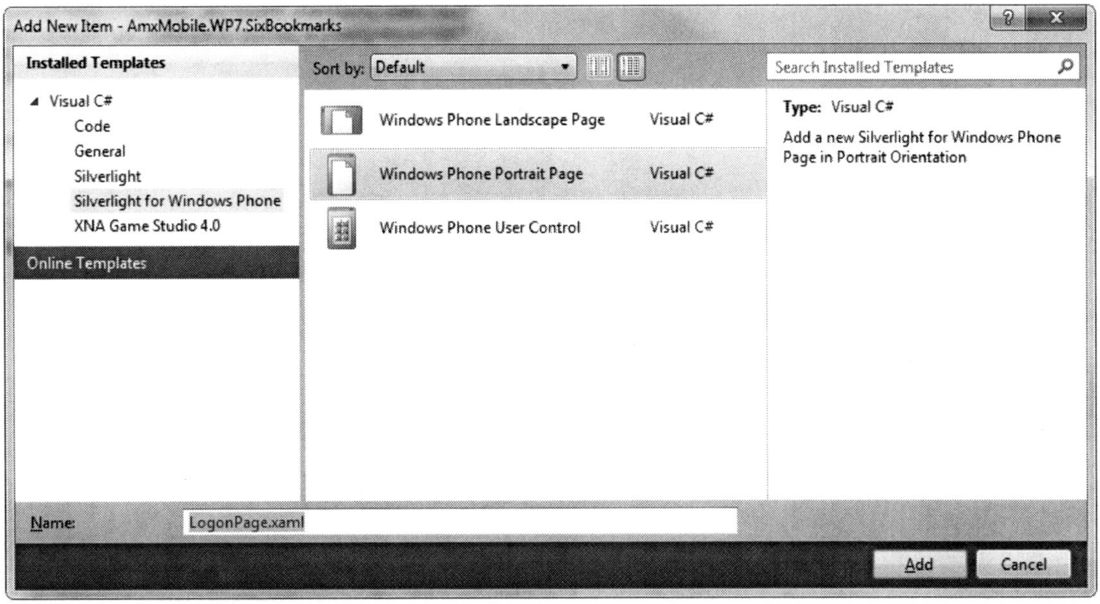

Figure 5-2. Adding a page to the project

Building the actual logon form is an issue of dragging controls onto the design surface from the toolbox. I won't go through in detail how you do this—it's likely that you've done it before. That said, a gotcha for me the first time I did this was that there is a separate control for capturing passwords (PasswordBox as opposed to TextBox). This should obviously be used for the control to capture the password.

Figure 5-3 illustrates the layout that we're looking for—and here's the listing for the XAML markup that makes up the page.

```
<phone:PhoneApplicationPage
    x:Class="AmxMobile.Phone7.SixBookmarks.LogonPage"
    xmlns="http://schemas.microsoft.com/winfx/2006/xaml/presentation"
    xmlns:x="http://schemas.microsoft.com/winfx/2006/xaml"
    xmlns:phone="clr-namespace:Microsoft.Phone.Controls;assembly=Microsoft.Phone"
    xmlns:shell="clr-namespace:Microsoft.Phone.Shell;assembly=Microsoft.Phone"
    xmlns:d="http://schemas.microsoft.com/expression/blend/2008"
    xmlns:mc="http://schemas.openxmlformats.org/markup-compatibility/2006"
    FontFamily="{StaticResource PhoneFontFamilyNormal}"
    FontSize="{StaticResource PhoneFontSizeNormal}"
    Foreground="{StaticResource PhoneForegroundBrush}"
    SupportedOrientations="Portrait" Orientation="Portrait"
    mc:Ignorable="d" d:DesignHeight="768" d:DesignWidth="480"
    shell:SystemTray.IsVisible="True">

    <!--LayoutRoot contains the root grid where all other page content is placed-->
    <Grid x:Name="LayoutRoot" Background="Transparent">
        <Grid.RowDefinitions>
```

```
            <RowDefinition Height="Auto"/>
            <RowDefinition Height="*"/>
        </Grid.RowDefinitions>

        <!--TitlePanel contains the name of the application and page title-->
        <StackPanel x:Name="TitlePanel" Grid.Row="0" Margin="24,24,0,12">
            <TextBlock x:Name="ApplicationTitle" Text="Six Bookmarks" Style="{StaticResource
PhoneTextNormalStyle}"/>
            <TextBlock x:Name="PageTitle" Text="Logon" Margin="-3,-8,0,0"
Style="{StaticResource PhoneTextTitle1Style}"/>
        </StackPanel>

        <!--ContentPanel - place additional content here-->
        <Grid x:Name="ContentGrid" Grid.Row="1">
            <TextBlock Margin="6,6,42,584" Name="textBlock1" Style="{StaticResource
PhoneTextNormalStyle}" Text="Username" />
            <TextBox Height="72" HorizontalAlignment="Left" Margin="0,28,0,0"
Name="textUsername" Text="" VerticalAlignment="Top" Width="480" />
            <TextBlock Margin="6,94,42,496" Name="textBlock2" Style="{StaticResource
PhoneTextNormalStyle}" Text="Password" />
            <PasswordBox Height="72" Margin="0,116,0,0" Name="textPassword"
VerticalAlignment="Top" />
            <CheckBox Content="Remember me" Height="72" HorizontalAlignment="Left"
Margin="0,180,0,0" Name="checkRememberMe" VerticalAlignment="Top" Width="480" IsChecked="True"
/>
            <Button Content="Logon" Height="72" HorizontalAlignment="Left" Margin="0,242,0,0"
Name="buttonLogon" VerticalAlignment="Top" Width="480" Click="buttonLogon_Click" />
        </Grid>
    </Grid>

</phone:PhoneApplicationPage>
```

Figure 5-3. *The design surface of the logon form*

Running the Logon Form

When the project was created, it was configured to boot the application using the `MainPage.xaml` page. We've created this, and so we need to reconfigure the application to boot using `LogonPage.xaml`. These settings are held in the `WMAppManifest.xml` file, which can be found in the `~/Properties` folder of the project. Open this file, and you will find an element with the path `Deployment/Task/DefaultTask`. You'll see `MainPage.xaml` in the `NavigationPage` attribute. Change this to `LogonPage.xaml`. Here's the revised configuration.

```
<Tasks>
  <DefaultTask  Name ="_default" NavigationPage="LogonPage.xaml"/>
</Tasks>
```

You can now run the project, and it will appear in the emulator. However, it won't do anything yet, as we have yet to code up any logic. Figure 5-4 illustrates.

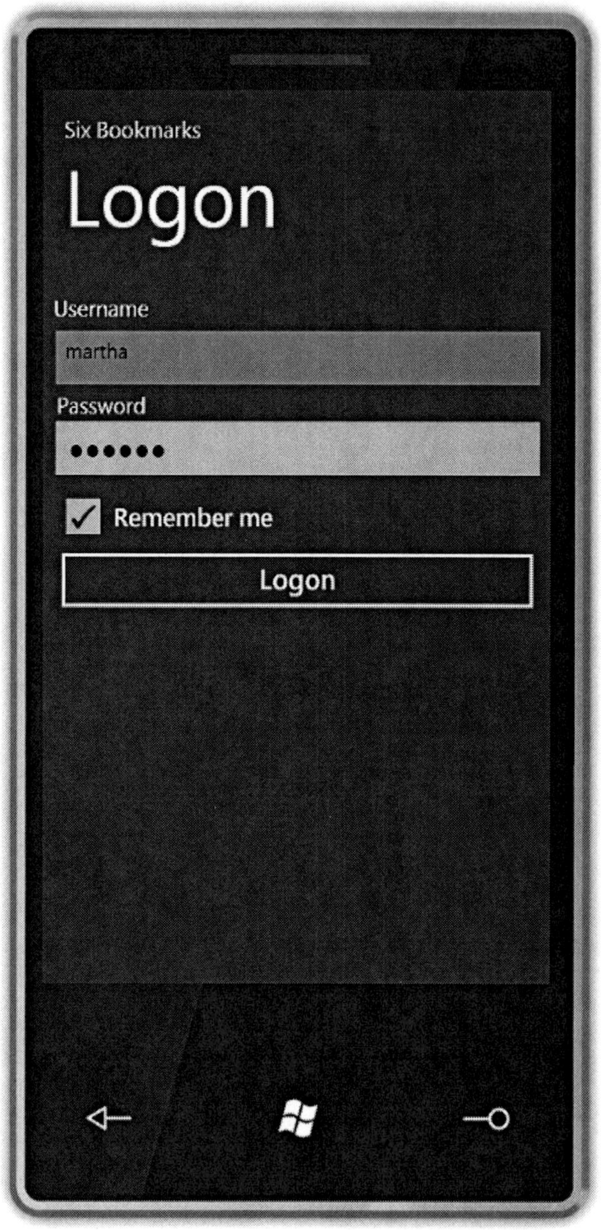

Figure 5-4. The logon screen running within the emulator

That was easy—as it should be—so now let's look at how we can call our services.

Calling the Services

We'll devote this first section to building the classes that can call up to our services. As discussed in the introduction to the chapter, we're interested only in authenticating against the API and logging in a user initially, and so, although we'll introduce all of the classes we'll build, we'll build only some of them here.

We need to create three service proxy classes that can communicate with each of the services at http://services.multimobiledevelopment.com/. Specifically we want to create ApiService, UsersService, and BookmarksService. As before, we'll need base classes for these, specifically ServiceProxy, RestServiceProxy, and ODataServiceProxy. Figure 5-5 illustrates.

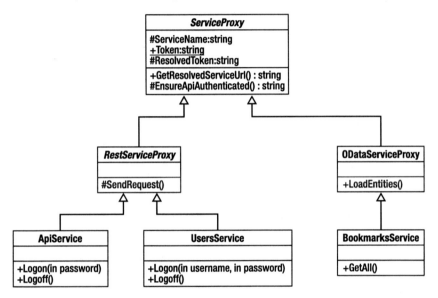

Figure 5-5. *UML static structure sketch of our service proxy classes*

The framework class that we're going to use to make the request is System.Net.HttpWebRequest, which has been part of .NET since version 1.0, has been on the .NET Compact Framework since .NET 1.0, and is also in the Silverlight for Windows Phone library. However, the version that is in the Silverlight library only supports asynchronous communications - blocking calls are not available.

As we've done before, we're going to create an HttpHelper class that can download HTTP resources for us using this library. HttpHelper will have two methods—one will request an HTTP resource and return a string. The second will request an HTTP resource and return a System.Xml.Linq.XDocument instance.

▨ **Note** Old-school Windows Mobile and desktop/server-side .NET developers will be more used to using the regular System.Xml.XmlDocument class. XmlDocument is not available on Windows Phone, and hence the only option to load a DOM object is to use the Linq API.

Before we build HttpHelper, we need a class that allows us to hold a list of headers that need to be added to any HTTP request. If you recall in Chapter 2, we discussed that to call into our services we needed to send up special x-amx-apiusername and x-amx-token HTTP headers. In previous chapters, we have built a class called DownloadSettings to do this, and we'll repeat this process here. Here's the implementation for DownloadSettings that needs to be added to the project:

```
using System;
using System.Collections.Generic;

namespace AmxMobile.Phone7.SixBookmarks
{
    public class DownloadSettings
    {
        public Dictionary<string, string> ExtraHeaders { get; private set; }

        public DownloadSettings()
        {
            this.ExtraHeaders = new Dictionary<string, string>();
        }
    }
}
```

We can now look at the implementation of the Download method on HttpHelper. This method uses regular practice for the System.Net.HttpWebRequest class to make the request, add any extra headers that we need, and then download any result.

Because the .NET HttpWebRequest class supports only asynchronous communication, we need to pass in delegates to the method that will be invoked on success or failure. The model I'm going to propose here is to use two callbacks—one for success and one for failure. This will allow us to use structured exception handling properly and pass back any exceptions that do occur to the caller in a safe and controlled manner. .NET provides a generic delegate called Action<T> that can be used to quickly scaffold up these kinds of callbacks. Using this in combination with anonymous methods makes for an arrangement whereby developing asynchronous code becomes actually quite rapid and natural. (Although I don't wish to lambast Objective-C, if Objective-C did have this sort of functionality, it would be hugely easier to write.)

We're going to use Action<T> as the default "success" delegate. For the default "failure" delegate, we're going to create a separate Failed delegate. The reasons will become apparent later, but for now add this type to your project in a separate file:

```
using System;

namespace AmxMobile.Phone7.SixBookmarks
{
    public delegate void Failed(Exception ex);
}
```

In a moment, we'll see the declaration of the HttpHelper class with the Download method in place. There are two things to note on this implementation. Firstly we designate a private method called HandleDownloadResult as the callback handler for the actual BeginGetResponse method call. We'll build this in a moment. Secondly, we pass an array of vanilla objects into the state for the callback. This allows us to pass the actual HttpWebRequest instance (which we need in order to unpack the asynchronous call at the other end) and the two callback delegates that we're provided. This isn't hugely natural or readable; however, it is highly practical. Another approach would be to create a specific class for passing the state around. My feeling on this is that it would lead to class bloat in the project and not really add anything, and thus I've gone with passing through an array. Here's the code:

```
using System;
using System.IO;
using System.Net;

namespace AmxMobile.Phone7.SixBookmarks
{
    public static class HttpHelper
    {
        public static void Download(string url, DownloadSettings settings, Action<string>
success, Action<Exception> failure)
        {
            // create the request stub...
            HttpWebRequest request = (HttpWebRequest)WebRequest.Create(url);

            // add...
            if (settings != null)
            {
                foreach (string name in settings.ExtraHeaders.Keys)
                    request.Headers[name] = settings.ExtraHeaders[name];
            }

            // call the server... we'll get notified at some point...
            request.BeginGetResponse(new AsyncCallback(HandleDownloadResult), new object[] {
request, success, failure });
        }
    }
}
```

The way that structured exception handling is done in these asynchronous framework methods is that if an exception occurs in the processing on the other thread, the exception is caught and rethrown at the point when the asynchronous call is "unpacked" when the "end" method is called. Thus we need to wrap the "end" method in a try…catch block and call out to our callback if necessary. Here's the code:

```
// Add method to HttpHelper…
        private static void HandleDownloadResult(IAsyncResult result)
        {
            // unpackage the state...
            object[] state = (object[])result.AsyncState;
            HttpWebRequest request = (HttpWebRequest)state[0];
            Action<string> success = (Action<string>)state[1];
            Failed failed = (Failed)state[2];

            // unwind...
            try
            {

                // get the response...
                HttpWebResponse response = (HttpWebResponse)request.EndGetResponse(result);
```

```
            using (Stream stream = response.GetResponseStream())
            {
                // read the html out...
                StreamReader reader = new StreamReader(stream);
                string html = reader.ReadToEnd();

                // callback the html...
                success(html);
            }
        }
        catch (WebException ex)
        {
            HandleDownloadException(request.RequestUri.ToString(), ex, failed);
        }
        catch (Exception ex)
        {
            // callback the error...
            failed(ex);
        }
    }
```

You'll notice there that we're specifically catching WebException and deferring to a yet-to-be-built method called HandleDownloadException. From experience, it's very helpful having a dump of the data that the server did send back for troubleshooting purposes. What HandleDownloadException will do is draw down the content from the server and package it in a new exception. It will then call the "failed" callback when complete. Here's the code:

```
// Add method to HttpHelper...
        private static void HandleDownloadException(string url, WebException ex, Failed
failed)
        {
            StringBuilder builder = new StringBuilder();
            builder.AppendFormat("Failed to download '{0}'.", url);
            builder.Append("\r\n");

            // do we have a response...
            if (ex.Response != null)
            {
                try
                {
                    Stream stream = ex.Response.GetResponseStream();
                    if (stream == null)
                        throw new InvalidOperationException("'stream' is null.");
                    using (stream)
                    {
                        builder.Append("Response data: ");

                        // reader...
                        using (StreamReader reader = new StreamReader(stream))
                            builder.Append(reader.ReadToEnd());
                    }
                }
```

```
            catch (Exception readEx)
            {
                builder.AppendFormat("An exception occurred when reading error data: " +
readEx.Message);
            }
        }
        else
            builder.Append("(No response)");

        // defer to the context...
        failed(new InvalidOperationException(builder.ToString(), ex));
    }
```

We've already got our form built, so we'll go back and wire up the logon button to call and test that so we're familiar with how the callbacks work.

Testing HttpHelper

Open the designer for the LogonPage.xaml file, and double-click the button. This will add an event handler for the click event on the button.

One of the peculiarities about .NET development on Windows Forms and Silverlight, both for desktop, Windows Mobile, and Windows Phones devices, is that you have to handle marshaling control between the thread that runs your asynchronous request and the thread that runs the controls. This has been a problem/feature of Windows since the very beginning. Windows is built on a message queuing system whereby the OS maintains a list of messages to send to windows that represent things like mouse movements, keypresses, and so on. The main thread in the process walks through this message queue and dispatches the message to the appropriate window. (A window in this context is any user interface object from an actual pop-up window down to a control.) Messages need to be pushed onto the queue from one thread and one thread only—if this rule is violated, horrible and nasty things happen.

The problem comes in that when an asynchronous method is completed, your callback is invoked on the worker thread, and thus if you want to interact with any controls, you need to marshal control back to the main thread first. In the very first version of .NET 1.0, there was no protection against this, but in .NET 1.1 protection was introduced such that an exception is thrown if the "no access from worker threads" rule is broken. This is actually very easy to do, but unless you get into the habit of it, you will forever be going back into and adding this marshaling code in when your application crashes. (Fortunately it is a very obvious crash, and you will typically shake them all down during debugging.)

In the other projects, we have created a MessageBox class to pop up an error. In .NET we already have a MessageBox class, and hence in this project we're going to build an Alert class that defers to MessageBox. We'll add two methods to this—one to show an arbitrary message string and one to show an exception.

In the Android chapter, we built an interface called IContextSource that could be used to pass around a reference to the Android application runtime. We're going to create an interface with the same name here, primarily to allow access to page objects without having to have a reference to the user interface. This is something I've added to illustrate best practice—we're not really going to take full advantage of it in this chapter. What I want to illustrate with this is loosely coupling the business and user interface tiers, especially in a world where we may well want to have device-agnostic, readily portable business tiers. The interface will provide access to an instance of System.Windows.Threading.Dispatcher. This class is the class that's used to marshal control back from worker threads to the main user interface thread, and hence it's a class that is extremely helpful to have around.

Here's the interface:

```
using System;
using System.Windows.Threading;

namespace AmxMobile.Phone7.SixBookmarks
{
    public interface IContextSource
    {
        Dispatcher Dispatcher
        {
            get;
        }
    }
}
```

For the Alert class, we need these two main methods. These will use the IContextSource to de-reference a Dispatcher instance and, if available, marshal control back to the main user interface thread. Otherwise we'll call MessageBox.Show directly and hope or assume that we're on the correct thread.

```
using System;
using System.Windows;
using System.Windows.Controls;

namespace AmxMobile.Phone7.SixBookmarks
{
    public static class Alert
    {
        private const string Caption = "Six Bookmarks";

        internal static void Show(object context, Exception ex)
        {
            if (ex == null)
                throw new ArgumentNullException("ex");

            // defer...
            Show(context, "An error occurred.", ex);
        }

        internal static void Show(object context, string message)
        {
            // defer...
            Show(context, message, null);
        }

        internal static void Show(object context, string message, Exception ex)
        {
            string toShow = message;
            if (ex != null)
                toShow = string.Concat(message, "\r\n", ex.ToString());

            // do we need to defer?
            if (context is Page)
            {
```

```
        ((Page)context).Dispatcher.BeginInvoke((Action)delegate()
        {
            MessageBox.Show(toShow, Caption, MessageBoxButton.OK);
        });
    }
    else
    {
        // show it, and hope we're on the right thread!
        MessageBox.Show(toShow, Caption, MessageBoxButton.OK);
    }
    }
  }
}
```

Recall that previously I said we would create a special `Failed` delegate and that the reason for this would become apparent. What we're going to do is add a helper function to `Alert` that creates a `Failed` delegate for us and is automatically rigged to show an error. Here's the code:

```
// Add method and private class to Alert...
    internal static Failed GetFailedHandler(IContextSource context)
    {
        // return...
        FailedHandler handler = new FailedHandler(context);
        return new Failed(handler.Failed);
    }

    private class FailedHandler
    {
        private IContextSource Context { get; set; }

        internal FailedHandler(IContextSource context)
        {
            this.Context = context;
        }

        internal void Failed(Exception ex)
        {
            Alert.Show(this.Context, "An error occurred.", ex);
        }
    }
```

We can run this all through by adding a handler to the button on `LogonPage`. If you open the designer and double-click the button, you can add an event handler. Add this code:

```
// Add method to LogonPage...
    private void buttonLogon_Click(object sender, RoutedEventArgs e)
    {
        HttpHelper.Download("http://www.google.co.uk/", new DownloadSettings(),
            delegate(string html)
            {
                Alert.Show(this, string.Format("Downloaded {0} bytes.", html.Length));
```

```
        }, Alert.GetFailedHandler(this));
    }
```

If you run the project and click the Logon button, you should see a successful result. Figure 5-6 illustrates.

Figure 5-6. A successful result!

This demonstrates that we can get an asynchronous HTTP request up to and back from the server and handle the result in the user interface. After a quick note about the MessageBox class, we'll look at making the operations more substantial.

Special Note on MessageBox

There is a rumor that MessageBox is going to be deprecated on Windows Phone. If you have problems compiling this, check out the support forums at http://forums.multimobiledevelopment.com/, because if there is a problem I will post a fix to that site.

It would not surprise me too much if it did. The behavior of the class is a little strange compared to the implementations on Android and iPhone. The Windows Phone implementation is modal, meaning that the application stops when a message box is shown waiting for input. The Android and iPhone implementations are not. This is relevant on a device that is primarily geared for asynchronous work. One of the problems of the way the Windows Phone implementation works is that if you marshal control from a worker thread to the UI thread like we have done, the worker thread is blocked and unable to do other work until the message box is cleared.

Building Out the API and User Service Proxies

We can go back to building our service classes now that we know the general principle of how we're going to make an HTTP request work.

Recall that the architecture of our Six Bookmarks services requires that we authenticate ourselves before we make any calls. Also recall that we have a "chicken and egg" situation in that we have to call up to the server to authenticate ourselves, but we need to be partly authenticated to do that. In the first instance, we need to make a call to the Logon operation of the API service, passing up a special HTTP header called x-amx-apiusername. This will return back a token that we store in global memory and pass up in x-amx-token in all future calls. To support this bit of functionality, we need to have ServiceProxy able to store the token in static memory, have it be able to build URLs, and also present the headers to anyone who needs them via a DownloadSettings instance. Here's the code:

```
using System;

namespace AmxMobile.Phone7.SixBookmarks
{
    public abstract class ServiceProxy
    {
        // YOU MUST CHANGE THESE VALUES IN ORDER TO USE THIS SAMPLE...
        internal const string ApiUsername = "amxmobile";
        internal const string ApiPassword = "password";

        private const string RootUrl = "http://services.multimobiledevelopment.com/services/";

        internal string ServiceName { get; private set; }
        internal static string Token { get; set; }

        protected ServiceProxy(string serviceName)
        {
            if (serviceName == null)
                throw new ArgumentNullException("serviceName");
            if (serviceName.Length == 0)
```

```
                    throw new ArgumentException("'serviceName' is zero-length.");

            // set...
            this.ServiceName = serviceName;
        }


        internal virtual bool IsAuthenticated
        {
            get
            {
                // we are not authenticated if we do not have a token...
                return !(string.IsNullOrEmpty(Token));
            }
        }

        public string ResolvedServiceUrl
        {
            get
            {
                return RootUrl + this.ServiceName;
            }
        }

        protected DownloadSettings GetDownloadSettings()
        {
            DownloadSettings settings = new DownloadSettings();
            settings.ExtraHeaders["x-amx-apiusername"] = ApiUsername;
            if (!(string.IsNullOrEmpty(Token)))
                settings.ExtraHeaders["x-amx-token"] = Token;

            // return...
            return settings;
        }
    }
}
```

In order to call the RESTful services, we need to build up URLs that have parameters specified in the query string. We'll therefore add a class called RestRequestArgs that can hold these parameters as a collection of name/value pairs and add a method to HttpHelper that can build a URL out of a collection of name/value pairs. Here's the code for RestRequestArgs:

```
using System;
using System.Collections.Generic;

namespace AmxMobile.Phone7.SixBookmarks
{
    internal class RestRequestArgs : Dictionary<string, string>
    {
        internal RestRequestArgs(string operation)
        {
            this["operation"] = operation;
```

```
        }
    }
}
```

And here's the method for HttpHelper that configures the query string of a URL with values from a name/value collection:

```
// Add method to HttpHelper…
        internal static string BuildUrl(string url, RestRequestArgs args)
        {
            StringBuilder builder = new StringBuilder();

            // remove the old query...
            int index = url.IndexOf("?");
            if(index != -1)
                builder.Append(url.Substring(0, index));
            else
                builder.Append(url);

            // add the arguments...
            if (args.Count > 0)
            {
                builder.Append("?");

                // params...
                bool first = true;
                foreach (string key in args.Keys)
                {
                    if (first)
                        first = false;
                    else
                        builder.Append("&");
                    builder.Append(key);
                    builder.Append("=");
                    builder.Append(HttpUtility.UrlEncode(args[key]));
                }
            }

            // return...
            return builder.ToString();
        }
```

RestServiceProxy will act as a base class for ApiService and UsersService. The class will have one method—SendRequest—that will call up to the server, download the XML, and check that the rules in the Six Bookmarks RESTful service protocol have been adhered to—specifically it will look to see if an exception has been sent back and raise an exception if it has.

The extra wrinkle to SendRequest is that if it detects that the API has not been authenticated it needs to go off and do that first. (For example, if we call Logon on the Users service, if Logon on the API service has not been called, it will automatically call the API service.) This is a little complicated because the service calls are asynchronous. If the API has not been authenticated, a new asynchronous call has to complete first *before* the original call can be made. Therefore we have to capture the arguments to the original call, hold them in memory until the API authentication call has completed, and then bring those original call arguments back and call the original operation as intended. This sounds ugly, but once you see it I hope you find that it's reasonably straightforward.

■ **Note** Again, this is really difficult to do neatly in Objective-C but much easier to do in C# because of the anonymous methods and delegates. I raise this point not to badmouth Objective-C but rather to illustrate the importance in bringing forward the toolset for iOS to make life easier for developers.

The code for `RestRequestProxy` is verbose, but it's hard to break down into smaller sections, and hence I will present it as a single chunk. Here's the overview:

- The `RestRequestProxy` class contains a private sub-class called `RequestState`. This holds the details of the original call. This will be used in situations where the API is not authenticated.

- `RequestState` has a method on it called `DoRequest`. This is the code that actually connects up to the server, downloads the XML, and processes it. If the call is successful, the "success" callback provided to `SendRequest` is invoked.

- On `SendRequest`, if the API is not authenticated, the `Authenticate` method on `ApiService` will be called, passing in a delegate to `RequestState.DoRequest`. Thus when the authenticate call is successful, the action of the "success" callback will be to invoke the original call.

- If the API has been authenticated when `SendRequest` is invoked, `DoRequest` is called directly.

- This code references a class called `XmlHelper`, which we'll build shortly. As background, this class simply extracts values from an XML document.

The upshot of the above is that we can divert of to do other setup operations without the original caller needing to be aware.

Here's the code:

```
using System;
using System.IO;
using System.Xml.Linq;
using System.Collections.Generic;

namespace AmxMobile.Phone7.SixBookmarks
{
    public abstract class RestServiceProxy : ServiceProxy
    {
        protected RestServiceProxy(string serviceName)
            : base(serviceName)
        {
        }
```

```
        internal void SendRequest(RestRequestArgs args, Action<XElement> success, Failed
failed)
        {
            // create a request state...
            RequestState state = new RequestState()
            {
                Owner = this,
                Args = args,
                Success = success,
                Failed = failed
            };

            // are we authenticated?  if we're not, we need to call that first...
            if (!(IsAuthenticated))
            {
                // call the authenticate routine, and ask it to call the state we just set up
                // if authentication works...
                ApiService.Authenticate(new Action(state.DoRequest), failed);
            }
            else
            {
                // call the method directly...
                state.DoRequest();
            }
        }

        private class RequestState
        {
            internal RestServiceProxy Owner { get; set; }
            internal RestRequestArgs Args { get; set; }
            internal Action<XElement> Success { get; set; }
            internal Failed Failed { get; set; }

            internal void DoRequest()
            {
                // get a url...
                string url = this.Owner.ResolvedServiceUrl;
                url = HttpHelper.BuildUrl(url, this.Args);

                // call download.  this is an async method, so we need to block...
                XDocument doc = null;
                HttpHelper.Download(url, this.Owner.GetDownloadSettings(), delegate(string
result)
                {
                    // we'll have some content - initialize XDocument and parse it...
                    using (TextReader reader = new StringReader(result))
                    {
                        doc = XDocument.Load(reader);
                        if (doc == null)
                            throw new InvalidOperationException("'doc' is null.");
                    }
```

```
                    // look for the response element...
                    var responseElements = new List<XElement>(doc.Descendants("AmxResponse"));
                    if (responseElements.Count == 0)
                        throw new InvalidOperationException("An AmxResponse element was not
returned.");

                    // select out "HasException"...
                    XElement responseElement = responseElements[0];
                    bool hasException = XmlHelper.GetElementBoolean(responseElement,
"HasException", true);
                    if (!(hasException))
                        this.Success(responseElement);
                    else
                    {
                        // get the error...
                        string message = XmlHelper.GetElementString(responseElement, "Error",
true);

                        throw new InvalidOperationException(string.Format("The server returned
an error: {0}.", message));
                    }

                }, this.Failed);
            }
        }
    }
}
```

To complete this work, we'll look at XmlHelper. The purpose of this class is to make working with the DOM-based XML a little easier. I've mentioned a few times now that I'm very keen on DOM-based XML manipulation; however, I'm the first to admit that the code is rather verbose, and so I tend to build helper classes to support the operation.

In the implementation, we'll see in this book that we'll add support for three data types—string, 32-bit integer, and Boolean. In a production implementation, you would need more data types supported; however, to keep the code down in the book, we'll keep it short. Here's an enumeration that defines the types:

```
using System;

namespace AmxMobile.Phone7.SixBookmarks
{
    public enum XmlDataType
    {
        String = 0,
        Int32 = 1,
        Boolean = 2
    }
}
```

For the actual XmlHelper implementation, we'll have one set of methods that find a child element given a name, and one set of methods that extract strongly typed values out of a given element. Here's the code:

```
using System;
using System.Xml.Linq;

namespace AmxMobile.Phone7.SixBookmarks
{
    public static class XmlHelper
    {
        public static string GetElementString(XElement element, string name, bool
throwIfNotFound)
        {
            return (string)GetElementValue(element, name, XmlDataType.String,
throwIfNotFound);
        }

        public static bool GetElementBoolean(XElement element, String name, bool
throwIfNotFound)
        {
                return (bool)GetElementValue(element, name, XmlDataType.Boolean,
throwIfNotFound);
            }

            public static int GetElementInt32(XElement element, String name, bool
throwIfNotFound)
            {
            return (int)GetElementValue(element, name, XmlDataType.Int32, throwIfNotFound);
            }

            private static Object GetElementValue(XElement element, String name, XmlDataType
dt, bool throwIfNotFound)
            {
                    // find it...
            XElement child = element.Element(name);
                    if(child != null)
                    {
                            if(dt == XmlDataType.String)
                                    return GetStringValue(child);
                            else if(dt == XmlDataType.Boolean)
                    return (bool)GetBooleanValue(child);
                            else if(dt == XmlDataType.Int32)
                    return (int)GetInt32Value(child);
                            else
                                    throw new Exception(string.Format("Cannot handle '{0}'.",
dt));
                    }
                    else
                    {
                            if(throwIfNotFound)
                                    throw new Exception(string.Format("An element with name
'{0}' was not found within an element with name '{1}'.", name, element.Name));
                            else
                                    return null;
                    }
```

```
        }

    public static String GetStringValue(XNode item)
        {
        if(item == null)
                throw new ArgumentNullException("item");

        if (item is XElement)
            return ((XElement)item).Value;
        else
            throw new Exception(string.Format("Cannot handle '{0}'.", item.GetType()));
        }

    public static int GetInt32Value(XNode item)
        {
                string asString = GetStringValue(item);
                return int.Parse(asString);
        }

    public static bool GetBooleanValue(XNode item)
        {
                string asString = GetStringValue(item);

        // check...
                if(asString == "0" || string.Compare(asString, "false",
StringComparison.InvariantCultureIgnoreCase) == 0)
                        return false;
            else if (asString == "1" || string.Compare(asString, "false",
StringComparison.InvariantCultureIgnoreCase) == 0)
                        return true;
                else
                        throw new Exception(string.Format("The value '{0}' could not be
recognised as valid Boolean value.", asString));
            }
        }
}
```

At this point, we're able to make a call to either of the RESTful services. Now we just have to call one.

Implementing the Authenticate Method

You may have noticed that the Authenticate method was called as a static method from within RestServiceProxy. What we're going to do is create an instance method on ApiService that calls the Logon operation and then have a static Authenticate method that acts as a wrapper.

The reason for this is to divide responsibility. We want Logon to be responsible just for communication with the server, and we want Authenticate to defer to Logon and interpret the result.

As we know, the actual logon operation runs asynchronously, and so when we call SendRequest we need to pass in two delegates. One will be an anonymous method that will do some processing with the result; the other will be a reference to the "failed" callback. Also, in this code, we'll use a to-be-built class called LogonResult that will interpret the result from the server and package it up. We'll reuse this class we call the UsersService later on.

Either of the two logon operations can return four results—OK, invalid username, invalid password, or account expired. We need an enumeration to represent these states—here it is:

```
using System;

namespace AmxMobile.Phone7.SixBookmarks
{
    public enum LogonResult
    {
        LogonOk = 0,
        InvalidUsername = 1,
        InvalidPassword = 2,
        UserInactive = 3
    }
}
```

The behavior of LogonResponse will be to look at the XML that comes back and package up properties to represent the result, any message that the server wishes to send, or any token that the server wishes to send. Here's the code:

```
using System;
using System.Xml.Linq;

namespace AmxMobile.Phone7.SixBookmarks
{
    public class LogonResponse
    {
        public LogonResult Result { get; private set; }
        public string Message { get; private set; }
        public string Token { get; private set; }

        internal LogonResponse(LogonResult result, string message, string token)
        {
            this.Result = result;
            this.Message = message;
            this.Token = token;
        }

        internal static LogonResponse FromXmlElement(XElement element)
        {
            if (element == null)
                throw new ArgumentNullException("element");

            // get the result...
            string asString = XmlHelper.GetElementString(element, "Result", true);
            LogonResult result = (LogonResult)Enum.Parse(typeof(LogonResult), asString, true);
            return new LogonResponse(result, XmlHelper.GetElementString(element, "Message",
false),
                XmlHelper.GetElementString(element, "Token", false));
        }
    }
}
```

Here's the implementation for ApiService with the Logon method in play. I've also overridden the operation of IsAuthenticated. This is very important—the base class will call Authenticate whenever it detects that the API has not been authenticated. We need to disable this function when calling up to the API service in order to set up the service.

```
using System;
using System.Xml.Linq;

namespace AmxMobile.Phone7.SixBookmarks
{
    public class ApiService : RestServiceProxy
    {
        public ApiService()
            : base("apirest.aspx")
        {
        }

        public void Logon(string password, Action<LogonResponse> result, Failed failed)
        {
            // create the request...
            RestRequestArgs args = new RestRequestArgs("logon");
            args["password"] = password;

            // send the request...
            this.SendRequest(args, (Action<XElement>)delegate(XElement element)
            {
                // walk...
                LogonResponse response = LogonResponse.FromXmlElement(element);
                if (response == null)
                    throw new InvalidOperationException("'response' is null.");

                // call...
                result(response);

            }, failed);
        }

        internal override bool IsAuthenticated
        {
            get
            {
                // make this return true, otherwise we'll get a stack overflow...
                return true;
            }
        }
    }
}
```

Within the Authenticate method, we need to look at the result from the server. If the logon operation was OK, we need to take the provided token and store it in the static Token property of ServiceProxy. This effectively puts the application into a state of "API authenticated," meaning that we don't need to call the Authenticate method for the duration of the application run. Here's the code:

```
// Add Authenticate method to ApiService.cs…
        internal static void Authenticate(Action callback, Failed failed)
        {
            ApiService service = new ApiService();
            service.Logon(ApiPassword, (Action<LogonResponse>)delegate(LogonResponse result)
            {
                // we have a result from *our* call to ApiService, if that works, call back to
the next
                // item in the chain...
                if (result.Result == LogonResult.LogonOk)
                {
                    // store the token in static memory...
                    Token = result.Token;

                    // call the caller...
                    callback();
                }
                else
                    throw new InvalidOperationException(string.Format("A response of '{0}' was
returned when authenticating the API.  Check that the the values of ApiUsername and
ApiPassword correspond to your unique API account.", result.Result));

            }, failed);
        }
```

Within the anonymous "success" method, you'll notice that we call the "success" callback that we were originally provided. This delegate will actually be a reference to the DoRequest method buried within the RestServiceProxy class. The upshot of this is that when the service layer has finished making its call to authenticate the API, the original call will be made. The chain then continues until the original caller has been satisfied.

To finish this piece of code off, we need to look at building the UsersService class. We'll do this next.

Making the Logon Button Work

We've already seen that the ApiService class makes its logon operation. The equivalent method on UsersService should hold no surprises. Here it is:

```
using System;
using System.Xml.Linq;

namespace AmxMobile.Phone7.SixBookmarks
{
    public class UsersService : RestServiceProxy
    {
        public UsersService()
            : base("usersrest.aspx")
        {
        }

        public void Logon(String username, String password, Action<LogonResponse> callback,
Failed failed)
```

```
        {
            // create the request...
            RestRequestArgs args = new RestRequestArgs("logon");

            // add the username and password...
            args["username"] = username;
            args["password"] = password;

            // send the request...
            SendRequest(args, delegate(XElement element)
            {
                // create a result from that...
                LogonResponse response = LogonResponse.FromXmlElement(element);
                if (response == null)
                    throw new InvalidOperationException("'response' is null.");

                // callback...
                callback(response);

            }, failed);
        }
    }
}
```

We can now call that method from the button handle on the logon form; however, the first thing we need to do is validate the user input. In previous chapters, we have built an "error bucket," and we're going to do the same thing here. This is going to be a very simple class—essentially just a generic collection of string instances with a couple of helper members. Here's the code:

```
using System;
using System.Text;
using System.Collections.Generic;

namespace AmxMobile.Phone7.SixBookmarks
{
    public class ErrorBucket : List<string>
    {
        public ErrorBucket()
        {
        }

        public bool HasErrors
        {
            get
            {
                if (this.Count > 0)
                    return true;
                else
                    return false;
            }
        }
```

```
        public string GetAllErrorsSeparatedByCrLf()
        {
            StringBuilder builder = new StringBuilder();
            foreach (string error in this)
            {
                if (builder.Length > 0)
                    builder.Append("\r\n");
                builder.Append(error);
            }

            // return...
            return builder.ToString();
        }
    }
}
```

The actual button handling code is now pretty easy. We get the username and password values off of the UI, and if validation is OK we create a new UsersService instance and call Logon. The result for us in this chapter will be to show a message box. In the next chapter, we'll go on and present the bookmarks as we had done previously.

Here's the code:

```
// Replace handle method in LogonPage.xaml.cs and add method…
        private void buttonLogon_Click(object sender, RoutedEventArgs e)
        {
                DoLogon();
        }

        private void DoLogon()
        {
            // validate...
            ErrorBucket bucket = new ErrorBucket();
            string username = this.textUsername.Text.Trim();
            if (string.IsNullOrEmpty(username))
                bucket.Add("Username is required.");
            string password = this.textPassword.Password.Trim();
            if(string.IsNullOrEmpty(password))
                bucket.Add("Password is required.");

            // error?
            if (bucket.HasErrors)
            {
                Alert.Show(this, bucket.GetAllErrorsSeparatedByCrLf());
                return;
            }

            // logon...
            UsersService users = new UsersService();
            users.Logon(username, password, delegate(LogonResponse response)
            {
                // we managed to get a response...
```

```
            if (response.Result == LogonResult.LogonOk)
    {
            // defer...
            LogonOk();
    }
            else
                Alert.Show(this, response.Message);

        }, Alert.GetFailedHandler(this));
    }

    private void LogonOk()
    {
            Alert.Show(this, "Logon OK.");
    }
```

You can now run the code and try to log on. Figure 5-7 shows a successful result.

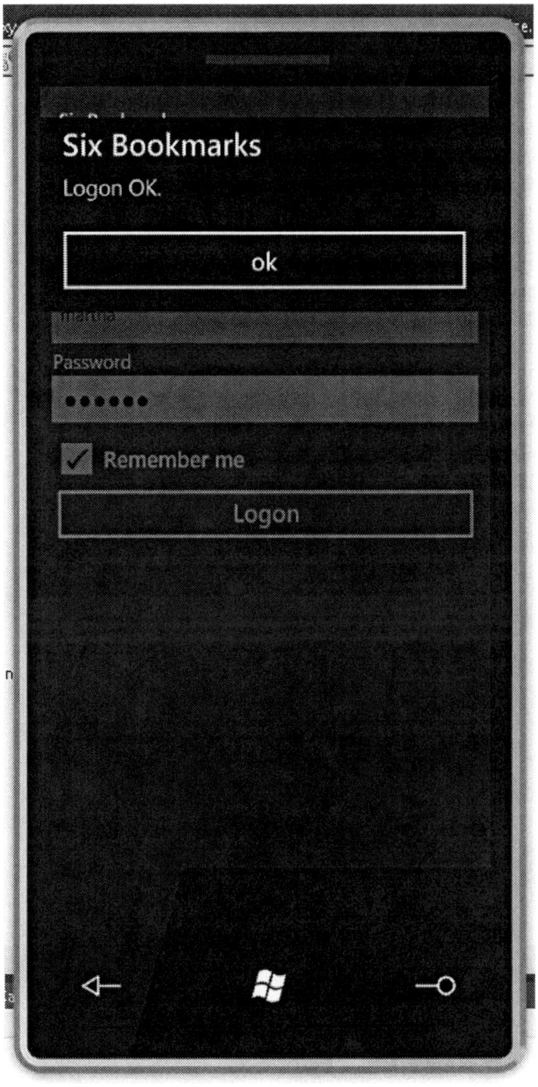

Figure 5-7. *Another sucessful result!*

Implementing "Remember Me"

The last feature to implement in this chapter is "remember me." This will store the user's username and password securely on the device.

On Android and iPhone, we have custom APIs for storing user settings. Perhaps oddly on WP7 we don't have this feature. I say "perhaps oddly" because we won't have this feature in the full-blown .NET Framework either. When solving this problem on the desktop, I have tended to create an XML file and store the values in there.

In the next two chapters, we're going to be looking quite intensively at working with XML files—as we've mentioned before, WP7 does not have a database and the only solution we have for storing data is to use files. To work with files, we need to use a .NET feature called "isolated storage." This feature has been around in .NET since version 1.0, but it's rarely used. Isolated storage was designed to support applications that downloaded .NET components over Internet Explorer and run in a special privilege mode that had limited access to the local disk. Isolated storage makes sense in the context of a phone because we do want to make sure that our applications are nicely isolated away from other apps that may be running.

In this section, we're going to build a class called SimpleXmlPropertyBag. I've named this class after a commonly used class in BootFX—simply, all it does is maintain a list of values and read and write them from an XML file. (The BootFX implementation can handle any type of data; the one that we're going to build works only with strings.) We will use the bag to store the user's username and password if the "remember me" option is checked.

The SimpleXmlPropertyBag class will hold a property containing the path that it was stored in. (In isolated storage, the path of the file is relative to the root of the store, which is then mapped to a "magic" folder on disk. On WP7 this magic folder is named for the unique ID of the application.)

Here's the basic implementation of SimpleXmlPropertyBag that sets the base class to be a generic dictionary and accepts a file path through the constructor:

```
using System;
using System.Collections.Generic;
using System.IO;
using System.IO.IsolatedStorage;
using System.Xml.Linq;

namespace AmxMobile.Phone7.SixBookmarks
{
    public class SimpleXmlPropertyBag : Dictionary<string, string>
    {
        private string Path { get; set; }

        internal SimpleXmlPropertyBag(string path)
        {
            if (path == null)
                throw new ArgumentNullException("path");
            if (path.Length == 0)
                throw new ArgumentException("'path' is zero-length.");

            // set...
            this.Path = path;
        }
    }
}
```

To create an XML document, we use the XDocument class again. By adding a method called ToXmlDocument to SimpleXmlPropertyBag, we can turn the values into XML at any point. Here's the implementation:

```
// Add method to SimpleXmlPropertyBag…
        private XDocument ToXmlDocument()
        {
```

```
        XDocument doc = new XDocument();

        // root...
        XElement root = new XElement("Root");
        doc.Add(root);

        // items...
        foreach (string key in this.Keys)
        {
            // create a child element...
            XElement element = new XElement(key);
            root.Add(element);

            // set...
            element.SetValue(this[key]);
        }

        // return...
        return doc;
    }
```

Once we have an XML document containing the values, we can save them to disk using the path that we captured when the class was instantiated. Here's the code for the Save method:

```
// Add method to SimpleXmlPropertyBag...
        public void Save()
        {
            IsolatedStorageFile store = IsolatedStorageFile.GetUserStoreForApplication();

            // get a document...
            XDocument doc = this.ToXmlDocument();

            // open a stream and recreate the file...
            if (store.FileExists(this.Path))
                store.DeleteFile(this.Path);
            using (Stream stream = store.OpenFile(this.Path, FileMode.Create,
FileAccess.Write))
                    doc.Save(stream);
        }
```

The Load method takes a parameter that indicates whether we should ignore missing files. If we're not ignoring files, we'll create a blank one. (The motivation for this will become apparent shortly.) If we do load a file, we'll walk the elements within the document and recreate the property bag to the state that it was in immediately prior to it being saved. Here's the code:

```
// Add method to SimpleXmlPropertyBag...
        internal static SimpleXmlPropertyBag Load(string path, bool throwIfNotFound)
        {
            IsolatedStorageFile store = IsolatedStorageFile.GetUserStoreForApplication();

            // does the file exist?
            if (store.FileExists(path))
```

```
        {
            // load it...
            XDocument doc = null;
            using(Stream stream = store.OpenFile(path, FileMode.Open, FileAccess.Read))
                doc = XDocument.Load(stream);

            // find the root...
            XElement root = doc.Element("Root");
            if(root == null)
                    throw new InvalidOperationException("'root' is null.");

            // load...
            SimpleXmlPropertyBag bag = new SimpleXmlPropertyBag(path);
            foreach(XElement element in root.Elements())
                bag[element.Name.LocalName] = element.Value;

            // return...
            return bag;
        }
        else
        {
            if(throwIfNotFound)
                throw new InvalidOperationException(string.Format("A file at '{0}' was not
found.", path));
            else
            {
                // return a new one...
                return new SimpleXmlPropertyBag(path);
            }
        }
    }
}
```

At the moment, we have an object that is able to save and load its settings at will. What we need is a globally available bag that can be used to store all user settings. We'll do this by creating a class called SixBookmarksRuntime that will persist for the life of the application. A property on this—Settings—will hold a SimpleXmlPropertyBag instance representing the user settings. We'll build SixBookmarksRuntime as a singleton class. Here's the code:

```
using System;

namespace AmxMobile.Phone7.SixBookmarks
{
    public class SixBookmarksRuntime
    {
        /// <summary>
            /// Private field to hold singleton instance.
            /// </summary>
            private static SixBookmarksRuntime _current = new SixBookmarksRuntime();

            // settings...
        public SimpleXmlPropertyBag Settings { get; private set; }
```

```
        /// <summary>
        /// Private constructor.
        /// </summary>
        private SixBookmarksRuntime()
        {
    // settings...
    this.Settings = SimpleXmlPropertyBag.Load("Settings.xml", false);
        }

        /// <summary>
        /// Gets the singleton instance of <see
cref="SixBookmarksRuntime">SixBookmarksRuntime</see>.
        /// </summary>
        internal static SixBookmarksRuntime Current
        {
            get
            {
                if(_current == null)
                        throw new
ObjectDisposedException("SixBookmarksRuntime");
                return _current;
            }
        }
    }
}
```

We'll use SixBookmarksRuntime a little more in the next chapter.

We can now change the behavior of the logon page so that it understands how to use the property bag exposed through Settings to save and load user options. (Although we've had to do a reasonable amount of work here, this is basically what iPhone and Android are doing with their custom user settings buckets.)

To LogonPage we'll add a new method called LogonOk. In the next chapter, when we start building the synchronization class, we'll shim in a call to LogonOk to kick off the sync operation. However, for now we'll just set the credentials if needed. As a wrinkle to this, we need to marshal control back to the main user interface thread, as our callback telling us that the logon operation has been successful will come in on a worker thread. We'll also add a method to clear the credentials. Here's the code:

```
// Replace LogonOk method and add ClearCredentials method to LogonPage...
        private void LogonOk()
        {
            // flip back - we're not on the right thread...
            this.Dispatcher.BeginInvoke(delegate()
            {
                // save...
                if (this.checkRememberMe.IsChecked.Value)
                {
                    SimpleXmlPropertyBag settings = SixBookmarksRuntime.Current.Settings;
                    settings[UsernameKey] = this.textUsername.Text.Trim();
                    settings[PasswordKey] = this.textPassword.Password.Trim();
                    settings.Save();
                }
                else
```

```
            this.ClearCredentials();

        // do sync will come here...

        // show...
        Alert.Show(this, "Logon (still) OK.");

    });
}

private void ClearCredentials()
{
    // set...
    SimpleXmlPropertyBag settings = SixBookmarksRuntime.Current.Settings;
    if (settings.ContainsKey(UsernameKey))
        settings.Remove(UsernameKey);
    if (settings.ContainsKey(PasswordKey))
        settings.Remove(PasswordKey);

    // save...
    settings.Save();
}
```

And that's it! If you run the application, you'll find that it remembers your credentials.

Conclusion

In this chapter, we've built the foundations of our Six Bookmarks application by creating classes that can communicate with our RESTful API and Users services and also capture and validate input to a form on the device. In the next chapter, we'll look at how we can store a persistent set of bookmarks on the device.

CHAPTER 6

■ ■ ■

Windows Phone 7: Persisting Bookmarks Locally

As I've mentioned several times now, as of the time of writing, there is no relational database available for third-party apps on Windows Phone 7. There is, in fact, an implementation of the SQL CE database on the devices, but this is locked down so that it is available only to Microsoft applications, notably the Office Hub applications available on the device. One can only assume that SQL CE will become available again given time. This would be a definite good thing—Microsoft has a proven track record in building synchronization frameworks that work between its full-on SQL Server database and devices. It would be nice to have this back again on its mobile devices. Over time we'll probably see close integration with its Azure cloud services.

All this means that this chapter is a bit of an oddball because it's the only one in the book in which we're not using a database at all, let alone SQLite, which features prominently on the other platforms.

■ **Note** Although I hope this chapter is of interest even when a full-on SQL database is available on Windows Phone 7, it's my intention to update this chapter online. Check the content on www.multimobiledevelopment.com/ for more information.

Approach

The approach we're going to take in this chapter is to store individual entities in individual files within a folder in isolated storage. We'll be reproducing the same entity-based scheme, including the metadata subsystem. We'll also have a `SqlFilter` class, although, unlike the name implies, this won't work with SQL statements. My rationale for doing this is that we want to aim for consistency across the different code bases wherever possible.

Entities

In Chapter 3, we looked at the structure of the entity model and its associated metadata subsystem, and we built an implementation on Android and iOS. In this section, we'll repeat this work in C# for Windows Phone 7. This code will more or less work unchanged on Windows Mobile, and also in the Mono implementations on Android and iOS. More importantly, it will also work if you do move over to a proper relational database.

The EntityType Class

The purpose of the EntityType class is to bundle together all of the information that you need in order to build code that can "magically" manipulate the underlying store and user interface depending on the structure of the data. In our case, instances of EntityType classes are going to group fields together, plus static memory on EntityType itself will hold a list of entity types. (But in this example we're going to have only one entity type.)

Each entity type will have two names—a programmatic name and a native name. Having separate values for the names makes it possible to smooth out other problems with the underlying store. For example, you may have a database table called TBL_CUST that you would like to refer to as Customer in code. In this case, TBL_CUST would be the native name, and Customer would be the programmatic name.

To this end, we'll create a class called EntityItem that will act as a base class for things that we want to store using the metadata system. Here's the code:

```
using System;

namespace AmxMobile.Phone7.SixBookmarks
{
    public abstract class EntityItem
    {
        public string Name { get; private set; }
        public string NativeName { get; private set; }

        protected EntityItem(string name, string nativeName)
        {
            this.Name = name;
            this.NativeName = nativeName;
        }
    }
}
```

We'll look at the fields first. Each field will store the following information:

- A native name and programmatic name

- A data type

- A size

- In this chapter, we're going to have only one, which indicates whether the field is a key field. In a full-on implementation, another example of a flag would be indicating whether the field could be nullable.

In this example, we're going to support just two data types; in a more full-on implementation, we'd obviously need to support all of the data types that the underlying database supports. (If we implement all of them now, half the book will be taken up with methods exposing out all of the data types.) Our server-side service used only strings and 32-bit integers, so we will need these, plus a Boolean type that we'll use on fields that are held locally and not on the server. Here's the SBDataType enumeration that we need to support those three types:

```
using System;

namespace AmxMobile.Phone7.SixBookmarks
{
    public enum DataType
    {
        String = 0,
        Int32 = 1,
        Boolean = 2
    }
}
```

Now that we have the enumeration, we can build `EntityField`. As well as supporting native name, name, data type, size, and an indication as to whether the field is a key, we'll have another property holding the ordinal of the field within the type. Here's the code:

```
using System;

namespace AmxMobile.Phone7.SixBookmarks
{
    public class EntityField : EntityItem
    {
        public DataType Type { get; private set; }
        public int Size { get; private set; }
        public int Ordinal { get; private set; }
        public bool IsKey { get; set; }

        internal EntityField(string name, string nativeName, DataType type, int size, int
ordinal)
            : base(name, nativeName)
        {
            this.Type = type;
            this.Size = size;
            this.Ordinal = ordinal;
        }
    }
}
```

One other thing we need `EntityField` to be able to do is return a default value for the given type. We need this in order to support the insert operation. We'll talk more about this at that time—for now, here's the `DefaultValue` property:

```
// Add property to EntityField…
        public object DefaultValue
        {
            get
            {
                if (this.Type == DataType.Int32)
                    return 0;
                else if (this.Type == DataType.String)
                    return null;
                else if (this.Type == DataType.Boolean)
```

```
                    return false;
                else
                    throw new NotSupportedException(string.Format("Cannot handle '{0}'.",
this.Type));
            }
        }
```

So that we can effectively work with entities, we need `EntityType` to be able to instantiate instances of individual entities and collections of entities. In this example, we're going to have only one entity—Bookmark. In any real-world application, you're likely to have many entity types. This will be done by holding references to the relevant .NET types. Our motivation for doing this is so that we can say to framework code "give me a list of bookmarks" and the framework code itself will be able to create an appropriate collection type and individual entities. (Of all the platforms that we've seen in this book, the reflection subsystem in .NET is far and away the best.)

In addition, we're going to add a method to `EntityType` called `AddField`. This will be used to programmatically define the fields available on an entity type. Here's the code:

```
using System;
using System.Collections.Generic;

namespace AmxMobile.Phone7.SixBookmarks
{
    public class EntityType : EntityItem
    {
        public List<EntityField> Fields { get; private set; }
        public Type InstanceType { get; private set; }

        public EntityType(Type instanceType, string nativeName)
            : base(instanceType.Name, nativeName)
        {
            // set...
            this.Fields = new List<EntityField>();
            this.InstanceType = instanceType;
        }

        public EntityField AddField(string name, string nativeName, DataType type, int size)
        {
            EntityField field = new EntityField(name, nativeName, type, size,
this.Fields.Count);
            this.Fields.Add(field);

            // return...
            return field;
        }
    }
}
```

An important part of the code there is that when we add a field using the `AddField` method, we need to assign each field a unique ordinal. By passing in the length of the array as the ordinal, we effectively do that.

Next we can look some of the other methods on `EntityType`. We're going to need to be able to find a field with a specific name, find the key field, or determine whether a field with a specified name actually exists. (This latter one is used for populating entities from data received over XML where the XML may reference fields that we don't know about.) Here are the three methods that also need to be added to `EntityType`:

```
// Add methods to EntityType...
        public EntityField GetField(String name, bool throwIfNotFound)
        {
                foreach(EntityField field in Fields)
                {
                        if(string.Compare(field.Name, name,
StringComparison.InvariantCultureIgnoreCase) == 0)
                                return field;
                }

                // throw...
                if(throwIfNotFound)
                        throw new Exception(string.Format("Failed to find a field with
name '{0}'.", name));
                else
                        return null;
        }

    public EntityField GetKeyField()
    {
        foreach (EntityField field in this.Fields)
        {
            if (field.IsKey)
                return field;
        }

        // nope...
        throw new InvalidOperationException("Failed to find a key field.");
    }

    public bool IsField(string name)
    {
        EntityField field = this.GetField(name, false);
        if (field != null)
            return true;
        else
            return false;
    }
```

Recall that the other function `EntityType` needs is the ability to hold a register of the available entity types. We'll do this by creating a static hashtable on `EntityType` and methods called `RegisterEntityType` and `GetEntityType`.

```
// Add static field and methods to EntityType...
        private static Dictionary<Type, EntityType> EntityTypes { get; set; }
```

```
static EntityType()
{
    EntityTypes = new Dictionary<Type, EntityType>();
}

public static void RegisterEntityType(EntityType entityType)
{
    EntityTypes[entityType.InstanceType] = entityType;
}

public static EntityType GetEntityType(Type type)
{
    if (EntityTypes.ContainsKey(type))
        return EntityTypes[type];
    else
        throw new Exception(string.Format("Failed to get entity type for '{0}'.",
type));
}
```

We can now use this class to create and store entity types. Let's look now at building the Entity base class.

The Entity Class

The basic functionality of an entity is to store a dynamic list of data that represents the columns in the underlying database table. An entity will be created either manually by the developer or by framework code that retrieves the data from some source. (In our application, the source of data is going to be either the local files on disk or the Bookmarks data service at http://services.multimobiledevelopment.com/.) At some point during the entity's life, the data stored within will either be read for display on a screen, or be used to issue some sort of change request to the underlying store.

In our entity, we are going to hold three sets of values. Firstly we're going to store a reference to our related EntityType instance. Secondly we're going to store an array of values that map 1:1 with the data in the underlying store. Thirdly and finally, we're going to store a bunch of flags that help the entity keep track of its internal state.

Storage of data within the entity will be done in "slots." You will notice on our EntityField instance we have a property called Ordinal. This ordinal value is the index of the slot in the entity. Thus if we have five fields, we'll have five slots numbered from zero to four inclusive.

■ **Note** Recall in Chapter 3 we spoke about the BootFX application framework and its ORM functionality. Internally within BootFX, this functionality is known as "storage."

To manage the lifetimes of values stored within the new Entity class, we need to create an enumeration that indicates the status of the slots. We'll call this enumeration EntityFieldFlags, and it needs to be defined prior to building Entity. Here's the listing:

```
using System;

namespace AmxMobile.Phone7.SixBookmarks
{
    [Flags()]
    public enum FieldFlags
    {
        NotLoaded = 0,
        Loaded = 1,
        Modified = 2
    }
}
```

Next we'll look at the definition for the basic "storage" capability of Entity. The first thing we do is capture the entity type in the constructor. We'll need this later to allow all of the methods on the base class to reflect against the metadata. The second thing that we do is create two arrays—one to hold the values of the slots, the other to hold the flags. Here's the code:

```
using System;

namespace AmxMobile.Phone7.SixBookmarks
{
    public abstract class Entity
    {
        public EntityType EntityType { get; private set; }
        private object[] _values { get; set; }
        private FieldFlags[] _flags { get; set; }
        public bool IsDeleted { get; private set; }

        protected Entity()
        {
            // get the entity type...
            this.EntityType = EntityType.GetEntityType(this.GetType());
            if (this.EntityType == null)
                throw new InvalidOperationException("'this.EntityType' is null.");

            // create the slots...
            _values = new object[this.EntityType.Fields.Count];
            _flags = new FieldFlags[this.EntityType.Fields.Count];
        }
    }
}
```

We'll now look at making our entity do something interesting.

Setting Values in an Entity

Whenever we set a value within an entity, we'll be doing one of two things—we'll be plugging in either a value that the user has provided through some form of input, or a value that we have retrieved from a database or service. It's important that we can distinguish between these two operations—if the user has changed something, we may need to update the underlying store with that value. Conversely, if the user has not changed something, we do not want to be issuing unnecessary update requests back to the underlying store.

To keep track of which operation we intend when we set a value, we'll create an enumeration called SetReason. Here's the code:

```
using System;

namespace AmxMobile.Phone7.SixBookmarks
{
    public enum SetReason
    {
        UserSet = 0,
        Load = 1
    }
}
```

As we add methods to the entity, we'll find that oftentimes we need to add overloads for each of the methods that take either the name of a field as a string or an actual instance of an EntityField class. This is going to create additional code, but there is a substantially higher level of utility in not requiring the caller to dig out an EntityField instance every time the caller wishes to access field data. Whenever one of the string-based "name" overloads is used, we'll defer to the EntityType for the field name. Here's a collection of methods that allow values to be set:

```
// Add methods to Entity…
        protected void SetValue(String name, Object value, SetReason reason)
            {
                    EntityField field = EntityType.GetField(name, true);
                    SetValue(field, value, reason);
            }

        public void SetValue(EntityField field, Object value, SetReason reason)
            {
                    int ordinal = field.Ordinal;
                    SetValue(ordinal, value, reason);
            }

        private void SetValue(int ordinal, Object value, SetReason reason)
            {
                    _values[ordinal] = value;

                    // if...
                    SetFlag(ordinal, FieldFlags.Loaded);
                    if(reason == SetReason.UserSet)
                SetFlag(ordinal, FieldFlags.Modified);
            }

        private void SetFlag(int ordinal, FieldFlags flag)
            {
                    _flags[ordinal] = _flags[ordinal] | flag;
            }
```

The function of SetValue is twofold. Firstly, it sets the value in the Values array to be the value passed in. Secondly, it sets the value in the Flags to indicate the state of the field. Regardless of the value of the reason parameter, it will indicate that the field has been loaded. If the value of reason indicates that the user changed a value, the field is marked as having been modified.

Retrieving the values is—oddly—a little trickier. In the first instance, we need to be able to behave differently depending on the state of the data. For example, if we're trying to retrieve the value for a field and we have not loaded it, we need to throw an error indicating that the value is not available. (Some implementations, including BootFX, will demand load data in this situation. However, for simplicity, we're not doing this here.)

Before we do that, we'll add a few methods that will help us understand whether fields have been loaded or modified, or whether the entity as a whole is new. We'll need these later on. Here's the implementation:

```
// Add methods to Entity…
        public bool IsNew
        {
        get
        {
            EntityField key = EntityType.GetKeyField();

            // state...
            if (!(IsLoaded(key)) && !(IsLoaded(key)))
                return true;
            else
                return false;
        }
        }

        public bool IsModified()
        {
        for (int index = 0; index < _flags.Length; index++)
        {
            if (IsModified(index))
                return true;
        }

        // nope...
        return false;
        }

        public bool IsLoaded(EntityField field)
        {
        return IsLoaded(field.Ordinal);
        }

    private bool IsLoaded(int index)
        {
                return IsFlagSet(index, FieldFlags.Loaded);
        }

        public bool IsModified(EntityField field)
```

```
        {
        return IsModified(field.Ordinal);
        }

    private bool IsModified(int index)
        {
                return IsFlagSet(index, FieldFlags.Modified);
        }

    private bool IsFlagSet(int index, FieldFlags flag)
        {
                if((_flags[index] & flag) == flag)
                        return true;
                else
                        return false;
        }

    public void MarkForDeletion()
    {
    // set the flag to indicate that we want to delete on the next save…
        this.IsDeleted = true;
    }
```

Those methods lay the groundwork for the GetValue method that we implied must exist when we created our SetValue earlier. One implementation point is that we have to add a rule whereby if we're not new and we don't have it, we have to throw an error as we can't demand-load the value. This is called "demand-loading." It's common enough in ORM tools, but to keep things simple, I have chosen not to implement it here. (Plus, seeing as we're not using a database at the moment on WP7, there's no mileage in not loading the whole entity in memory.)

We've touched a few times on this idea that we have deliberately limited data type support in this application to keep the code simple. We're about to see an example—there's quite a lot of code here to support just the few data types that we do support. Here's the code:

```
    public Object GetValue(String name)
        {
                EntityField field = EntityType.GetField(name, true);
                return GetValue(field.Ordinal);
        }

    public Object GetValue(EntityField field)
        {
                return GetValue(field.Ordinal);
        }

    private Object GetValue(int index)
        {
                // do we need to demand load?
                if(!(IsLoaded(index)) && !(this.IsNew))
                        throw new Exception("Demand loading is not implemented.");

                // return...
```

```
        return _values[index];
}

public String GetStringValue(String name)
{
        EntityField field = EntityType.GetField(name, true);
        return GetStringValue(field);
}

public String GetStringValue(EntityField field)
{
        Object value = GetValue(field);
        if(value != null)
                return value.ToString();
        else
                return null;
}

public int GetInt32Value(String name)
{
        EntityField field = EntityType.GetField(name, true);
        return GetInt32Value(field);
}

public int GetInt32Value(EntityField field)
{
        Object value = GetValue(field);
if (value == null)
    return 0;
else if (value is Int32)
    return (int)value;
else
    throw new Exception(string.Format("Cannot handle '%s'.", value.GetType()));
}

public bool GetBooleanValue(String name)
{
        EntityField field = EntityType.GetField(name, true);
        return GetBooleanValue(field);
}

public bool GetBooleanValue(EntityField field)
{
        Object value = GetValue(field);
        if(value == null)
                return false;
    else if (value is bool)
            return (bool)value;
        else if(value is int)
        {
                int asInt = (int)value;
                if(asInt == 0)
```

```
                                              return false;
                              else
                                              return true;
                      }
                      else
                              throw new Exception(string.Format("Cannot handle '{0}'.",
value.GetType())));
                      }
```

Now that we can get data into and out of our base entity, let's look at creating a strongly typed Bookmark class.

Building Bookmark

The point of ORM is that you're looking to get the entity layer to do most of the hard work of managing the data for you—i.e., it's easier to call a property called Name and know you're getting a string value back than it is to request an item with the name "name" out of a bucket of values returned over a SQL interface. Thus we need to add a bunch of properties to Bookmark that abstract calls to GetValue and SetValue.

Before we do that, though, there's one thing to consider. As discussed in Chapter 2, the database stores against each bookmark an internal ID, the user ID, the name, the URL, and ordinal values. In our database, in order to support the synchronization functionality that we'll build in the next chapter, we also need to store flags to indicate whether the item has been modified or deleted locally. We'll add IsLocalModified and IsLocalDeleted to achieve this.

Here's the definition of Bookmark:

```
using System;

namespace AmxMobile.Phone7.SixBookmarks
{
    public class Bookmark : Entity
    {
        public const String BookmarkIdKey = "BookmarkId";
        public const String OrdinalKey = "Ordinal";
        public const String NameKey = "Name";
        public const String UrlKey = "Url";
        public const string IsLocalModifiedKey = "IsLocalModified";
        public const string IsLocalDeletedKey = "IsLocalDeleted";

        public Bookmark()
        {
        }

        public int BookmarkId
        {
            get
            {
                return this.GetInt32Value(BookmarkIdKey);
            }
            set
            {
```

```csharp
            this.SetValue(BookmarkIdKey, value, SetReason.UserSet);
    }
}

public string Name
{
    get
    {
        return this.GetStringValue(NameKey);
    }
    set
    {
        this.SetValue(NameKey, value, SetReason.UserSet);
    }
}

public string Url
{
    get
    {
        return this.GetStringValue(UrlKey);
    }
    set
    {
        this.SetValue(UrlKey, value, SetReason.UserSet);
    }
}

public int Ordinal
{
    get
    {
        return this.GetInt32Value(OrdinalKey);
    }
    set
    {
        this.SetValue(OrdinalKey, value, SetReason.UserSet);
    }
}

public bool IsLocalModified
{
    get
    {
        return this.GetBooleanValue(IsLocalModifiedKey);
    }
    set
    {
        this.SetValue(IsLocalModifiedKey, value, SetReason.UserSet);
    }
}
```

```
    public bool IsLocalDeleted
    {
        get
        {
            return this.GetBooleanValue(IsLocalDeletedKey);
        }
        set
        {
            this.SetValue(IsLocalDeletedKey, value, SetReason.UserSet);
        }
    }
}
}
```

As well as the singleton entity, we'll create a strongly typed collection. (I'm always a fan of building strongly typed collections when building entities, as it makes building a strong API on your business tier easier.) Here's the code:

```
using System;
using System.Collections.Generic;

namespace AmxMobile.Phone7.SixBookmarks
{
    public class List<Bookmark> : List<Bookmark>
    {
    }
}
```

When we built our `EntityType` class previously, we missed a couple of methods—specifically ones that would dynamically create singleton entity instances and collections. Here's the code to add to `EntityType`:

```
    internal Entity CreateInstance()
    {
        return (Entity)Activator.CreateInstance(this.InstanceType);
    }
```

Creating SBEntityType Instances

Before we can create instances of `Bookmark` and use them, we need to be able to create an instance of `EntityType` that supports it. In more sophisticated ORM layers, it's commonplace to build the metadata up from some sort of decoration in the code (this is very easy to do using attributes in .NET). In this implementation, we're going to add code to the `SixBookmarksRuntime` that we built in the last chapter and have it register the entity type on start. Here's the code to the constructor of `SixBookmarksRuntime`:

```
// Add code to SixBookmarksRuntime…
        private SixBookmarksRuntime()
        {
        // settings...
        this.Settings = SimpleXmlPropertyBag.Load("Settings.xml", false);
```

```
            // register the entity type...
            EntityType bookmark = new EntityType(typeof(Bookmark), "Bookmark");
            bookmark.AddField(Bookmark.BookmarkIdKey, Bookmark.BookmarkIdKey,
DataType.Int32, -1).IsKey = true;
            bookmark.AddField(Bookmark.NameKey, Bookmark.NameKey, DataType.String, 128);
            bookmark.AddField(Bookmark.UrlKey, Bookmark.UrlKey, DataType.String, 128);
            bookmark.AddField(Bookmark.OrdinalKey, Bookmark.OrdinalKey, DataType.Int32, -
1);
            bookmark.AddField(Bookmark.IsLocalModifiedKey, Bookmark.IsLocalModifiedKey,
DataType.Boolean, -1);
            bookmark.AddField(Bookmark.IsLocalDeletedKey, Bookmark.IsLocalModifiedKey,
DataType.Boolean, -1);
            EntityType.RegisterEntityType(bookmark);
                }
```

We're essentially done here—we can now move on to creating some fake bookmarks and showing them on the device.

Displaying Some Fake Bookmarks

To keep us going until we have real data on the device, we'll display some fake bookmarks on the screen. To do this, we'll need a form that in previous incarnations of the application we have called the "navigator."

Note The name "navigator" is a little unfortunate in Silverlight, as Silverlight has a thing called a "navigation service" that is used to move the user around features of the application, and hence we have a little bit of a naming collision. However, as you know by now, to me the most important thing is consistency across the applications, and hence we'll keep the name "navigator."

To the project, add a new Windows Phone Portrait Page called NavigatorPage.xaml. We'll add nine buttons to the form, one for each of the six buttons and one for each of the three options—configure, logoff, and about. These can be dragged and dropped onto the design surface in the usual way. For each of the buttons, change the Content value as per Figure 6-1, and set the Name properties to be buttonNavigate1, buttonNavigate2, etc., buttonConfigure, buttonLogoff, and buttonAbout.

Figure 6-1. The design surface for the Navigation page

Here's the XAML that creates this view:

```
<navigation:PhoneApplicationPage
    x:Class="AmxMobile.Phone7.SixBookmarks.NavigatorPage"
    xmlns="http://schemas.microsoft.com/winfx/2006/xaml/presentation"
    xmlns:x="http://schemas.microsoft.com/winfx/2006/xaml"
    xmlns:navigation="clr-
namespace:Microsoft.Phone.Controls;assembly=Microsoft.Phone.Controls.Navigation"
    xmlns:d="http://schemas.microsoft.com/expression/blend/2008"
    xmlns:mc="http://schemas.openxmlformats.org/markup-compatibility/2006"
    SupportedOrientations="Portrait"
    mc:Ignorable="d" Loaded="PhoneApplicationPage_Loaded" d:DesignHeight="800"
d:DesignWidth="480">
```

```xml
<Grid x:Name="LayoutRoot" Background="{StaticResource PhoneBackgroundBrush}">
    <Grid.RowDefinitions>
        <RowDefinition Height="170"/>
        <RowDefinition Height="*"/>
    </Grid.RowDefinitions>

    <!--This is the name of the application and page title-->
    <Grid Grid.Row="0" x:Name="TitleGrid">
        <TextBlock x:Name="ApplicationName" Text="Six Bookmarks" Style="{StaticResource
PhoneTextPageTitle1Style}"/>
        <TextBlock x:Name="ListName" Text="Bookmarks" Style="{StaticResource
PhoneTextPageTitle2Style}"/>
    </Grid>

    <!--This section is empty. Place new content here Grid.Row="1"-->
    <Grid Grid.Row="1" x:Name="ContentGrid">
        <Button Content="..." Height="70" HorizontalAlignment="Left"
Name="buttonNavigate1" VerticalAlignment="Top" Width="480" />
        <Button Content="..." Height="70" HorizontalAlignment="Left" Margin="0,59,0,0"
Name="buttonNavigate2" VerticalAlignment="Top" Width="480" />
        <Button Content="..." Height="70" HorizontalAlignment="Left" Margin="0,116,0,0"
Name="buttonNavigate3" VerticalAlignment="Top" Width="480" />
        <Button Content="..." Height="70" HorizontalAlignment="Left" Margin="0,174,0,0"
Name="buttonNavigate4" VerticalAlignment="Top" Width="480" />
        <Button Content="..." Height="70" HorizontalAlignment="Left" Margin="0,231,0,0"
Name="buttonNavigate5" VerticalAlignment="Top" Width="480" />
        <Button Content="..." Height="70" HorizontalAlignment="Left" Margin="0,289,0,0"
Name="buttonNavigate6" VerticalAlignment="Top" Width="480" />
        <Button Content="Configure" Height="70" HorizontalAlignment="Left"
Margin="0,383,0,0" Name="buttonConfigure" VerticalAlignment="Top" Width="480" />
        <Button Content="Logoff" Height="70" HorizontalAlignment="Left" Margin="0,441,0,0"
Name="buttonLogoff" VerticalAlignment="Top" Width="480" />
        <Button Content="About" Height="70" HorizontalAlignment="Left" Margin="0,500,0,0"
Name="buttonAbout" VerticalAlignment="Top" Width="480" />
    </Grid>
</Grid>
</navigation:PhoneApplicationPage>
```

This gets as far as having a view that we can actually show. What we need to do now is create our set of fake bookmarks and update the view.

Creating Fake Bookmarks

Creating the fake bookmarks is very straightforward—we just need to create instances of the Bookmark class that we built earlier and populate the properties accordingly.

To add a little finesse, we'll add a static method to Bookmark called GetBookmarksForDisplay. This will make more sense in the next chapter, but for now what we're looking to do is provide a mechanism whereby we can "soft-delete" bookmarks from the local data store by marking them as deleted. The real implementation of GetBookmarksForDisplay will return a list of bookmarks that are *not* soft-deleted. For now, here's the implementation that returns the fakes:

```
// Add method to Bookmark...
        internal static List<Bookmark> GetBookmarksForDisplay()
        {
            List<Bookmark> results = new List<Bookmark>();

            // add...
            Bookmark bookmark = new Bookmark();
            bookmark.Name = ".NET 247";
            bookmark.Url = "http://www.dotnet247.com/";
            bookmark.Ordinal = 0;
            results.Add(bookmark);

            // again...
            bookmark = new Bookmark();
            bookmark.Name = "Apress";
            bookmark.Url = "http://www.apress.com/";
            bookmark.Ordinal = 1;
            results.Add(bookmark);

            // return...
            return results;
        }
```

Showing and Populating the View

To use the bookmarks, we need to firstly modify the logon form so that it launches the navigator form, and we also need to implement a page load handler on the navigator form so that it displays the buttons. We do the logon form changes first.

As I alluded to earlier, Silverlight uses an approach of exposing out a class that provides navigation services to the application as a whole, which in this context means providing access to different views. These are done via URIs. In order to move from the logon form to the navigator form, we need to construct a URI for the navigator form and ask the Silverlight navigation service to show it. This is actually pretty straightforward—as the forms are in the root of the project, we create a URI relative to the root of the application that specifies the name of the .xaml file that drives the form. Here's the code that shows the change to the LogonOk method in the LogonPage class:

```
// Modify LogonOk method on LogonPage...
        private void LogonOk()
        {
            // flip back - we're not on the right thread...
            this.Dispatcher.BeginInvoke(delegate()
            {
                // save...
                if (this.checkRememberMe.IsChecked.Value)
                {
                    SimpleXmlPropertyBag settings = SixBookmarksRuntime.Current.Settings;
                    settings[UsernameKey] = this.textUsername.Text.Trim();
                    settings[PasswordKey] = this.textPassword.Password.Trim();
                    settings.Save();
                }
                else
```

```
                this.ClearCredentials();

            // do sync will come here...

            // ask the navigation service to show the form...
            NavigationService.Navigate(new Uri("/NavigatorPage.xaml",
UriKind.RelativeOrAbsolute));
        });
    }
```

Those are all the changes that we need to make to the logon form.

Going back to the navigator form, in the designer, double-click the white background of the design surface. This will add a Loaded event handler, like this one:

```
// This is added by the designer when you double-click the background of the design surface…
    private void PhoneApplicationPage_Loaded(object sender, RoutedEventArgs e)
    {
    }
```

The approach we'll take on this form is that we'll create a property called Bookmarks that will hold a List<Bookmark>. When this property is set, we will refresh the view. This will involve going through each of the six buttons and resetting them to a "not set" state, which in our case will mean returning them to having an ellipsis ("…") for their text. For each bookmark that we do have, we'll find the appropriate button and set the text to be the name. Here's the code to be added to NavigatorPage.

```
// Modify Loaded handler, add field, properties and methods on NavigatorPage…
    private List<Bookmark> _bookmarks = null;

    private void PhoneApplicationPage_Loaded(object sender, RoutedEventArgs e)
    {
        // get a list of bookmarks and bind it...
        this.Bookmarks = Bookmark.GetBookmarksForDisplay();
    }

    private List<Bookmark> Bookmarks
    {
        get
        {
            return _bookmarks;
        }
        set
        {
            _bookmarks = value;
            this.RefreshView();
        }
    }

    private void RefreshView()
    {
        // reset...
        for (int index = 0; index < 5; index++)
            ResetButton(index);
```

```csharp
    // configure...
    foreach (Bookmark bookmark in this.Bookmarks)
        ConfigureBookmark(bookmark);
}

private void ConfigureBookmark(Bookmark bookmark)
{
    if (bookmark == null)
        throw new ArgumentNullException("bookmark");

    // get...
    Button button = this.GetButton(bookmark.Ordinal);
    if (button == null)
        throw new InvalidOperationException("'button' is null.");

    // set it...
    button.Content = bookmark.Name;
}

private void ResetButton(int ordinal)
{
    Button button = this.GetButton(ordinal);
    button.Content = "...";
}

private Button GetButton(int ordinal)
{
    if (ordinal == 0)
        return this.buttonNavigate1;
    else if (ordinal == 1)
        return this.buttonNavigate2;
    else if (ordinal == 2)
        return this.buttonNavigate3;
    else if (ordinal == 3)
        return this.buttonNavigate4;
    else if (ordinal == 4)
        return this.buttonNavigate5;
    else if (ordinal == 5)
        return this.buttonNavigate6;
    else
        throw new NotSupportedException(string.Format("Cannot handle '{0}'.",
ordinal));
    }
```

■ **Note** You'll notice that the code to return the button given an ordinal (GetButton) is kinda clunky (if you've read along during the iOS and Android implementations, you'll notice something similar). There are slicker ways to handle a set of controls that operate in a similar fashion, but my view on the code for this book was that this was easier to follow than something slicker.

You can now run the code and log on. Figure 6-2 shows you what to expect.

Figure 6-2. The Navigation form running and displaying fake bookmarks

Implementing Button Clicks

Those of you familiar with .NET and a particular product in its ancestry called Visual Basic will know that when you double-click a button on a design surface, it will give you a handler method for that button. This is the case with the toolset we're using now. However, we want to create just a single handler method for the navigation buttons. One way to do this is to change the XAML for all six buttons with the name of the handler that we want and double-click one of the buttons to create an appropriate handler in code.

The XAML is changed by adding a Click attribute. This snippet of the XAML from the designer shows the method reference in place:

```
<!--markup removed for brevity… -->
        <Button Content="..." Height="70" HorizontalAlignment="Left"
Name="buttonNavigate1" VerticalAlignment="Top" Width="480" Click="buttonNavigate_Click" />
        <Button Content="..." Height="70" HorizontalAlignment="Left" Margin="0,59,0,0"
Name="buttonNavigate2" VerticalAlignment="Top" Width="480" Click="buttonNavigate_Click" />
        <Button Content="..." Height="70" HorizontalAlignment="Left" Margin="0,116,0,0"
Name="buttonNavigate3" VerticalAlignment="Top" Width="480" Click="buttonNavigate_Click" />
        <Button Content="..." Height="70" HorizontalAlignment="Left" Margin="0,174,0,0"
Name="buttonNavigate4" VerticalAlignment="Top" Width="480" Click="buttonNavigate_Click" />
        <Button Content="..." Height="70" HorizontalAlignment="Left" Margin="0,231,0,0"
Name="buttonNavigate5" VerticalAlignment="Top" Width="480" Click="buttonNavigate_Click" />
        <Button Content="..." Height="70" HorizontalAlignment="Left" Margin="0,289,0,0"
Name="buttonNavigate6" VerticalAlignment="Top" Width="480" Click="buttonNavigate_Click" />
<!--markup removed for brevity… -->
```

If you double-click one of these buttons, you will get a method handler stub. Here's the listing for the stub. This code goes back into the Bookmarks property and extracts the bookmark with the matching ordinal. (Again the code to de-reference the button could be slicker—I'm biased toward ease of reading.)

```
// Add methods to NavigatorPage…
    private void buttonNavigate_Click(object sender, RoutedEventArgs e)
    {
        int ordinal = GetOrdinalForButton((Button)sender);

        // find it...
        Bookmark bookmark = GetBookmarkForOrdinal(ordinal);
        if (bookmark != null)
            SixBookmarksRuntime.Current.ShowUrl(bookmark.Url);
        else
            HandleConfigure();
    }

    private int GetOrdinalForButton(Button button)
    {
        if (button == buttonNavigate1)
            return 0;
        else if (button == buttonNavigate2)
            return 1;
        else if (button == buttonNavigate3)
            return 2;
        else if (button == buttonNavigate4)
```

```
            return 3;
        else if (button == buttonNavigate5)
            return 4;
        else if (button == buttonNavigate6)
            return 5;
        else
            throw new NotSupportedException(string.Format("Cannot handle '{0}'.",
button.Name));
    }

    private Bookmark GetBookmarkForOrdinal(int ordinal)
    {
        foreach (Bookmark bookmark in this.Bookmarks)
        {
            if (bookmark.Ordinal == ordinal)
                return bookmark;
        }

        // return...
        return null;
    }

    private void HandleConfigure()
    {
        Alert.Show("TBD.");
    }
```

You'll notice that the way we open a web resource is to defer to a to-be-built method on SixBookmarksRuntime called ShowUrl. Here's what this method this looks like:

```
// Add method to SixBookmarksRuntime…
    internal void ShowUrl(string url)
    {
        WebBrowserTask task = new WebBrowserTask();
        task.URL = url;
        task.Show();
    }
```

This method, as you can see, uses the WebBrowserTask class. The operation of this class is to open the instance of Internet Explorer installed on the phone.

If you run the application and click one of the links, IE will launch and show the page. Figure 6-3 illustrates.

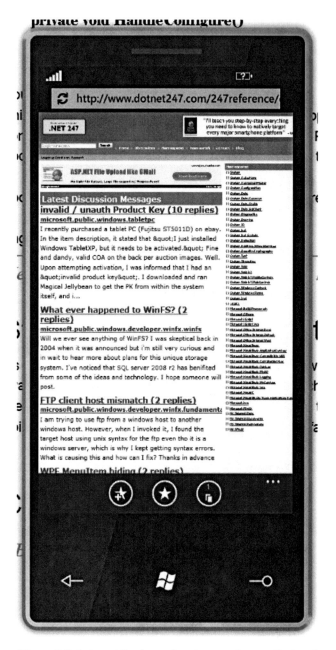

Figure 6-3. Internet Explorer showing a web page that we have navigated to

Tombstoning—A Brief Word

At this point, it's worth introducing the idea of "tombstoning." Windows Phone 7 has a feature whereby rather than having proper multitasking, when you switch to a new application (as we have done by opening the web browser), your application is dumped out of memory. Should you click the phone's back button, your application will be brought back to life. The only wrinkle with this is that you are the one responsible for saving and restoring your application's global state when this happens. Windows Phone 7 is unique in this regard—none of the other phones works in this way.

I personally think this is a neat idea—it keeps memory usage and processor cycles on the device down to a minimum. What I don't think is neat is that you have to manage this yourself (i.e., you have to open a file of some kind and dump your static data into it)! You would think that in the OS design they would have built in a mechanism for serializing the application state down to the disk itself.

But I digress—for now, we're not going to look at tombstoning, but we will come back to it toward the end of the chapter. We're going to use the ORM subsystem to store data, and we can't do that until we've been through getting the ORM system working.

Storing Entities in the Data Box

As you know by now, as of the time of writing, a database management system is not available for Windows Phone 7, and, as such, we need to store our entities on disk. In the rest of this chapter, we'll examine how to do this by storing entities into what I'm going to call a "data box." (This isn't a fabulous name, but it will do!)

We've already seen in the last chapter how we can use .NET's isolated storage feature to store files on disk. We'll use this feature again as part of our data box.

The design that we're going to aim for is one whereby we will create exactly one XML file per entity and we'll use the ID of the entity as the file name. When we create a data box, we'll give it an entity type, and it will use this entity type as part of the name of the folder. So, if we want to store a bookmark with ID 27, it would have a path like this:

```
~/Entities/Bookmark/27.xml
```

One complication with this arrangement is that we cannot rely on the store to manage the IDs for us. (With SQLite, or any relational DBMS we have an "autonumbering" scheme that manages the IDs of values as we put them into the store.)

Finally, as mentioned before, we'll build the SQL filter and change processor implementations as we have done on the other implementations with a proper SQL database.

Data Box Basics

The basics of a data box are a class with a property that holds a reference to an entity type and another that holds a reference to a folder. As mentioned before, we'll be using isolated storage for this. I'm also proposing creating a folder underneath a root Entities folder—this is analogous to a table. In our case, it makes it easier to get all the entities of a given type in a single hit. Here's the code:

```
using System;
using System.IO;
using System.IO.IsolatedStorage;
using System.Xml.Linq;
```

```
namespace AmxMobile.Phone7.SixBookmarks
{
    internal class DataBox
    {
        public EntityType EntityType { get; private set; }
        internal string FolderName { get; private set; }

        internal DataBox(EntityType et)
        {
            this.EntityType = et;

            // create a folder...
            IsolatedStorageFile store = GetStore();
            this.FolderName = "Entities/" + et.NativeName;
            if (!(store.DirectoryExists(FolderName)))
                store.CreateDirectory(FolderName);
        }

        internal IsolatedStorageFile GetStore()
        {
            return IsolatedStorageFile.GetUserStoreForApplication();
        }
    }
}
```

The first things we'll look at are methods to insert and update entities. These are actually the same operation—if we're doing an insert, we do not have a file to insert into, and if we're doing an update, we have an existing file that we wish to overwrite.

In both cases, we need to be able to transform the ID of an entity of a known type into a full file path within isolated storage. This is one example where the metadata system pays dividends. We can ask the entity type to return the key value for a given entity. We can then use this in the file name. Here's a method called GetFilePath that, when given an entity, de-references the ID and transforms it into a file name:

```
// Add method to DataBox...
        private string GetFilePath(Entity entity)
        {
            return string.Format("{0}/{1}.xml", this.FolderName,
entity.GetValue(EntityType.GetKeyField()));
        }
```

This means that we can now take a bookmark entity with an ID of, say, 27 and turn it into a file path, such as ~/Entities/Bookmark/27.xml.

If we need to insert an entity, we need to obtain the next ID in the set. As alluded to earlier, if we were using a proper relational database management system (RDBMS) to do this, we could ask it to retrieve an ID from its internal table. We don't have as much luck—what we need to do is ask isolated storage to return a list of file names to us. We can then walk these file names and look for the largest ID. The result of GetNextId would be this largest ID value plus one. Here's the code:

```
        private int GetNextId()
        {
```

```
        IsolatedStorageFile store = this.GetStore();
        int max = 0;
        foreach (string path in store.GetFileNames(this.FolderName + "/*.*"))
        {
            string filename =
System.IO.Path.GetFileNameWithoutExtension(System.IO.Path.GetFileName(path));
            int id = int.Parse(filename);
            if (id > max)
                max = id;
        }

        // return...
        return max + 1;
    }
```

As a thought on this method, this is fine if you don't mind potentially repeating IDs. For example, if you had bookmark 27 and asked for the next ID, you would get 28. If you created 28.xml and deleted it, if you called GetNextId again, the largest ID would be 27, and hence you be given 28 again. This almost certainly works OK for our method here, but this behavior does not mimic that of a regular database, which, without explicit instruction, will not return the same ID twice.

As just mentioned, Insert and Update are pretty similar. Insert will retrieve an ID value and set that ID value into the entity before deferring to Update. (This process ensures not only that the ID is written to the internals of the file, but also that Entity.IsNew will return false after SaveChanges is called.) The Update method will obtain a file path and then save the entity via SaveEntity. (We'll build SaveEntity shortly.)

There is one special thing that Insert has to do that Update does not. When we write an entity to disk for the first time, we need to make sure that all of the fields are populated. If we don't do this, if we later rely on a field being there (for example, we want to select out entities by constraining on the field's values), we'll get an error. Therefore, after we have set the ID, we loop through all of the fields and find any not marked as modified. If we find any that are not modified, we set the value of the field to be the default value for that field type. (Recall that when we built EntityField field, we added the DefaultValue property.)

Here's the code:

```
// Add methods to DataBox…
        internal void Insert(Entity entity)
        {
            // get an ID by walking files...
            int id = GetNextId();

            // set the id into the entity...
            entity.SetValue(this.EntityType.GetKeyField(), id, SetReason.UserSet);

            // when we create an entity, all of the values have to be set as "modified"
otherwise we get
            // a problem when reading them back...
            foreach (EntityField field in entity.EntityType.Fields)
            {
                if (!(entity.IsModified(field)))
                {
                    object defaultValue = field.DefaultValue;
```

```
                    entity.SetValue(field, defaultValue, SetReason.UserSet);
            }
        }

        // ...and then update it, because that operation is basically just a save...
        Update(entity);
    }

    internal void Update(Entity entity)
    {
        // get the filename...
        string path = GetFilePath(entity);

        // save it...
        SaveEntity(entity, path);
    }
```

The operation of SaveEntity will be to call a method called EntityToXml, which will return back to us an XDocument instance. After we have the XML, we save it by asking isolated storage to give us a file stream. The operation of EntityToXml is straightforward—it uses the metadata on the entity type to enumerate the fields and simply dumps the entity's current value for that field to the XML document. Here's the code:

```
// Add methods to DataBox...
    private void SaveEntity(Entity entity, string path)
    {
        // create a document...
        XDocument doc = EntityToXml(entity);

        // save the file...
        IsolatedStorageFile store = this.GetStore();
        using (IsolatedStorageFileStream stream = store.CreateFile(path))
            doc.Save(stream);
    }

    private XDocument EntityToXml(Entity entity)
    {
        // save...
        XDocument doc = new XDocument();
        XElement root = new XElement(EntityType.NativeName);
        doc.Add(root);

        // walk the fields...
        foreach (EntityField field in EntityType.Fields)
        {
            XElement element = new XElement(field.NativeName);
            root.Add(element);

            // get...
            object value = entity.GetValue(field);
            if (value != null)
```

```
                element.Value = value.ToString();
        }

        // return...
        return doc;
    }
```

For completeness, we'll also build the Delete method. Here's the code:

```
    internal void Delete(Entity entity)
    {
        string path = this.GetFilePath(entity);

        // delete...
        IsolatedStorageFile store = this.GetStore();
        if(store.FileExists(path))
            store.DeleteFile(path);
    }
```

Creating the Entity Change Processor

In this section, we're going to build the change processor. However, the approach I'm going to propose is to build it so that we can swap out the data box implementation for a proper RDBMS implementation at a future point. To do this, we'll build a strategy class that knows how to work with data boxes and a base class that is strategy-agnostic. When the time comes, we can create a new strategy class for the database.

Here's the implementation for the base class. All it needs to do is look at the state of the entity and decide whether to insert, update, delete, or take no action.

```
using System;

namespace AmxMobile.Phone7.SixBookmarks
{
    internal abstract class EntityChangeProcessor
    {
        public EntityType EntityType { get; private set; }

        protected EntityChangeProcessor(EntityType et)
        {
            if (et == null)
                throw new ArgumentNullException("et");
            this.EntityType = et;
        }

        internal void SaveChanges(Entity entity)
        {
            if (entity == null)
                throw new ArgumentNullException("entity");

            // new?
            if (entity.IsNew)
                Insert(entity);
            else if (entity.IsModified())
```

```
                    Update(entity);
                else if (entity.IsDeleted)
                    Delete(entity);
        }

        internal abstract void Insert(Entity entity);

        internal abstract void Update(Entity entity);

        internal abstract void Delete(Entity entity);
    }
}
```

You may notice that on the EntityChangeProcessor class we have Insert, Update, and Delete methods. What we'll do is implement a DataBoxEntityChangeProcessor class that defers to an instance of a DataBox. Here's the implementation:

```
using System;

namespace AmxMobile.Phone7.SixBookmarks
{
    internal class DataBoxEntityChangeProcessor : EntityChangeProcessor
    {
        private DataBox DataBox { get; set; }

        internal DataBoxEntityChangeProcessor(EntityType et)
            : base(et)
        {
            this.DataBox = new DataBox(et);
        }

        internal override void Insert(Entity entity)
        {
            // defer...
            this.DataBox.Insert(entity);
        }

        internal override void Update(Entity entity)
        {
            // defer...
            this.DataBox.Update(entity);
        }

        internal override void Delete(Entity entity)
        {
            // defer...
            this.DataBox.Delete(entity);
        }
    }
}
```

All that remains now is to add a SaveChanges method to Entity. We'll hard-code the DataBoxEntityChangeProcessor instantiation in here. In a more sophisticated implementation, we would look at this being a factory method of some sort, but for our purposes here, this is fine. Here's the code:

```
public void SaveChanges()
{
    DataBoxEntityChangeProcessor processor = new
DataBoxEntityChangeProcessor(this.EntityType);
        processor.SaveChanges(this);
}
```

Now that we can write entities onto disk, we'll look at building our Sync class. In this chapter, we'll implement this so that it will download bookmarks from the OData service. In the next chapter, we'll modify this implementation so that we can transmit changes back.

Building the Sync Class

The Sync class will be the provider of the functionality to our application that downloads bookmarks from the server and pushes changes back again. We'll call it when we log on, and we'll also call it in the next chapter in response to the user actually changing bookmarks.

If you've followed along during the Android and iOS implementations, you'll know that we had to handcrank the code to talk to the OData service. *Ideally*, back in the Microsoft "we'll give you a wizard to do everything" world, we should not have to do this. However, it transpires that there is no support for the kind of OData operation that we wish to build on Windows Phone 7.

Interesting story—when the first draft of this chapter was written against the CTP bits for Windows Phone 7, this support was there! However, by the time it went to release, support was dropped. There is some support available through open source efforts, but the major initiative in this space approaches the problem in a way that's not directly compatible with the other platforms. Therefore, in this chapter and the next, we're going to roll our own OData support, just as we have done for the other chapters. Let's get started and build a class called Sync that we'll use whenever we need to upload changes to the server or download the definitive set of bookmarks from the server. (In this chapter, we're not going to upload changes—that'll happen in the next chapter.)

As you know from the last chapter, when we communicate with the server, we do so asynchronously. While this adds extra difficulty to building the application, it's worth doing so because the effect is much nicer for the user. (Plus on Windows Phone you do not have a non-asynchronous—i.e., synchronous—option.)

Each of the calls that we build will use the pattern we saw last time of providing one callback delegate for the successful path and another callback delegate for the error path. Moreover we'll reuse the Failed delegate that we introduced last time.

Let's look now at consuming the OData service. First of all, here's the code for ODataServiceProxy. We'll add more to this later.

```
using System;
using System.Data.Services.Client;

namespace AmxMobile.Phone7.SixBookmarks
{
    internal abstract class ODataServiceProxy : ServiceProxy
    {
        protected ODataServiceProxy(string serviceName)
            : base(serviceName)
```

```
            {
            }
          }
    }
```

On our `BookmarksService` class, we need to add a method called `GetAll`. The method ultimately needs to call up to the server and retrieve a set of bookmarks. This is done by building and issuing a query to the server.

As you know from our work on the basic REST services, all HTTP requests happen asynchronously, and hence, when we call the `GetAll` method, we will pass in a success callback and a failure callback. We'll make the success delegate accept a list of bookmarks by way of a return value. In order to pass these callbacks through to the delegate that gets called when the query has executed, we'll create a private class in `BookmarksService` called `ODataFetchState` that holds the state that we need, and has some methods on it to help interpret and package the results. (This class in a real-world implementation would be internal rather than private, but this would mean making it more generic, and this seems overkill for this example.) Here's the basic implementation of `BookmarksService`:

```csharp
using System;
using System.Data.Services.Client;
using AMX = AmxMobile.Services;

namespace AmxMobile.Phone7.SixBookmarks
{
    internal class BookmarksService : ODataServiceProxy
    {
        internal BookmarksService()
            : base("Bookmarks.svc/")
        {
        }

        private string GetServiceUrl(EntityType et)
        {
            return HttpHelper.CombineUrlParts(this.ResolvedServiceUrl, et.NativeName);
        }
    }
}
```

Let's look at how to build the `ODataFetchState` class first. This class will be a generic class and will accept a type related to an entity that we support (the `Bookmark` instance in this case). As part of its state, we need to track a callback to call when we have data (which will be passed into the `GetAll` method), and a callback if there's a failure (again, passed into the `GetAll` method).

The `GetAll` method itself will run asynchronously and will retrieve XML from the server. This will be passed into a method called `ReceiveXml` on the state class. Here's the implementation of `GetAll` first:

```csharp
// Add to ODataServiceProxy…
        public void GetAll<T>(Action<List<T>> callback, Failed failed)
            where T : Entity
        {
            EntityType et = EntityType.GetEntityType(typeof(T));

            // create a state object...
```

```
            ODataFetchState<T> state = new ODataFetchState<T>();
            state.Callback = callback;
            state.Failed = failed;

            // run...
            String url = GetServiceUrl(et);
            HttpHelper.DownloadXml(url, GetDownloadSettings(), new
Action<XDocument>(state.ReceiveXml), failed);
        }
```

And here's the stub implementation of the state class and its `ReceiveXml` method:

```
// Add to ODataServiceProxy…
        private class ODataFetchState<T>
            where T : Entity
        {
            internal Action<List<T>> Callback;
            internal Failed Failed;

            internal void ReceiveXml(XDocument doc)
            {
                Debug.WriteLine("Received XML from server...");

                // got...
                List<T> items = LoadEntities(doc, EntityType.GetEntityType(typeof(T)));

                // debug...
                Debug.WriteLine(string.Format("{0} item(s) loaded.", items.Count));

                // callback...
                this.Callback(items);
            }
        }
```

You can see there that `ReceiveXml` actually defers to a method called `LoadEntities`, and it's this `LoadEntities` call that actually does the work. This will reel through the XML from the server, creating entities as it goes.

By way of a reminder, here's what the XML from the server typically looks like (I've included only one bookmark here for brevity, but a larger snippet is shown in Chapter 2).

```
<?xml version="1.0" encoding="iso-8859-1" standalone="yes"?>
<feed xml:base="http://services. multimobiledevelopment.com/services/Bookmarks.svc/"
xmlns:d="http://schemas.microsoft.com/ado/2007/08/dataservices"
xmlns:m="http://schemas.microsoft.com/ado/2007/08/dataservices/metadata"
xmlns="http://www.w3.org/2005/Atom">
  <title type="text">Bookmark</title>
  <id>http://services. multimobiledevelopment.com/services/bookmarks.svc/Bookmark</id>
  <updated>2010-04-18T10:54:32Z</updated>
  <link rel="self" title="Bookmark" href="Bookmark" />
  <entry>
    <id>http://services. multimobiledevelopment.com/services/Bookmarks.svc/Bookmark(1002)</id>
    <title type="text"></title>
    <updated>2010-04-18T10:54:32Z</updated>
```

```
  <author>
    <name />
  </author>
  <link rel="edit" title="Bookmark" href="Bookmark(1002)" />
  <category term="AmxMobile.Services.Bookmark"
scheme="http://schemas.microsoft.com/ado/2007/08/dataservices/scheme" />
  <content type="application/xml">
    <m:properties>
      <d:BookmarkId m:type="Edm.Int32">1002</d:BookmarkId>
      <d:UserId m:type="Edm.Int32">1001</d:UserId>
      <d:Name>.NET 247</d:Name>
      <d:Url>http://www.dotnet247.com/</d:Url>
      <d:Ordinal m:type="Edm.Int32">1</d:Ordinal>
    </m:properties>
  </content>
  </entry>
</feed>
```

Thus, to read in a bookmark, all we have to do is find the entry elements and then walk the properties contained within the m:properties element. Here's the code that does that:

```
// Add to the private ODataFetchState class within ODataServiceProxy…
  protected List<T> LoadEntities(XDocument doc, EntityType et)
        {
            // feed...
            XElement feed = doc.Element(XName.Get("feed", AtomNamespace));

            // walk...
            List<T> results = et.CreateCollectionInstance<T>();
            var entries = feed.Elements(XName.Get("entry", AtomNamespace));
            foreach (XElement entry in entries)
            {
                // get the content item...
                XElement content = entry.Element(XName.Get("content", AtomNamespace));

                // then get the properties element...
                XElement properties = content.Element(XName.Get("properties",
MsMetadataNamespace));

                // create an item...
                T item = (T)et.CreateInstance();

                // then get the fields...
                Dictionary<string, object> values = new Dictionary<string, object>();
                foreach (XElement fieldElement in properties.Elements())
                {
                    if (fieldElement.Name.Namespace == MsDataNamespace)
                    {
                        // do we have that field?
                        EntityField field = et.GetField(fieldElement.Name.LocalName,
false);

                        if (field != null)
```

```
            {
                // get the value...
                object value = this.GetValue(fieldElement);
                item.SetValue(field, value, SetReason.UserSet);
            }
        }
    }

    // add...
    results.Add(item);
}

// return...
return results;
}
```

During the read process, LoadEntities calls a helper method called GetValue. This latter method's job is to interpret the data type and return strongly typed values back to the caller, ready to store within the entity. We're going to support only two data types here—a real-world implementation would contain more first-class support for different types.

```
private Object GetValue(XElement field)
{
    // fields are provided with a data element, like this....
    // <d:BookmarkId m:type="Edm.Int32">1002</d:BookmarkId>

    // look up the type name...
    string typeName = null;
    XAttribute attr = field.Attribute(XName.Get("type", MsMetadataNamespace));
    if (attr != null)
        typeName = attr.Value;

    // nothing?
    if (string.IsNullOrEmpty(typeName))
        return XmlHelper.GetStringValue(field);
    else if (string.Compare(typeName, "Edm.Int32",
StringComparison.InvariantCultureIgnoreCase) == 0)
        return XmlHelper.GetInt32Value(field);
    else
        throw new Exception(string.Format("Cannot handle '%s'.", typeName));
}
```

Calling GetAll

The operations of the Sync class have to run asynchronously, as we've already stated that all server communication has to be done in this way. As a result, the DoSync method on the Sync class will also need to accept a success callback and a failed callback. As we'll need to use these from various places in the code, we'll store these callbacks as properties on the Sync class.

Internal to the Sync class will be a GetLatest method. The operation of this method will be to call the GetAll method and wait until some bookmarks are returned. The bookmarks that are returned will be ready for committal to disk via a change to SaveChanges. In addition to this, we also need to delete the existing bookmarks from disk; however, we cannot do this part yet as we have not built the code that retrieves the bookmarks back. (We'll do this shortly.)

As a result, the Sync method is actually pretty simple. Here's the code:

```
using System;

namespace AmxMobile.Phone7.SixBookmarks
{
    public class Sync
    {
        private Action Callback { get; set; }
        private Failed Failed { get; set; }

        public Sync()
        {
        }

        public void DoSync(Action callback, Failed failed)
        {
            // set...
            this.Callback = callback;
            this.Failed = failed;

            // get latest...
            GetLatest();
        }

        private void GetLatest()
        {
            BookmarksService service = new BookmarksService();
            service.GetAll((Action<List<Bookmark>>)delegate(List<Bookmark> bookmarks) {

                // go through and save them...
                foreach (Bookmark bookmark in bookmarks)
                    bookmark.SaveChanges();

                // signal that we've finished...
                this.Callback();

            }, this.Failed);
        }
    }
}
```

If you recall, when we built the logon form, we added a method called LogonOk, and also added a comment indicating where the code to the synchronization code would go. We can now add this in—on success what we want to do is navigate over to the navigator form using the Silverlight NavigationService.

There's one wrinkle that we have to deal with, however. When our success callback is invoked, we'll be running on a worker thread and not on the main user interface thread. As a result, we have to use the

Silverlight `Dispatcher` class to marshal control back to the main thread before using the `NavigationService`.

Here's the modified implementation of `LogonOk`:

```
// Change implementation of LogonOk on LogonForm…
        private void LogonOk()
        {
            // flip back - we're not on the right thread...
            this.Dispatcher.BeginInvoke(delegate()
            {
                // save...
                if (this.checkRememberMe.IsChecked.Value)
                {
                    SimpleXmlPropertyBag settings = SixBookmarksRuntime.Current.Settings;
                    settings[UsernameKey] = this.textUsername.Text.Trim();
                    settings[PasswordKey] = this.textPassword.Password.Trim();
                    settings.Save();
                }
                else
                    this.ClearCredentials();

                // do sync will come here...
                Sync sync = new Sync();
                sync.DoSync(delegate() {

                    // we worked...
                    Dispatcher.BeginInvoke(delegate()
                    {
                        NavigationService.Navigate(new Uri("/NavigatorPage.xaml",
UriKind.RelativeOrAbsolute));
                    });

                }, Alert.GetFailedHandler(this));
            });
        }
```

Now you can run the application, and the sync code will complete. However, you won't be able to see anything different, as all we're doing is writing files to disk and there's no way of browsing those files on the device. In the next section, we'll look at reading the files back out.

Selecting Entities

In this section, we're going to create a class called `DataBoxFilter` that can be used to read entities from disk.

If you've been reading along the Android and iOS implementations, you'll know that we built a class called `SqlFilter` that was able to select data out of a table in a relational store. This class worked by assuming that when you created a filter you wanted all entities of a given type. You could then add constraints to limit the entities that were returned.

In `DataBoxFilter`, we're going to do much the same thing. This class will be bound to a data box and initially be configured to return back a list of all entities of a given type. We can add constraints to limit the results returned. (Because we are trying to move to a world where we have a relational store, I'm going to call the constraint class `SqlConstraint`, as ultimately we'd like to do away with `DataBoxFilter` and use `SqlFilter` instances instead.) In terms of how we're going to do the filtering, we'll always load all entities from disk and walk them one by one to see if they are included based on the constraints. This is the easiest way to achieve what we want, but it is the least efficient. Given that we need to keep this code easy to read in order to make the book more comprehendable, and given that our dataset is small, this approach is suitable in this case. If you were looking to work with a larger set of data, you'd need to be more sophisticated with your approach.

■ **Note** I've avoided trying in this case to create a provider pattern-like approach here, whereby we abstract the user away from knowing whether he or she is using a data box or a relational store, primarily to reduce complexity. What I've tried to do is take a stab in the direction of making it easier to move over to a relational database, rather than create something that lets the developer move between the two at will.

The first method we'll need is one that returns all of the entities out of the data box. We'll implement this on `DataBox` itself and use it from within `DataBoxFilter`. This method will need to be able to create a strongly typed, generic collection of entities for a given entity type, and therefore we'll add a method called `CreateCollectionInstance` to `EntityType`. This method uses some semi-advanced .NET magic to create an appropriate collection type at runtime—suffice it to say that if we call this method on the entity type that represents `Bookmark`, we'll get a `List<Bookmark>` returned. Here's the code:

```
// Add method to EntityType…
        internal List<T> CreateCollectionInstance<T>()
            where T : Entity
        {
            Type listType = typeof(List<>);
            Type genericType = listType.MakeGenericType(new Type[] { typeof(T) });

            // return...
            return (List<T>)Activator.CreateInstance(genericType);
        }
```

We can now implement our `GetAll` method on `DataBox`. The operation of this method will be to ask isolated storage for a list of file names. These file names will then be turned into full paths (e.g., 27.xml → ~/Entities/Bookmark/27.xml) and passed to a method called `EntityFromXml` for rehydration back into an instance. Here's the implementation of the basic `GetAll` method:

```
// Add method to DataBox…
        internal List<T> GetAll<T>()
            where T : Entity
        {
            IsolatedStorageFile store = this.GetStore();

            // load them all...
            List<T> results = this.EntityType.CreateCollectionInstance<T>();
            foreach (string filename in store.GetFileNames(this.FolderName + "/*.xml"))
            {
```

```
            // get the xml...
            XDocument doc = null;
            using (Stream stream = store.OpenFile(this.FolderName + "/" + filename,
FileMode.Open, FileAccess.Read))
                    doc = XDocument.Load(stream);

            // turn it into an entity...
            T entity = (T)EntityFromXml(doc);
            results.Add(entity);
        }

        // return...
        return results;
    }
```

The EntityFromXml method is intended to be able to be able to hydrate any form of entity (i.e., it's not Bookmark-specific). Its operation is to use the field definition within the entity type to identify elements contained within the document. If there is a match between a field and an element, the field's value is set and marked as loaded. If there is no match, no error occurs. Here's the code:

```
// Add method to DataBox…
        private Entity EntityFromXml(XDocument doc)
        {
            Entity entity = this.EntityType.CreateInstance();

            // walk...
            List<XElement> elements = new
List<XElement>(doc.Descendants(this.EntityType.NativeName));
            if (elements.Count == 0)
                    throw new InvalidOperationException(string.Format("An element with name '{0}'
was not found.", this.EntityType.NativeName));

            // walk the fields...
            XElement root = elements[0];
            foreach (EntityField field in this.EntityType.Fields)
            {
                // find an element...
                XElement element = root.Element(field.NativeName);
                if (element != null)
                {
                    if (field.Type == DataType.String)
                        entity.SetValue(field, XmlHelper.GetStringValue(element),
SetReason.Load);
                    else if (field.Type == DataType.Int32)
                        entity.SetValue(field, XmlHelper.GetInt32Value(element),
SetReason.Load);
                    else if (field.Type == DataType.Boolean)
                        entity.SetValue(field, XmlHelper.GetBooleanValue(element),
SetReason.Load);
                    else
                        throw new NotSupportedException(string.Format("Cannot handle '{0}'.",
field.Type));
```

```
            }
        }

        // return...
        return entity;
    }
```

Now that we can load the entities, we can turn our attention to creating a filter. The first class we need to support our filter is SqlConstraint. This class exists simply as a pair of properties—specifically an EntityField instance and the value be constrained. (In more sophisticated implementations, this may include an operator, such as "not equal to" or "greater than." Our implementation will support only "equal to.")

Here's the code:

```
using System;

namespace AmxMobile.Phone7.SixBookmarks
{
    public class SqlConstraint
    {
        internal EntityField Field { get; private set; }
        internal object Value { get; private set; }

        internal SqlConstraint(EntityField field, object value)
        {
            this.Field = field;
            this.Value = value;
        }
    }
}
```

For our actual DataBoxFilter, we'll hold a DataBox instance and set of constraints in instance fields. For our ExecuteEntityCollection method, we'll call GetAll to get them all back and then go through and "black ball" any in the collection that do not meet the constraints. For extra flexibility, when we know we're matching string fields, we'll do the matching in a case-insensitive fashion. Here's the code:

```
using System;
using System.Collections.Generic;

namespace AmxMobile.Phone7.SixBookmarks
{
    internal class DataBoxFilter
    {
        private DataBox Box { get; set; }
        private List<SqlConstraint> Constraints { get; set; }

        internal DataBoxFilter(DataBox box)
        {
            this.Box = box;
            this.Constraints = new List<SqlConstraint>();
        }
```

```csharp
internal List<T> ExecuteEntityCollection<T>()
    where T : Entity
{
    // get them all from the box...
    List<T> all = this.Box.GetAll<T>();

    // create a new collection to put the filtered results in...
    List<T> results = this.Box.EntityType.CreateCollectionInstance<T>();

    // walk the master list...
    foreach (T item in all)
    {
        bool ok = true;

        // look for non-matches...
        foreach (SqlConstraint constraint in this.Constraints)
        {
            if (constraint.Field.Type == DataType.String)
            {
                string value = item.GetStringValue(constraint.Field);
                if (string.Compare(value, (string)constraint.Value,
StringComparison.InvariantCultureIgnoreCase) != 0)
                    ok = false;
            }
            else if (constraint.Field.Type == DataType.Int32)
            {
                int value = item.GetInt32Value(constraint.Field);
                if (value != (int)constraint.Value)
                    ok = false;
            }
            else
                throw new InvalidOperationException(string.Format("Cannot handle
{0}.", constraint.Field.Type));

            // stop early?
            if(!(ok))
                break;
        }

        // add if we're OK...
        if (ok)
            results.Add(item);
    }

    // return...
    return results;
}

internal T ExecuteEntity<T>()
    where T : Entity
{
    List<T> items = ExecuteEntityCollection<T>();
```

```
            if (items.Count > 0)
                return items[0];
            else
                return null;
        }

        internal void AddConstraint(string name, object value)
        {
            EntityField field = this.Box.EntityType.GetField(name, true);
            if (field == null)
                throw new InvalidOperationException("'field' is null.");

            // defer...
            AddConstraint(field, value);
        }

        internal void AddConstraint(EntityField field, object value)
        {
            if (field == null)
                throw new ArgumentNullException("field");

            // add...
            this.Constraints.Add(new SqlConstraint(field, value));
        }
    }
}
```

Now all that remains is to create a filter, configure it, and call the ExecuteEntityCollection method.

At this point, we already have a method on Bookmark called GetBookmarksForDisplay. At the moment, this returns a list of fake bookmarks; what we can do now is change it so that it returns the bookmarks from the data box. At this stage, we're going to return all of them—in the next chapter, we're going to add an additional flag to the bookmark and make a further change to GetBookmarksForDisplay to constrain against that field. For now, here's the revised implementation of GetBookmarksForDisplay:

```
// Modify implementation of GetBookmarksForDisplay...
        internal static List<Bookmark> GetBookmarksForDisplay()
        {
            // create a filter...
            DataBoxFilter filter = new DataBoxFilter(GetDataBox());
            return filter.ExecuteEntityCollection<Bookmark>();
        }
```

With that method in place, all we have to do is run the project, and it will load the real bookmarks and display them. Figure 6-4 shows the result.

Figure 6-4. The Navigation form showing real bookmarks from the server

That's it! The whole thing works from end to end. We can connect up to the server, download the bookmarks, and show them on the screen. There's just one housekeeping task missing, which we'll do next.

Implementing Delete All on the Sync

The synchronization routine needs to delete all of the bookmarks off of the local device before the new bookmarks are downloaded. Although it's not obvious, at this stage we're actually creating an ever-increasing list of bookmarks on the device. It's not obvious because when the UI is built, the ordinal of the bookmark is used to choose the button to associate the bookmark with. Hence we can have multiple bookmarks with the same ordinal, and the result is to just keep reconfiguring the same bookmark again and again.

Here's the code:

```
// Add method to Bookmark…
    internal static void DeleteAll()
    {
        DataBoxFilter filter = new DataBoxFilter(GetDataBox());
        foreach(Bookmark bookmark in filter.ExecuteEntityCollection<Bookmark>())
        {
            bookmark.MarkForDeletion();
            bookmark.SaveChanges();
        }
    }
```

All we have to do once we have that method is call DeleteAll from within the GetLatest method on Sync. Here's the code:

```
// Modify GetLatest method on Sync…
    private void GetLatest()
    {
        BookmarksService service = new BookmarksService();
        service.GetAll((Action<List<Bookmark>>)delegate(List<Bookmark> bookmarks)
        {
            // delete first...
            Bookmark.DeleteAll();

            // go through and save them...
            foreach (Bookmark bookmark in bookmarks)
                bookmark.SaveChanges();

            // signal that we've finished...
            this.Callback();

        }, this.Failed);
    }
```

Using the ORM Subsystem to Support Tombstoning

Before we finish the chapter, we should clear up the issue related to tombstoning the applications.

As discussed previously, when we switch to another application (of which Internet Explorer is one), we will get dismissed from memory automatically. The state of our application is not preserved when this happens—we are responsible for serializing and deserializing whatever state we want to keep in order to maintain our application. The only state that we *absolutely* need to keep in this fashion is our logon token to the services.

Various bits of documentation related to tombstoning suggest using isolated storage to keep the data safe. We already use isolated storage with our ORM subsystem, so it seems logical to reuse this for this purpose. Specifically we'll build a new entity called TombstoneItem and create a related entity type. The format of TombstoneItem will be as a basic name/value pair.

Without further ado, we'll define our TombstoneItem class like this:

```
using System;
using System.Collections.Generic;

namespace AmxMobile.Phone7.SixBookmarks
{
    public class TombstoneData : Entity
    {
        public const string TombstoneDataIdKey = "TombstoneDataId";
        public const string NameKey = "Name";
        public const string ValueKey = "Value";

        public TombstoneData()
        {
        }

        public int TombstoneDataId
        {
            get
            {
                return this.GetInt32Value(TombstoneDataIdKey);
            }
            set
            {
                this.SetValue(TombstoneDataIdKey, value, SetReason.UserSet);
            }
        }

        public string Name
        {
            get
            {
                return this.GetStringValue(NameKey);
            }
            set
            {
                this.SetValue(NameKey, value, SetReason.UserSet);
            }
        }

        public string Value
        {
```

```
    get
    {
        return this.GetStringValue(ValueKey);
    }
    set
    {
        this.SetValue(ValueKey, value, SetReason.UserSet);
    }
}

private static DataBox GetDataBox()
{
    EntityType et = EntityType.GetEntityType(typeof(TombstoneData));
    return new DataBox(et);
}
    }
}
```

To use this name/value collection, we'll need to be able to get a TombstoneItem instance for a given name. We'll do this via a method called GetTombstoneItem, which will use the DataBoxFilter that we built earlier, plus it will have the capability to create a new item, should one not be found. Here's the code:

```
// Add to TombstoneItem…
    internal static TombstoneData GetTombstoneItem(string name, bool createIfNotFound)
    {
        DataBoxFilter filter = new DataBoxFilter(GetDataBox());
        filter.AddConstraint(NameKey, name);

        // return...
        TombstoneData data = filter.ExecuteEntity<TombstoneData>();
        if (data == null && createIfNotFound)
        {
            data = new TombstoneData();
            data.Name = name;
        }

        // return...
        return data;
    }
```

As you know, in order to use entities, we need to define an entity type. As before, we'll do this within the SixBookmarksRuntime class. Here's the modified code:

```
// Modified SixBookmarksRuntime constructor…
        private SixBookmarksRuntime()
        {
        // settings...
        this.Settings = SimpleXmlPropertyBag.Load("Settings.xml", false);

        // register the entity type...
        EntityType bookmark = new EntityType(typeof(Bookmark), "Bookmark");
```

```
            bookmark.AddField(Bookmark.BookmarkIdKey, Bookmark.BookmarkIdKey, DataType.Int32,
-1).IsKey = true;
            bookmark.AddField(Bookmark.NameKey, Bookmark.NameKey, DataType.String, 128);
            bookmark.AddField(Bookmark.UrlKey, Bookmark.UrlKey, DataType.String, 128);
            bookmark.AddField(Bookmark.OrdinalKey, Bookmark.OrdinalKey, DataType.Int32, -1);
            bookmark.AddField(Bookmark.IsLocalModifiedKey, Bookmark.IsLocalModifiedKey,
DataType.Boolean, -1).IsOnServer = false;
            bookmark.AddField(Bookmark.IsLocalDeletedKey, Bookmark.IsLocalDeletedKey,
DataType.Boolean, -1).IsOnServer = false;
            EntityType.RegisterEntityType(bookmark);

            // create a tombstone data entity type...
            EntityType tombstone = new EntityType(typeof(TombstoneData),
"TombstoneData");
            tombstone.AddField(TombstoneData.TombstoneDataIdKey,
TombstoneData.TombstoneDataIdKey, DataType.Int32, -1).IsKey = true;
            tombstone.AddField(TombstoneData.NameKey, TombstoneData.NameKey,
DataType.String, 64);
            tombstone.AddField(TombstoneData.ValueKey, TombstoneData.ValueKey,
DataType.String, 256);
            EntityType.RegisterEntityType(tombstone);
        }
```

To support tombstoning, the Windows Phone 7 runtime will call events on our application class—specifically `Activated` and `Deactivated`. When we're deactivated, we need to store the user token held in static memory within the `RestServiceProxy` base class. (For a more elegant solution, each class that you know should be storing state could be enlisted in some sort of chain, and each class given responsibility for storing its own state. However, this is probably good enough for this example.) Here's the "deactivated" event handler:

```
// Add to App…
    private void Application_Deactivated(object sender, DeactivatedEventArgs e)
    {
        // get a tombstonedata item...
        TombstoneData data = TombstoneData.GetTombstoneItem("UserToken", true);
        if (data == null)
            throw new InvalidOperationException("'data' is null.");
        data.Value = RestServiceProxy.Token;
        data.SaveChanges();
    }
```

The "activated" handler is a similar shape, although, on top of restoring the data, we also have to "reboot" the application runtime. This is done by using a method called `EnsureInitialized`, which we'll build in a moment. Here's the "activated" handler:

```
// Add to App…
    private void Application_Activated(object sender, ActivatedEventArgs e)
    {
        SixBookmarksRuntime.EnsureInitialized();

        // load up the token...
        TombstoneData data = TombstoneData.GetTombstoneItem("UserToken", false);
```

```
        if (data != null)
            RestServiceProxy.Token = data.Value;
    }
```

The operation of EnsureInitialized is very straightforward. By calling any static method on the class, we'll end up calling the constructor as we did before. Here's the code:

```
// Add to SixBookmarksRuntime...
    internal static void EnsureInitialized()
    {
        // called after we have been "tombstoned"... all we have to do here is check that
we
        // have Current defined.  this will re-establish our state...
        if (Current == null)
            throw new InvalidOperationException("'Current' is null.");
    }
```

There's one final thing to consider. Our state is persistently stored on disk; therefore we have to reset it when the application starts. We can listen out for the "launching" event and delete the tombstone item out at this stage. Here's the code:

```
// Add to App...
    private void Application_Launching(object sender, LaunchingEventArgs e)
    {
        // check...
        SixBookmarksRuntime.EnsureInitialized();

        // delete any old token that we may have...
        TombstoneData data = TombstoneData.GetTombstoneItem("UserToken", false);
        if (data != null)
        {
            data.MarkForDeletion();
            data.SaveChanges();
        }
    }
```

That's all we need to do! Now we can flip back and forth between our application and Internet Explorer with impunity.

Conclusion

In this chapter, we have seen how, despite the lack of a relational database management system on Windows Phone, we can still use the object-relational mapping approach we outlined in the system architecture chapter and implemented on iOS and Android. We saw how we could create a "data box" and entities in it as individual files. We also saw how to communicate with the standard OData service in order to download entities from the cloud service. In the next chapter, we'll look at how to push up changes to the server.

CHAPTER 7

■ ■ ■

Windows Phone 7: Pushing Changes Back to the Server

In this last chapter on Windows Phone, we're going to look at allowing the user to configure his or her bookmarks and then push those bookmarks back up to the server. This will involve building two forms—one for displaying a list of the bookmarks and one for editing and modifying the Sync class that we built in the last chapter to allow for changes to be sent back. We'll look at the user interface first.

The Configuration User Interface

The new wave of phones (Android, iOS, and Windows Phone) has a common user interface metaphor whereby the user is presented with lists of items. This metaphor is particularly prevalent on iOS; Apple did a lot of work on the iPhone to make these lists particularly flexible and attractive to the users (although we don't cover iOS in this book, obviously—but you can follow along in the sister book). Android picked up the lists when designing its UI, and now Windows Phone has a list metaphor too.

■ **Note** A control called ListBox has been around since version 1.0 of Windows, but the Windows Phone implementation is tweaked to create a particularly "phone-y" experience.

Another feature of Silverlight that we're going to be using in this chapter is databinding. Windows Phone has the best databinding story out of all of the major platforms, probably because Microsoft has been continually improving its databinding story on all of its toolsets since before the days of the original Visual Basic. Databinding makes it much easier to get information onto and off of the screen by allowing data to be pushed onto the view declaratively, rather than having to write code that explicitly pushes data onto the screen.

Let's start by building the core view.

Building ConfigurePage.xaml

To start, add a new page to the project called ConfigurePage.xaml. This will create a new page with the usual header containing two labels. Change the small text in the header to Six Bookmarks and the large text in the header to Configure.

From the toolbox, drag a ListBox control on the grid surface and size it so that it occupies all of the available space. Set the Name property of the control to listBookmarks. You'll have something that looks like Figure 7-1.

Figure 7-1. The ListBox control on the design surface

ASP.NET developers will find this next part familiar—we need to define a "template" that items within the list box will use to create items for display.

This is done by adding markup to the XAML code. What we're going to do is define an item template as using a StackPanel control. The StackPanel control is a standard Silverlight layout control that allows you to arrange items horizontally or vertically. The details of how to use it are beyond the scope of this book, but essentially what we're going to do is define a container stack panel with the items arranged horizontally. The left-hand control will show an icon, and the right-hand control will be another stack panel. This second stack panel will be arranged vertically and contain two text boxes, one for the name and one for the URL of the bookmark.

This is also the first time that we're going to see databinding in Silverlight. The principle of Silverlight databinding is that you can specify any property in XAML as being data bound by enclosing an expression in curly brackets and using the keyword Binding. For example, this expression binds the Text value to the Name member of the object that is being bound:

```
Text="{Binding Name}"
```

Later we're going to bind the ListBox control to a list of bookmarks (List<Bookmark>). As the view is being built, it will walk each bookmark in turn and binding expressions will be evaluated on an item-by-item basis; hence the {Binding Name} expression will evaluate against Bookmark.

To create the stack panels and contained controls, specify the following XAML markup within the ListBox element created when you dropped the ListBox control onto the design surface:

```
<ListBox x:Name="listBookmarks">
    <ListBox.ItemTemplate>
        <DataTemplate>
            <StackPanel x:Name="DataTemplateStackPanel"
Orientation="Horizontal">
                <Image x:Name="ItemImage"
Source="/AmxMobile.Phone7.SixBookmarks;component/Images/ArrowImg.png" Height="43"
Width="43" VerticalAlignment="Top" Margin="10,0,20,0"/>
                <StackPanel>
                    <TextBlock x:Name="ItemText" Text="{Binding Name}"
Margin="-2,-13,0,0" Style="{StaticResource PhoneTextExtraLargeStyle}"/>
                    <TextBlock x:Name="DetailsText" Text="{Binding Url}"
Margin="0,-6,0,3" Style="{StaticResource PhoneTextSubtleStyle}"/>
                </StackPanel>
            </StackPanel>
        </DataTemplate>
    </ListBox.ItemTemplate>
</ListBox>
```

You'll notice in that markup that we specified an Image element. The Source attribute of this element points to a local URI within the application that references an image. This image and others that we'll see later are not standard Windows Phones resources and need to be included manually. You can obtain the images by downloading the Visual Studio solution from http://code.multimobiledevelopment.com/. In this case, the images have to be created in an Images folder in the root of the project and have a Build Action value of Resource.

▓ **Note** It's important that the Build Action is set to Resource. If it isn't, it won't load.

Binding the List

To make the list do something, we have to bind it to some data. This is where the view model approach of Silverlight development comes in.

Silverlight, and by extension Windows Phone development, is supposed to be done using something called MVVM, or Model-View-ViewModel. The principle is that you have a "model" containing the data that you wish to display, the "view," which is the code and markup that drives the user interface, and a "view model," which is a specialized model that is tailored to the view that you are building. For example, our model contains the entire list of bookmarks stored locally on the device. Some of these bookmarks will be marked as "locally deleted," meaning that the user has indicated that they should be deleted but that the delete instruction has not yet been passed to the server. Thus our view model for our configuration page needs to select all bookmarks apart from those that have been locally deleted. Further, our bookmarks need to be presented ordered by the ordinal value specified on each bookmark.

That said, although MVVM is strongly recommended as a standard for Silverlight applications, my own view is that you need to feel your way through these things and find an approach that makes the most sense to you. It's certainly true to say that data binding in Silverlight is easier if you adopt an MVVM approach, but it's equally true to say that the tools are flexible enough so that you will not get horrendously stuck if you choose to go your own way.

We're going to create a class in our project called ConfigurePageViewModel, which, as the name implies, will be the view model for our configure page. On instantiation this will load the appropriate bookmarks from disk and sort them by ordinal. Here's the code:

```
using System;
using System.Collections.Generic;

namespace AmxMobile.Phone7.SixBookmarks
{
    public class ConfigurePageViewModel
    {
        public List<Bookmark> Items { get; private set; }

        internal ConfigurePageViewModel()
        {
            // set...
            List<Bookmark> items = new List<Bookmark>(Bookmark.GetBookmarksForDisplay());

            // sort...
            items.Sort(new OrdinalComparer());

            // set...
            this.Items = items;
        }

        private class OrdinalComparer : IComparer<Bookmark>
        {
            public int Compare(Bookmark x, Bookmark y)
            {
                if (x.Ordinal < y.Ordinal)
                    return -1;
                else if (x.Ordinal > y.Ordinal)
                    return 1;
```

```
                else
                    return 0;
            }
        }
    }
}
```

The important thing there is the Items property. Note how this is a public property and that the ConfigurePageViewModel is a public class. Silverlight databinding will bind to any public property on any public type; thus if we set the list box to bind to the model and specify a binding expression of Items, when it's time to retrieve the data, the ListBox control will query the Items property, find that it's of type IEnumerable, and walk through the bookmarks, creating list items as it goes. Further, because the items themselves are specified with binding expressions as each list item is created, the properties specified in the per-item bindings will be queried and pushed through to the relevant controls.

To specify that we want the list to bind to something called Items, we need to change the XAML to include a binding expression. This is done by specifying an expression in the ItemSource attribute. Here's a snippet of the XAML:

```xml
<!-- markup omitted for brevity… -->
        <ListBox x:Name="listBookmarks" ItemsSource="{Binding Items}">
            <ListBox.ItemTemplate>
                <DataTemplate>
                    <StackPanel x:Name="DataTemplateStackPanel" Orientation="Horizontal">
                        <Image x:Name="ItemImage"
Source="/AmxMobile.Phone7.SixBookmarks;component/Images/Arrow.png" Height="43" Width="43"
VerticalAlignment="Top" Margin="10,0,20,0"/>
                        <StackPanel>
                            <TextBlock x:Name="ItemText" Text="{Binding Name}" Margin="-
2,-13,0,0" Style="{StaticResource PhoneTextExtraLargeStyle}"/>
                            <TextBlock x:Name="DetailsText" Text="{Binding Url}"
Margin="0,-6,0,3" Style="{StaticResource PhoneTextSubtleStyle}"/>
                        </StackPanel>
                    </StackPanel>
                </DataTemplate>
            </ListBox.ItemTemplate>
        </ListBox>
<!-- markup omitted for brevity… -->
```

It's not necessary to bind the view model directly to the control. The page itself has a DataContext property. If we set this property to be our view model, when the list box notices that it was an ItemSource value set, it will go to the page to discover the value in DataContext. To make this happen, all we have to do is override the OnNavigatedTo method and set DataContext to be a new instance of the view model. Here's the code:

```csharp
// Add method to ConfigurePage…
        protected override void OnNavigatedTo(System.Windows.Navigation.NavigationEventArgs e)
        {
            base.OnNavigatedTo(e);
```

```
        // set the context...
        this.DataContext = new ConfigurePageViewModel();
    }
```

The final step in making this work is to modify the HandleConfigure method on the navigator page so that it opens the new configuration page. Here's the modified method:

```
// Modify method in NavigatorPage
    private void HandleConfigure()
    {
        NavigationService.Navigate(new Uri("/ConfigurePage.xaml",
UriKind.RelativeOrAbsolute));
    }
```

Run the application now, and you'll be able to access the configuration page. Figure 7-2 illustrates.

Figure 7-2. The configuration screen running on the emulator

Configuring the Application Bar

One of the user interface metaphors that Microsoft is very keen to promote on Windows Phone is the application bar. This is a bar that is shown at the bottom of a page, offers commonly used functions by way of "always on" buttons, and allows the user to access more options via an ellipsis button shown to the right of the bar. Figure 7-3 illustrates the application bar from Internet Explorer.

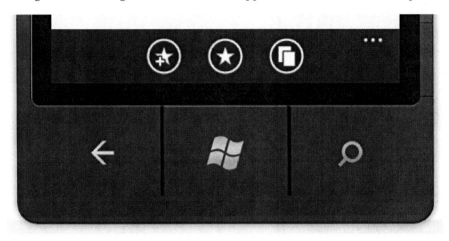

Figure 7-3. *IE's application bar*

If we press the ellipsis button, we get more options—plus we also get some text describing the "always on" buttons. Figure 7-4 illustrates.

Figure 7-4. The expanded application bar

In our application, we're going to add a couple of buttons—one for adding a bookmark and one for saving changes and returning to the navigator form.

Adding the buttons is a little bit fiddly—you have to get the images exactly right. The rules are that you need to create a 48x48 pixel image, and design the actual image so that it fits exactly within a 26x26 pixel square within the middle of that image. The image has to be white, and the background has to be transparent (which is fun, because when you're looking at the images in preview mode in Explorer with a default background of white, you end up looking through images that are white rendered on white.) The circle is rendered by the Windows Phone runtime itself—you only have to worry about the central image.

As mentioned before, Windows Phone doesn't have any stock images that we can reuse, and so we have to add them manually. In the solution that you can download from http://code.multimobiledevelopment.com/, you will find three images for buttons: Add.png, Finish.png, and Delete.png. Add these to the Images folder within your project, and make sure that the Build Action for each is set to Content. Copy to Output Directory should be set to Copy always.

■ **Note** It's important that the Build Action is set to Content, otherwise the image will not load. Recall that we set the Arrow.png image to a Build Action of Resource. Because the images are referenced in different ways, they need different Build Actions.

In terms of code, the easiest way to configure the application bar is to do so programmatically by first creating an `ApplicationBar` instance and then creating and adding `ApplicationBarIconButton` instances to the bar's `Buttons` collection. For each button, we can also create an event handler that will be called when the button is pressed. Here's the revised version of the constructor for `ConfigurePage`:

```
// Modified constructor and stub event handlers within ConfigurePage...
        public ConfigurePage()
        {
            InitializeComponent();

            // application bar...
            this.ApplicationBar = new ApplicationBar();
            this.ApplicationBar.IsVisible = true;
            this.ApplicationBar.IsMenuEnabled = true;

            // add...
            ApplicationBarIconButton add = new ApplicationBarIconButton(new
Uri("/Images/Add.png", UriKind.Relative));
            add.Text = "add";
            add.Click += new EventHandler(add_Click);
            this.ApplicationBar.Buttons.Add(add);

            // finish...
            ApplicationBarIconButton finish = new ApplicationBarIconButton(new
Uri("/Images/Finish.png", UriKind.Relative));
            finish.Text = "finish";
            finish.Click += new EventHandler(finish_Click);
            this.ApplicationBar.Buttons.Add(finish);
        }

        void finish_Click(object sender, EventArgs e)
        {
        Alert.Show(this, "TBD");
        }

        void add_Click(object sender, EventArgs e)
        {
        Alert.Show(this, "TBD");
        }
```

Now, if you run the project, you will see the application bar with the two buttons shown in all their glory. Figure 7-5 illustrates.

Figure 7-5. The application bar on a running configuration page

Now that we have the buttons, we can wire up the functionality.

Implementing the Button and List Selection Handler

When the user clicks one of the items in the list, we want to take the user to a page where he or she can edit that individual bookmark. To do this, we need to subscribe to the SelectionChanged event on the list box.

The easiest way to add a handler is to double-click the list box in the designer view. Once there, add this code:

```
// Methods in ConfigurePage…
        private void listBookmarks_SelectionChanged(object sender, SelectionChangedEventArgs
e)
        {
            Bookmark selected = (Bookmark)this.listBookmarks.SelectedItem;
            if (selected != null)
                ConfigureBookmark(selected.Ordinal);
        }

        private void ConfigureBookmark(int ordinal)
        {
            NavigationService.Navigate(new
Uri(string.Format("/ConfigureSingletonPage.xaml?ordinal={0}", ordinal),
UriKind.RelativeOrAbsolute));
        }
```

The magic here happens in the ConfigureBookmark method. When we want to configure a bookmark, we'll pass in the ordinal through a query string variable (in this case, called ordinal). The singleton page that edits a single bookmark will de-reference the ordinal and find the appropriate bookmark. If a bookmark with a given ordinal cannot be found, a new one will be created. This approach makes it easy to write some relatively simple code that can handle working with existing bookmarks or creating new ones.

Therefore, for the "add" button handler, we need to find the next available bookmark ordinal. If an ordinal can be found, a call to ConfigureBookmark will redirect the user appropriately. If all six slots are taken, we can show an error. Here's the code:

```
// Replace add_Click method in ConfigurePage…
        void add_Click(object sender, EventArgs e)
        {
            // get the next ordinal...
            bool[] taken = new bool[6];
            foreach (Bookmark bookmark in this.listBookmarks.Items)
                taken[bookmark.Ordinal] = true;

            // walk...
            for (int index = 0; index < taken.Length; index++)
            {
                if (!(taken[index]))
                {
                    ConfigureBookmark(index);
                    return;
                }
            }
```

```
        // show...
        MessageBox.Show("There are no more slots available.");
    }
```

The final thing to do on the configuration page is handle the user clicking the "finish" button. When he does this, we want to call the sync routine to push the changes back up to the server. Although, at the moment, the sync routine is not able to push changes back, if we call the method here, it'll save us a job later on. Here's the code:

```
// Replace finish_Click method in ConfigurePage…
    void finish_Click(object sender, EventArgs e)
    {
        // sync...
        Sync sync = new Sync();
        sync.DoSync((Action)delegate()
        {
            Dispatcher.BeginInvoke((Action)delegate()
            {
                NavigationService.Navigate(new Uri("/NavigatorPage.xaml",
UriKind.RelativeOrAbsolute));
            });

        }, Alert.GetFailedHandler(this));
    }
```

The next thing we have to do is create the page for modifying a single bookmark. We'll do this in the next section.

The ConfigureSingletonPage Page

To configure a single bookmark, we need a page (called ConfigureSingletonPage) that has one text box for the name and another for the URL. We'll also need a Save Changes button and labels to suit. Figure 7-6 illustrates.

Figure 7-6. The singleton view design surface

In terms of things that you cannot see from the screenshot, the name text box needs to have a Name value of textName and the URL text box needs to have a Name value of textUrl. The Text property of textName needs to be set to {Binding Name}, and similarly the Text property of textural needs to be set to {Binding Url}. Here's the markup:

```
<phone:PhoneApplicationPage
    x:Class="AmxMobile.Phone7.SixBookmarks.ConfigureSingletonPage"
    xmlns="http://schemas.microsoft.com/winfx/2006/xaml/presentation"
    xmlns:x="http://schemas.microsoft.com/winfx/2006/xaml"
    xmlns:phone="clr-namespace:Microsoft.Phone.Controls;assembly=Microsoft.Phone"
    xmlns:shell="clr-namespace:Microsoft.Phone.Shell;assembly=Microsoft.Phone"
    xmlns:d="http://schemas.microsoft.com/expression/blend/2008"
    xmlns:mc="http://schemas.openxmlformats.org/markup-compatibility/2006"
    FontFamily="{StaticResource PhoneFontFamilyNormal}"
    FontSize="{StaticResource PhoneFontSizeNormal}"
    Foreground="{StaticResource PhoneForegroundBrush}"
    SupportedOrientations="Portrait" Orientation="Portrait"
    mc:Ignorable="d" d:DesignHeight="768" d:DesignWidth="480"
    shell:SystemTray.IsVisible="True">
```

```xml
    <!--LayoutRoot contains the root grid where all other page content is placed-->
    <Grid x:Name="LayoutRoot" Background="Transparent">
        <Grid.RowDefinitions>
            <RowDefinition Height="Auto"/>
            <RowDefinition Height="*"/>
        </Grid.RowDefinitions>

        <!--TitlePanel contains the name of the application and page title-->
        <StackPanel x:Name="TitlePanel" Grid.Row="0" Margin="24,24,0,12">
            <TextBlock x:Name="ApplicationTitle" Text="Six Bookmarks" Style="{StaticResource
PhoneTextNormalStyle}"/>
            <TextBlock x:Name="PageTitle" Text="Configure" Margin="-3,-8,0,0"
Style="{StaticResource PhoneTextTitle1Style}"/>
        </StackPanel>

        <!--ContentPanel - place additional content here-->
        <Grid x:Name="ContentGrid" Grid.Row="1">
            <TextBlock Margin="6,4,42,586" Name="textBlock1" Style="{StaticResource
PhoneTextNormalStyle}" Text="Name" />
            <TextBox Height="72" Text="{Binding Name}" HorizontalAlignment="Left"
Margin="0,26,0,0" Name="textName" VerticalAlignment="Top" Width="480" />
            <TextBlock Margin="6,97,42,493" Name="textBlock2" Style="{StaticResource
PhoneTextNormalStyle}" Text="URL" />
            <TextBox Height="72" Text="{Binding Url}" HorizontalAlignment="Left"
Margin="0,119,0,0" Name="textUrl" VerticalAlignment="Top" Width="480" />
            <Button Content="Save Changes" Height="72" HorizontalAlignment="Left"
Margin="0,197,0,0" Name="buttonSaveChanges" VerticalAlignment="Top" Width="480"
Click="buttonSaveChanges_Click" />
        </Grid>
    </Grid>

</phone:PhoneApplicationPage>
```

I'll go through the code for this page quite quickly, as it's pretty straightforward. Recall that previously we said that when we navigated the user to this page, we were going to provide the ordinal in the URL. We also said that if we were unable to load a bookmark for the given ordinal, we would create a new one. The dependency in this is a business method that loads a bookmark for a given ordinal. Here's the code for the GetByOrdinal method:

```csharp
// Add method to Bookmark...
    internal static Bookmark GetByOrdinal(int ordinal)
    {
        DataBoxFilter filter = new DataBoxFilter(GetDataBox());
        filter.AddConstraint("ordinal", ordinal);

        // return...
        return filter.ExecuteEntity<Bookmark>();
    }
```

Here's the implementation for the Bookmark property on ConfigureSingletonPage. You'll also need a private field called _bookmark to hold the item that we're working on.

```
// Add property to ConfigureSingletonPage…
        private Bookmark Bookmark
        {
            get
            {
                if (_bookmark == null)
                {
                    string asString = NavigationContext.QueryString["ordinal"];
                    int ordinal = int.Parse(asString);

                    // get...
                    _bookmark = Bookmark.GetByOrdinal(ordinal);

                    // if we don't have one, we must be new...
                    if (_bookmark == null)
                    {
                        Bookmark newBookmark = new Bookmark();
                        newBookmark.Ordinal = ordinal;
                        newBookmark.IsLocalDeleted = false;
                        newBookmark.IsLocalModified = true;

                        // set...
                        _bookmark = newBookmark;
                    }
                }
                return _bookmark;
            }
        }
```

By overriding the OnNavigatedTo method, we can set the DataContext property of the page to initialize the databinding. Thanks to the {Binding <name>} declarations that we added to the markup, this will push the values onto the page. Here's the code:

```
// Add method to ConfigureSingletonPage…
        protected override void OnNavigatedTo(System.Windows.Navigation.NavigationEventArgs e)
        {
            base.OnNavigatedTo(e);

            // show...
            if (Bookmark == null)
                throw new InvalidOperationException("'Bookmark' is null.");
            this.DataContext = this.Bookmark;
        }
```

To add a click handler to the Save Changes button, double-click the button in the designer view, and one will be created for you. In this method, we're going to do validation of the data, push the values onto the bookmark, and save them back. When we save the bookmark, we'll set the IsLocalModified and IsLocalDeleted properties so that we know we have to write the changes back to the server. Note that here we're not using Silverlight databinding to pull data from the control. My motivation for this is that I'm trying to keep the logic between the different platforms the same, and, as iOS and Android do not have Silverlight-style databinding, I have kept this manual. Here's the code for the Save Changes handler.

```
// Add method (and wire up handler via designer) to ConfigureSingletonPage…
    private void buttonSaveChanges_Click(object sender, RoutedEventArgs e)
    {
        ErrorBucket errors = new ErrorBucket();
        string name = this.textName.Text.Trim();
        if (string.IsNullOrEmpty(name))
            errors.Add("Name is required.");
        string url = this.textUrl.Text.Trim();
        if (string.IsNullOrEmpty(url))
            errors.Add("URL is required.");

        // ok?
        if(!(errors.HasErrors))
        {
            // set...
            if (Bookmark == null)
                throw new InvalidOperationException("'Bookmark' is null.");
            this.Bookmark.Name = name;
            this.Bookmark.Url = url;

            // set...
            this.Bookmark.IsLocalModified = true;
            this.Bookmark.IsLocalDeleted = false;

            // save...
            this.Bookmark.SaveChanges();

            // back...
            NavigationService.Navigate(new Uri("/ConfigureForm.xaml",
UriKind.RelativeOrAbsolute));
        }

        // show...
        if(errors.HasErrors)
            Alert.Show(this, errors.GetAllErrorsSeparatedByCrLf());
    }
```

The only thing that remains now is the "delete" functionality.

On Android we have a "long click" on the list, from which we can pop up a context menu. On iOS we can put the list into "edit" mode, where each item has a delete item. Windows Phone does not have either of these—specifically there is no support for context menus. Therefore, to implement the delete option, we have to put it as an application bar option on the singleton edit page itself. Here's the implementation:

```
// Modify constructor on and add button handler to ConfigureSingletonPage…
    public ConfigureSingletonPage()
    {
        InitializeComponent();
```

```
        // application bar...
        this.ApplicationBar = new ApplicationBar();
        this.ApplicationBar.IsVisible = true;
        this.ApplicationBar.IsMenuEnabled = true;

        // add...
        ApplicationBarIconButton delete = new ApplicationBarIconButton(new
Uri("/Images/Delete.png", UriKind.Relative));
        delete.Text = "delete";
        delete.Click += new EventHandler(delete_Click);
        this.ApplicationBar.Buttons.Add(delete);
    }

    void delete_Click(object sender, EventArgs e)
    {
        // delete...
        if (Bookmark == null)
            throw new InvalidOperationException("'Bookmark' is null.");
        this.Bookmark.IsLocalDeleted = true;
        this.Bookmark.SaveChanges();

        // navigate...
        NavigationService.Navigate(new Uri("/ConfigureForm.xaml",
UriKind.RelativeOrAbsolute));
    }
```

That's it! We can now add, edit, and delete bookmarks. Figure 7-7 illustrates the singleton page in operation. Now that we're able to make changes to the bookmarks locally, let's look now at pushing the changes up to the server.

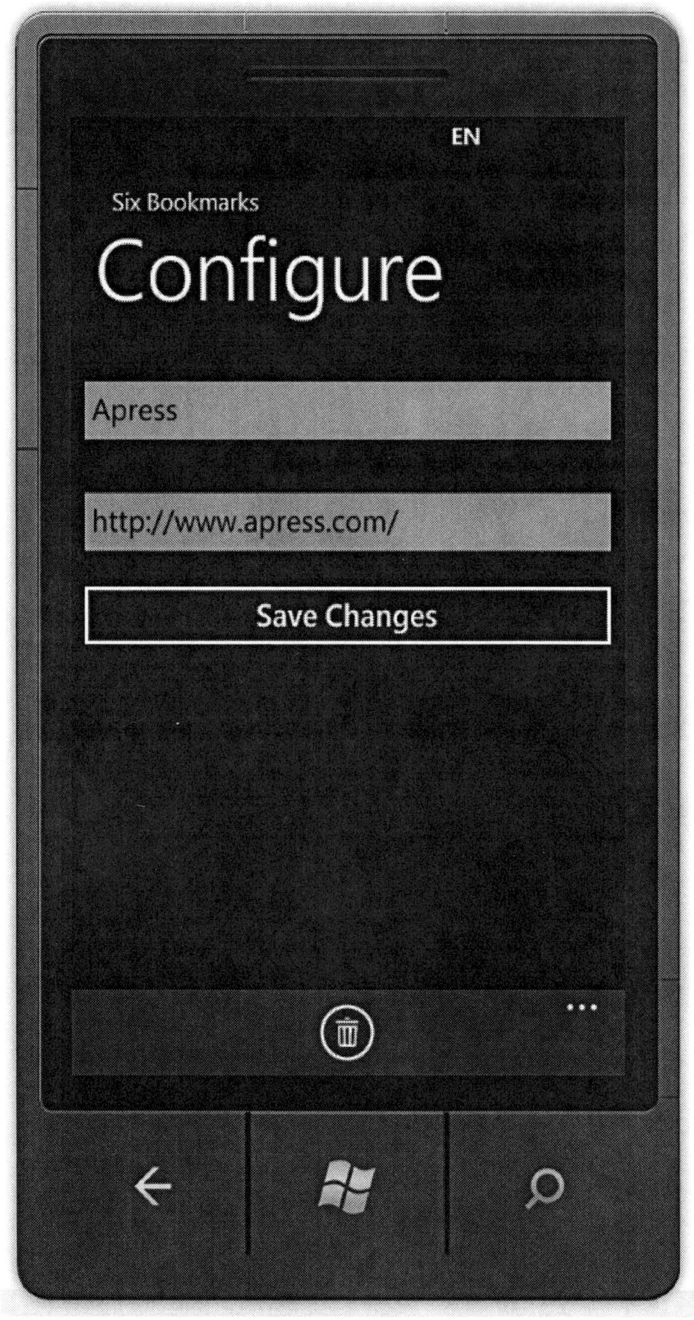

Figure 7-7. The running singleton page

Sending Changes to the Server

In the last chapter, we discussed how there was limited support in Windows Phone 7 for directly consuming the OData service via one of Microsoft's classic "magic wizards." Although I'm not a fan of these sorts of wizards and never have been (you can't write a "proper" application without rolling your sleeves up and getting down and dirty in code), it is helpful to be able to shortcut some of the plumbing. But, no matter—the approach we're going to take in the remainder of this chapter is to roll our own OData client implementation.

The sync operation will run in two phases, and in this order: it will detect and push local changes to the server, and it will then download the latest version of the bookmarks from the server using the method that we have already built. We can be confident that by the time we get through this process, not only have our changes been merged, but also our local database contains an up-to-date set of what is on the server.

Building the PushUpdates Method

We'll start by building the PushUpdates method. There's going to be quite a lot of work here. In this section, we'll first look at the algorithm for detecting changes, and then we'll look at how we physically send changes up.

The algorithm for detecting changes looks like this:

- Download the latest set of bookmarks from the server.

- Walk each change detected on the client, and find the matching server item based on the ordinal of the item.

- If a local change is found and that change *can* be mapped to a server item, issue an update to the server.

- If a local change is found and that change *cannot* be mapped to a server item, issue an insert to the server.

- If we delete a bookmark locally and a bookmark with that ordinal *is* in the server's set, issue a delete to the server.

To support this operation, we'll need a method that updates a server bookmark, a second that inserts a server bookmark, and a third that deletes a server bookmark. If none of those applies, nothing will happen. We'll add these stub methods to the ODataServiceProxy class now—recall that we built this class in the last chapter.

▩ **Note** Although this implementation is going to be used only with bookmarks in this book, this approach will work with any sort of OData entity (with the caveat that for BlackBerry we're going to send the requests through a shim).

Here are the stub methods that we'll add to ODataServiceProxy to help us along. Note that these methods take callbacks for success and failure—we have to do this because we're working within an asynchronous programming model.

```
// Add methods to ODataServiceProxy…
    public void PushUpdate(Entity entity, int serverId, Action callback, Failed failed)
    {
            throw new NotImplementedException("TBD.");
}

    public void PushInsert(Entity entity, Action callback, Failed failed)
    {
            throw new NotImplementedException("TBD.");
}

    public void PushDelete(Entity entity, int serverId, Action callback, Failed failed)
    {
            throw new NotImplementedException("TBD.");
}
```

Moving back onto the PushChanges method in Sync, one thing it's going to need to be able to do is get back the changed local bookmarks and the local deleted (i.e., "soft deleted") bookmarks. I'm going to propose building these as separate methods. Although it's easy enough to build them as a single method, the discussion is easier to follow if they are separate. To do this, we'll add static methods to the Bookmark class itself.

The code for GetBookmarksForServerUpdate will return a list of the bookmarks that have been flagged as having local changes but not flagged as having been deleted. Here's the code:

```
// Add method to Bookmark…
    internal static List<Bookmark> GetBookmarksForServerUpdate()
    {
        DataBoxFilter filter = new DataBoxFilter(GetDataBox());
        filter.AddConstraint("islocalmodified", true);
        filter.AddConstraint("islocaldeleted", false);

        // return...
        return filter.ExecuteEntityCollection<Bookmark>();
    }
```

Likewise, the code for GetBookmarksForServerDelete will return a list of only those bookmarks that have been specifically flagged for deletion. Here's the code:

```
// Add method to Bookmark…
    internal static List<Bookmark> GetBookmarksForServerDelete()
    {
        DataBoxFilter filter = new DataBoxFilter(GetDataBox());
        filter.AddConstraint("islocaldeleted", true);

        // return...
        return filter.ExecuteEntityCollection<Bookmark>();
    }
```

We now have everything that we need to build PushChanges. The fact that we're working in an asynchronous world makes this a little harder than it would in a synchronous world. For one thing, in a synchronous world, you would make one call to a method called PushChanges and immediately after it call a method called GetLatest. We can't do that if we're coding up asynchronously. Instead we have to chain the calls by passing delegates around.

More onerously, because each change itself will block, we actually have to chain the individual change commands (insert, update, or delete) together. The approach I'm going to propose for doing that is a "unit of work" pattern. PushChanges will formulate a list of work units based on what it discovers about the changes. We'll then build a work unit processor that will rattle through these in turn, all the time doing so in a synchronous fashion.

Here's the code for SyncWorkItem. All it needs to do is store the bookmark, the ID on the server (for example, we might have a local ID of "5" referring to a server bookmark with an ID of "105"), and a reference to the type of operation that we're going to do.

```
internal enum ODataOperation
{
    Insert = 0,
    Update = 1,
    Delete = 2
}

internal class SyncWorkItem
{
    internal ODataOperation Operation { get; private set; }
    internal Bookmark Bookmark { get; private set; }
    internal int ServerId { get; private set; }

    internal SyncWorkItem(ODataOperation op, Bookmark bookmark, int serverId)
    {
        if (bookmark == null)
            throw new ArgumentNullException("bookmark");

        this.Operation = op;
        this.Bookmark = bookmark;
        this.ServerId = serverId;
    }
}
```

We'll go through the code for PushChanges in chunks, as it's a little complicated. The first thing we need to do is get the latest version of the bookmarks from the server. This itself is an asynchronous call, so we'll do this using an anonymous method.

```
// Add method to Sync...
    private void PushChanges()
    {
        // need to get all from the server - we need to calculate a delta...
        BookmarksService service = new BookmarksService();
        service.GetAll<Bookmark>((Action<List<Bookmark>>)delegate(List<Bookmark>
fromServer)
        {
```

Once we've got our value back from the server, we'll have a look at our local state and store the results in updates and deletes, like so:

```
// get the local set...
List<Bookmark> updates = Bookmark.GetBookmarksForServerUpdate();
List<Bookmark> deletes = Bookmark.GetBookmarksForServerDelete();
```

Next, for neatness later, we'll get and store the EntityType instance that maps to our Bookmark class. We'll also create a place to store our work units.

```
// et...
EntityType et = EntityType.GetEntityType(typeof(Bookmark));
if (et == null)
    throw new InvalidOperationException("'et' is null.");

// reset the work items...
this.WorkItems = new List<SyncWorkItem>();
```

Now we can get into the change detection code proper. We'll set up one loop that walks each local change, and for each local change, we'll first find a matching server change:

```
// walk the local updates...
foreach (Bookmark local in updates)
{
    // find it in our server-side set...
    Bookmark toUpdate = null;
    foreach (Bookmark server in fromServer)
    {
        if (local.Ordinal == server.Ordinal)
        {
            toUpdate = server;
            break;
        }
    }
}
```

If we do detect a change (i.e., toUpdate is not null), we need to create a new Bookmark instance and populate every field on it, bar the key. When we encounter the key, we'll set the ID to be the ID of the server's copy instead of the local copy. This doesn't matter too much, as when we issue the update request, we won't send up the ID, but it feels appropriate. If we do not detect a change (i.e., toUpdate is null), we'll call insert as opposed to update. Here's the code that makes that choice and also closes off the local bookmark loop. Remember, as we go, we're just tracking changes in work units for later processing.

```
// did we have one to change?
    if (toUpdate != null)
    {
        // walk the fields...
        int serverId = 0;
        foreach (EntityField field in et.Fields)
        {
            if (!(field.IsKey))
                toUpdate.SetValue(field, local.GetValue(field),
SetReason.UserSet);

            else
```

```
                    serverId = toUpdate.BookmarkId;
                }

                // send that up...
                this.WorkItems.Add(new SyncWorkItem(ODataOperation.Update, toUpdate,
serverId));
            }
            else
            {
                // we need to insert it...
                this.WorkItems.Add(new SyncWorkItem(ODataOperation.Insert, local, 0));
            }
        }
```

Once we've done that work, we can look at the deletes, which is the last thing we need to do on the method. The rule here is that if we have marked a bookmark as deleted and we can find a bookmark with a matching ordinal on the server, we'll delete it from the server. This code could be improved by deleting it only if no changes were detected; however, I've chosen to keep it simple. Here's the code.

```
            // what about ones to delete?
            foreach (Bookmark local in deletes)
            {
                // find a matching ordinal on the server...
                foreach (Bookmark server in fromServer)
                {
                    if (local.Ordinal == server.Ordinal)
                        this.WorkItems.Add(new SyncWorkItem(ODataOperation.Delete, server,
server.BookmarkId));
                }
            }
```

The last thing to do in this method is kick off the work unit processor. How this will work is that we'll maintain a pointer in instance memory (WorkItemIndex) of the "to-be-done" work units (WorkItems). We'll start the index at zero and call a method we'll build shortly, called PushNextWorkItem. If the pointer references a valid work unit, it'll do the work, otherwise it will call the next phase of the update chain—GetLatest. (But as I say, we'll do this in a moment.)

```
            // reset the queue and run it...
            this.WorkItemIndex = 0;
            this.PushNextWorkItem();

            // this is the hanging end of the call to get the server bookmarks...
        }, this.Failed);
    }
```

That's all of the changes that we need to make to make the sync run. All that we have to do now is replace the stubs for PushInsert, PushUpdate, and PushDelete with real logic as well as build the work unit processor.

Issuing Server Requests to Insert, Update, and Delete

In the last chapter, we requested XML data from the server that described our server-side entities in OData format. When we send insert and update requests back to the server, we need to create XML documents that adhere to that format. (Delete does not have a payload, so you do not need to send an XML document.)

The three operations we need to fire can be described thus:

- For insert operations, we issue an HTTP POST to the base URL of the entity's service and supply XML that describes the initial value of the fields, e.g., http://services.multimobiledevelopment.com/services/Bookmarks.svc/Bookmark.

- For update operations, we issue an HTTP MERGE to the URL of the item in question and supply XML that describes the changed fields, e.g., http://services.multimobiledevelopment.com/services/Bookmarks.svc/Bookmark (1000).

- For delete operations, we issue an HTTP DELETE to the URL of the item in question and provide no payload, e.g., http://services.multimobiledevelopment.com/services/Bookmarks.svc/.

The OData standard allows us to issue an HTTP MERGE or an HTTP PUT to send an "update" instruction. MERGE is better (in this case at least) because it will update the provided fields but leave the remaining fields. PUT requires all of the fields to be sent, as any missing fields are reset to their default values. As a general principle of designing systems that have this kind of intraconnected messaging, it's always a good idea to try to keep things loosely coupled, and MERGE feels looser to me.

We've already stubbed in methods for each of the three operations, so let's build them now.

Building PushNextWorkItem

Hopefully this method is easy to understand—I happen to feel this approach is quite elegant, although I can take no credit for it, as it's an obvious idea. As mentioned before, if WorkItemIndex refers to a valid piece of work, it will call the operation. Once the end of the operation (itself being asynchronous) is signaled, we'll increment the counter and call PushNextWorkItem again. Eventually the queue will be exhausted and our work will be done. Here's the code:

```
// Add to Sync…
private void PushNextWorkItem()
    {
        Debug.WriteLine(string.Format("Pushing work item {0}...", this.WorkItemIndex));

        // have we reached the end?  if so, branch off and get the latest...
        if (this.WorkItemIndex == this.WorkItems.Count)
        {
            this.GetLatest();
            return;
        }

        // get it...
        SyncWorkItem item = this.WorkItems[this.WorkItemIndex];

        // callback...
```

```
        Action callback = new Action(HandleWorkItemCompleted);

        // run...
        BookmarksService service = new BookmarksService();
        if (item.Operation == ODataOperation.Insert)
            service.PushInsert(item.Bookmark, callback, this.Failed);
        else if (item.Operation == ODataOperation.Update)
            service.PushUpdate(item.Bookmark, item.ServerId, callback, this.Failed);
        else if (item.Operation == ODataOperation.Delete)
            service.PushDelete(item.Bookmark, item.ServerId, callback, this.Failed);
        else
            throw new NotSupportedException(string.Format("Cannot handle '{0}'.",
item.Operation));
    }

    private void HandleWorkItemCompleted()
    {
        Debug.WriteLine("Work item completed.");

        // increment the index...
        this.WorkItemIndex++;

        // run the next one...
        this.PushNextWorkItem();
    }
```

Update via HTTP MERGE and Insert via HTTP POST

We're going to create one main method for doing updates and tweak its operation so that it also works for inserts.

Marking Fields As Being Available on the Server

We're now going to have to make a change to the application to get around an aspect of the OData protocol, namely, that if we try to update a field on the server that does not exist, we'll get an error back. The LocalModified and LocalDeleted columns that we added do not exist on the server, so any update or insert server operations that mention those will fail. (I'm not a fan of this—it seems wrong. It would seem better to me to ignore this situation much as the old SOAP protocol would. It implies it's possible to keep all of the clients that use the service in sync, or makes deprecation of server-side functionality harder than it should be.)

To do this, we'll add a property to EntityField that indicates whether the property is on the server.

▧ **Note** This is one of these application design aspects that end up in a messy design. It's not brilliant to have a metadata layer and the application have this "special" behavior in it—it would be better if this flag did not exist. But as a corollary, I'm not keen on having two classes do roughly the same thing—e.g., a server representation of a bookmark and a local representation. Essentially, there has to be a compromise somewhere…

Firstly, we'll add an `IsOnServer` property to `EntityField` (default true), like so:

```
// Add IsOnServer property and field to EntityField...
  public class EntityField : EntityItem
  {
      public DataType Type { get; private set; }
      public int Size { get; private set; }
      public int Ordinal { get; private set; }
      public bool IsKey { get; set; }
      public bool IsOnServer { get; set; }
```

And when we come to define the fields on `Bookmark` in our constructor on `SixBookmarksRuntime`, we'll set the flag for the two applicable fields:

```
// Modify Start method on SixBookmarksRuntime...
          private SixBookmarksRuntime()
          {
          // settings...
          this.Settings = SimpleXmlPropertyBag.Load("Settings.xml", false);

          // register the entity type...
          EntityType bookmark = new EntityType(typeof(Bookmark), "Bookmark");
          bookmark.AddField(Bookmark.BookmarkIdKey, Bookmark.BookmarkIdKey, DataType.Int32,
-1).IsKey = true;
          bookmark.AddField(Bookmark.NameKey, Bookmark.NameKey, DataType.String, 128);
          bookmark.AddField(Bookmark.UrlKey, Bookmark.UrlKey, DataType.String, 128);
          bookmark.AddField(Bookmark.OrdinalKey, Bookmark.OrdinalKey, DataType.Int32, -1);
          bookmark.AddField(Bookmark.IsLocalModifiedKey, Bookmark.IsLocalModifiedKey,
DataType.Boolean, -1).IsOnServer = false;
          bookmark.AddField(Bookmark.IsLocalDeletedKey, Bookmark.IsLocalDeletedKey,
DataType.Boolean, -1).IsOnServer = false;
          EntityType.RegisterEntityType(bookmark);

          // create a tombstone data entity type...
          EntityType tombstone = new EntityType(typeof(TombstoneData), "TombstoneData");
          tombstone.AddField(TombstoneData.TombstoneDataIdKey,
TombstoneData.TombstoneDataIdKey, DataType.Int32, -1).IsKey = true;
          tombstone.AddField(TombstoneData.NameKey, TombstoneData.NameKey, DataType.String,
64);
          tombstone.AddField(TombstoneData.ValueKey, TombstoneData.ValueKey,
DataType.String, 256);
          EntityType.RegisterEntityType(tombstone);
      }
```

Now we can use this property when building the messages to send to the server.

Building the XML

The documentation on the OData web site gives an example of an insert as the following listing:

```
POST /OData/OData.svc/Categories HTTP/1.1
Host: services.odata.org
DataServiceVersion: 1.0
MaxDataServiceVersion: 2.0
accept: application/atom+xml
content-type: application/atom+xml
Content-Length: 634

<?xml version="1.0" encoding="utf-8"?>
<entry xmlns:d="http://schemas.microsoft.com/ado/2007/08/dataservices"
       xmlns:m="http://schemas.microsoft.com/ado/2007/08/dataservices/metadata"
       xmlns="http://www.w3.org/2005/Atom">
    <title type="text"></title>
    <updated>2010-02-27T21:36:47Z</updated>
    <author>
        <name />
    </author>
    <category term="DataServiceProviderDemo.Category"
        scheme="http://schemas.microsoft.com/ado/2007/08/dataservices/scheme" />
    <content type="application/xml">
        <m:properties>
            <d:ID>10</d:ID>
            <d:Name>Clothing</d:Name>
        </m:properties>
    </content>
</entry>
```

If you refer back to the XML retrieved from the server in the last chapter, you can see that this is basically just a rehash of the data that we provided. Our job, then, is to replicate this request.

▓ **Note** As of the time of writing, the site at www.odata.org/ is showing the entry elements in the preceding listing as having an uppercase "E," e.g., Entry. The interface will not work with Entry compared to entry; hence I have edited it here, assuming a typo on the OData site.

In our request, we're going to trim it down slightly and omit the title, updated, author, and category elements. These are not required to make the request work. We'll also omit the DataServiceVersion and MaxDataServiceVersion headers, but we'll add in our special x-amx-apiusername and x-amx-token headers. If we patch in bookmark data rather than the sample data from the OData site, we'll have something like this:

```
POST /services/bookmarks.svc/Bookmark HTTP/1.1
Host: services.multimobiledevelopment.com
accept: application/atom+xml
content-type: application/atom+xml
content-encoding: UTF-8
content-length: 384
x-amx-apiusername: amxmobile
```

```
x-amx-token: 961c8c1b9d4ddd5799e7f0a7b4a5ee8b

<entry xmlns:d="http://schemas.microsoft.com/ado/2007/08/dataservices"
       xmlns:m="http://schemas.microsoft.com/ado/2007/08/dataservices/metadata"
       xmlns="http://www.w3.org/2005/Atom">
    <content type="application/xml">
        <m:properties>
            <d:Name>Apress</d:Name>
            <d:Url>http://www.apress.com/</d:Url>
            <d:Ordinal>0</d:Ordinal>
        </m:properties>
    </content>
</entry>
```

I personally feel that Microsoft's XML implementation in the XmlDocument class and others is the best part of .NET. The LINQ implementation that we have to use for Windows Phone is also solid and straightforward. For this reason, I'm just going to let the elegance of the API speak for itself in the following implementation!

Here's the listing for the ODataServiceProxy class:

```
// Replace stub method on ODataServiceProxy…
        public void PushUpdate(Entity entity, int serverId, Action callback, Failed failed)
    {
        XDocument doc = new XDocument();

        // entry...
        XElement entryElement = new XElement(XName.Get("entry", AtomNamespace));
        doc.Add(entryElement);

        // content...
        XElement contentElement = new XElement(XName.Get("content", AtomNamespace));
        contentElement.Add(new XAttribute(XName.Get("type", string.Empty),
"application/xml"));
        entryElement.Add(contentElement);

        // properties...
        XElement propertiesElement = new XElement(XName.Get("properties",
MsMetadataNamespace));
        contentElement.Add(propertiesElement);

        // walk the fields...
        EntityType et = entity.EntityType;
        if (et == null)
            throw new InvalidOperationException("'et' is null.");
        foreach (EntityField field in et.Fields)
        {
            if (!(field.IsKey) && field.IsOnServer)
            {
                // create...
                XElement element = new XElement(XName.Get(field.Name, MsDataNamespace));
                object value = entity.GetValue(field);
                if (value != null)
```

```
                        element.Value = value.ToString();

                    // add...
                    propertiesElement.Add(element);
                }
            }

            // run...
            String url = null;
            ODataOperation op = ODataOperation.Update;
            String xmlAsString = doc.ToString();
            if (serverId != 0)
                url = GetEntityUrlForPush(entity, serverId);
            else
            {
                url = this.GetServiceUrl(et);
                op = ODataOperation.Insert;
            }

            // run...
            ExecuteODataOperation(op, url, xmlAsString, callback, failed);
        }

        private string GetEntityUrlForPush(Entity entity, int serverId)
        {
            return string.Format("{0}({1})", GetServiceUrl(entity.EntityType), serverId);
        }
```

The code at the bottom of the PushUpdate defers to ExecuteODataOperation, which we will build in a moment. Notice as well that we have sneaked in a helper method—GetEntityUrlForPush. This builds the URL for the item.

The final argument to PushUpdate is the ID of the item on the server. If this is non-zero, we'll assume that we're updating and format the URL and set the operation as appropriate. Conversely, if it is, we'll use the base service URL and specify a different value in op.

Now that we have our PushUpdate method, we'll quickly add PushInsert and PushDelete so that we have a complete set. Here's the listing:

```
// Replace stub methods on ODataServiceProxy…
        public void PushInsert(Entity entity, Action callback, Failed failed)
        {
            // an insert is an update but with a different url...
            PushUpdate(entity, 0, callback, failed);
        }

        public void PushDelete(Entity entity, int serverId, Action callback, Failed failed)
        {
            // get...
            string url = GetEntityUrlForPush(entity, serverId);
            ExecuteODataOperation(ODataOperation.Delete, url, null, callback, failed);
        }
```

Building ExecuteODataOperation

The last thing we have to do is build ExecuteODataOperation. This method will take all of that information and build a request to issue to the server.

Here's what ExecuteODataOperation needs to do:

- We'll ensure that the API has been set up by calling EnsureApiAuthenticated.

- We'll choose the type of HTTP Client operation we want to run, dependent on what we're looking to achieve.

- To make the request, we need to pass up our special x-amx-apiusername and x-amx-token headers. We'll obtain these from the GetDownloadSettings method that we built earlier and pass those on.

- If we have anything other than a DELETE request, we'll add the XML to the request.

- We'll then execute the request.

There is one slightly complicated part, and—as usual—it relates to anonymous programming.

When we have to send XML up to the server, we have to access a "request stream." There's no blocking call to get this stream, so, when the time comes, we'll call BeginGetRequestStream on the HttpWebRequest class and handle the result in a callback. We can then send up the XML and get the response, again waiting for a callback.

To facilitate all this, we have to create an ODataRequestState class that can hold references to the callbacks that were passed into us (these ultimately relate back to the callbacks the caller gave us right at the top of the chain), a reference to the XML to send, and a reference to the request. If you recall, we had a similar class called ODataFetchState in the last chapter that was involved in getting data from the server.

Here's the private ODataRequestState class:

```
// Add as a private class within ODataServiceProxy...
    private class ODataRequestState
    {
        internal HttpWebRequest Request;
        internal Action Callback;
        internal Failed Failed;
        internal string OutboundXml;
    }
```

Oddly, because nothing really magic happens in ExecuteODataOperation, it's quite a simple method. We set up the HTTP method as appropriate, set up the headers, and then either branch off and get our request stream to send up the XML, or branch off and wait for the response from the server in the case of a "delete." Here's the code:

```
// Add to ODataServiceProxy...
    private void ExecuteODataOperation(ODataOperation opType, String url, String xml,
Action callback, Failed failed)
    {
        // create the request...
        HttpWebRequest request = (HttpWebRequest)WebRequest.Create(url);

        // set the method...
```

```
            if (opType == ODataOperation.Insert)
                request.Method = "POST";
            else if (opType == ODataOperation.Update)
                request.Method = "MERGE";
            else if (opType == ODataOperation.Delete)
                request.Method = "DELETE";
            else
                throw new NotSupportedException(string.Format("Cannot handle '{0}'.",
opType));

            // headers... (including our special tokens)...
            DownloadSettings settings = this.GetDownloadSettings();
            foreach (string name in settings.ExtraHeaders.Keys)
                request.Headers[name] = settings.ExtraHeaders[name];

            // create a state object...
            ODataRequestState state = new ODataRequestState();
            state.Request = request;
            state.Callback = callback;
            state.Failed = failed;
            state.OutboundXml = xml;

            // do we have xml?
            if (!(string.IsNullOrEmpty(xml)))
            {
                byte[] bs = Encoding.UTF8.GetBytes(xml);
                request.ContentType = "application/atom+xml";
                request.BeginGetRequestStream(new AsyncCallback(HandleOutboundXmlRequest),
state);
            }
            else
                request.BeginGetResponse(new AsyncCallback(HandleODataOperationResponse),
state);
        }
```

The last bit of the work is just to finish off that HandleOutboundXmlRequest callback. (This could have been done anonymously, but I felt this was easier to read.) Here's the code:

```
        private void HandleOutboundXmlRequest(IAsyncResult result)
        {
            // state...
            ODataRequestState state = (ODataRequestState)result.AsyncState;
            try
            {
                Stream stream = state.Request.EndGetRequestStream(result);
                if (stream == null)
                    throw new InvalidOperationException("'stream' is null.");
                using (stream)
                {
                    // send it...
                    StreamWriter writer = new StreamWriter(stream);
                    writer.Write(state.OutboundXml);
```

```
                    writer.Flush();
                }

                // ok... next...
                state.Request.BeginGetResponse(new
AsyncCallback(HandleODataOperationResponse), state);
            }
            catch (Exception ex)
            {
                state.Failed(ex);
            }
        }
    }
```

That's it! The changes we made to the Sync class earlier will run when the logon operation succeeds, or when the user manually chooses the Finish option on the configuration screen. When the code runs, the changes will be sent up and new versions downloaded. You can see the results by examining the database directly by managing the appropriate user at http://services.multimobiledevelopment.com/.

Conclusion

In this chapter, we have covered a lot of ground. We have looked at how to modify the ORM functionality to bring back selections of data. We have also looked at building a comprehensive user interface for editing the bookmarks, including how to handle standard UI elements such as lists and menus. Finally, we completed our synchronization routine so that we can send back updates to the server using the OData protocol.

CHAPTER 8

■■■

Six Bookmarks on Windows Mobile

In this chapter, we're going to look at the Windows Mobile version of the Six Bookmarks application. This chapter will be unique in that I'm not going to show you how to build the Six Bookmarks application on Windows Mobile. Instead, I'm going to take you through the highlights of the implementation that you can download from http://code.multimobiledevelopment.com/. The reason for this is twofold. Firstly, with Microsoft deprecating this platform, it's more likely that you will have Windows Mobile code that you wish to port, as opposed to you wanting to build the application from scratch. Secondly, the code is so similar to the Windows Phone implementation covered in Chapters 4 through 7 that it would be a couple of hundred pages of repeated text.

That said, I will go into more detail in the section on SQL CE since, as of the time of writing, the Windows Phone chapter did not feature a relational database. My anticipated path of least resistance to getting a relational database on Windows Phone is for Microsoft to switch SQL CE back on again, although there are some currently active community efforts to bring SQLite to Windows Phone.

■ **Note** To get the most out of this chapter, make sure that you have gone through the Windows Phone section so that you have a good picture of how the application hangs together.

Migrating/Porting

In terms of migrating, if you do have an app to migrate, you will most likely be moving to Android, iOS, or Windows Phone. As of the time of writing, Android and iOS look to be the dominant players for the medium term, and Windows Phone is an attractive choice for those with an existing investment in Microsoft's mobile working solutions.

Whatever migration path you choose, you will have to rewrite the user interface. While some validation logic can probably be salvaged, the difference in approaches between Windows Mobile and any of the other platforms is extreme.

In terms of business logic (in this context, "anything that's not UI"), when moving to iOS, you will almost certainly need to rewrite the code. Intellectual property in terms of algorithms and architecture you can probably take with you—but actual lines of code will be hard to port because Objective-C and C# are so vastly different. The story with Android is a little better—there is enough overlap between C# and Java to make it possible to move lines of code over. (This will be a degree harder if your code base is VB.NET.) The story with Windows Phone is better as you're still using native .NET, but most frustrating in some ways because it's *so* close, yet so far away.

> ■ **Note** As we go through, I shall endeavor to tell you where breaking changes are introduced between Windows Mobile and Windows Phone. I won't do this with iOS and Android—the appropriate sections in this book will stand as a resource for achieving this sort of migration. Look for boxes like this one by way of summaries.

Of course, there is a third way, which is to use Mono for the business logic. By the time you read this, MonoDroid (Android) will be out of beta and into release. MonoTouch (iOS) is available, but there are questions about whether applications based on this will continue to be smiled upon in the Apple App Store. (They are currently, and there have been some very public noises about Mono being OK for iOS apps.) Personally I feel that Mono is a very attractive option. (I would be a very happy man if I woke up and found an announcement that Apple was moving to MonoTouch as the de facto method for iOS development.) There are some community efforts to move SQLite over to Windows Phone—what an ideal world it would be to be able to use the same database on all three platforms and have one core code base in C# that you could compile against Windows Phone, Android, and iOS.

Finally, there is also a fourth way, in that you could use an intermediate layer that you can target and then execute on any of the platforms; however, such layers are explicitly not the remit of this book.

The Toolset

I won't show you how to install the toolset, as I'm assuming you already have a code base that you wish to port over. For reference, I have created a Smart Device Project using Visual Studio 2008 for both the "Hello, world" and Six Bookmarks applications. It's not possible to create Smart Device Projects in Visual Studio 2010—only Windows Phone can be targeted from this version of Visual Studio. Likewise, although the .NET Compact Framework was available in VS.NET 2003, we don't support this because the version of the Framework that we need (2.0) was not available then.

Out-of-the-box, Visual Studio 2008 does not support the Windows Mobile 6.0 SDK. You will need to download and install this separately.

> ■ **Note** This SDK is becoming increasingly hard to find on Google, as Google tries to make sense of the increasing "windows phone" traffic. This URL linking to the SDK was correct as of the time of going to print: `http://tinyurl.com/ynlobc`.

Hello, World

I'm not going to take you through a "Hello, world" application on Windows Mobile—again, I'm assuming that you have some experience of this platform. However, you can download a "Hello, world" application from `http://code.multimobiledevelopment.com/`.

Six Bookmarks

You can download the Six Bookmarks application from `http://code.multimobiledevelopment.com/`. You should download this and confirm that it is working before proceeding.

In the rest of this section, I'll go through the functional specification presented in Chapter 3, introduce some salient code, and link off into other platforms.

How the Windows Mobile Application Was Built

It may help to understand how I built the Windows Mobile application.

When building the applications for the other platforms, I started from scratch each time. On occasion I may have copied some code from some classes, but generally they were all hand-done.

For the Windows Mobile application, I created a new project and copied the code from the Windows Phone application. As SQL CE is supported on Windows Mobile, I removed the data box implementation and created a specific class called SqlCeHelper to talk to the SQL CE database. In addition, there is no OData proxy for Windows Mobile (unlike Windows Phone), and this was written from scratch, based on the Android implementation.

Logging On and Calling RESTful Services

One of the strengths of Windows Mobile is that the user interface is based on Windows Forms; hence, if you know how to build an application in Windows Forms, you already know how to target Windows Mobile devices. (Unfortunately for Microsoft, this cut both ways and painted it into a corner, insofar as new devices used different and slicker UI metaphors.)

We can start by designing the logon form. This is just an issue of dragging and dropping controls onto the form. The class in the project we're referring to here is the LogonForm. Figure 8-1 illustrates.

Figure 8-1. The logon form

We'll look at the operation of the logon form shortly, but now I want to talk about asynchronous programming.

One thing that I have brought forward from the Windows Phone implementation is the asynchronous programming model. For example, here's the code from HttpHelper that makes an asynchronous download request using BeginRequest:

```
// Method within HttpHelper class…
        public static void Download(string url, DownloadSettings settings, Action<string>
success, Failed failure)
        {
            // create the request stub...
            HttpWebRequest request = (HttpWebRequest)WebRequest.Create(url);
            request.UserAgent = "Mozilla/5.0 (Windows; U; Windows NT 6.1; en-GB; rv:1.9.2.7)
Gecko/20100713 Firefox/3.6.7";

            // add...
            if (settings != null)
            {
                foreach (string name in settings.ExtraHeaders.Keys)
                    request.Headers[name] = settings.ExtraHeaders[name];
            }

            // call the server... we'll get notified at some point...
            request.BeginGetResponse(new AsyncCallback(HandleDownloadResult), new object[] {
request, success, failure });
        }
```

In Windows Mobile, we do have the GetRequest method that runs synchronously and blocks the caller. It's likely that if you are porting code over that does HTTP communications, you will have this sort of blocking, synchronous call. You have two options in this case.

The first option, which is preferable, is to rewrite the code as asynchronous calls. However, this is likely to be a big change, requiring lots of dependent code to be reworked, and it could be highly unattractive. The second option, which is not preferable, is to build a layer on top of the asynchronous calls that block and make it appear that the original call was synchronous. This is a perfectly workable idea and is very attractive in that you do not have to rewrite large quantities of dependent code. That said, the user will not get as good an experience if the application is making blocking network calls all over the place. (A hidden third option would therefore be to use both techniques.)

■ **Note** When moving from Windows Mobile to Windows Phone, you have no synchronous/blocking HTTP calls. These would therefore have to be reengineered as asynchronous calls, or you would need to write an intermediate layer that behaved synchronously from the caller's perspective, despite the calls being asynchronous.

Back on the logon form, the code to initiate the logon is the same as the Windows Phone implementation, specifically as follows:

```
// Method handler and implementation within LogonForm class…
        private void menuLogon_Click(object sender, EventArgs e)
        {
            this.DoLogon();
        }

        private void DoLogon()
        {
            // validate...
            ErrorBucket bucket = new ErrorBucket();
            string username = this.textUsername.Text.Trim();
            if (string.IsNullOrEmpty(username))
                bucket.Add("Username is required.");
            string password = this.textPassword.Text.Trim();
            if (string.IsNullOrEmpty(password))
                bucket.Add("Password is required.");

            // error?
            if (bucket.HasErrors)
            {
                Alert.Show(bucket.GetAllErrorsSeparatedByCrLf());
                return;
            }

            // clear the credentials...
            this.ClearCredentials();

            // logon...
            UsersService users = new UsersService();
            users.Logon(username, password, delegate(LogonResponse response)
            {
                // we managed to get a response...
                if (response.Result == LogonResult.LogonOk)
                {
                    // we did it...
                    this.LogonOk();
                }
                else
                    Alert.Show(response.Message);

            }, Alert.GetFailedHandler());
        }
```

Let's look now in more detail at making RESTful calls.

Making RESTful Calls

The RESTful service calls are done in the same way as per Windows Phones—namely a custom request constructed using the .NET System.Net.HttpWebRequest class. (The service protocol is device-agnostic, and so the way we make the calls and the data that we need to provide have not changed.)

RestRequestArgs contains the arguments that need to be passed up to the RESTful services. This is used to create a URL with the arguments expressed as query string values—for example, `http://services.multimobiledevelopment.com/services/apirest.aspx?operation=logon&password=password`.

As we know, the call has to be done asynchronously, and so whenever we make a service call, we pass in a "success" delegate and a "failed" delegate. Here's the `Logon` method on `UsersService` that shows how to make one of these calls:

```
// Method within UsersService class…
    public void Logon(String username, String password, Action<LogonResponse> callback,
Failed failed)
    {
        // create the request...
        RestRequestArgs args = new RestRequestArgs("logon");

        // add the username and password...
        args["username"] = username;
        args["password"] = password;

        // send the request...
        SendRequest(args, delegate(XElement element)
        {
            // create a result from that...
            LogonResponse response = LogonResponse.FromXmlElement(element);
            if (response == null)
                throw new InvalidOperationException("'response' is null.");

            // callback...
            callback(response);

        }, failed);
    }
```

SendRequest is implemented in the base `RestServiceProxy` class. This method takes care of the problem of needing to authenticate the API before any RESTful calls can be made. What happens is that SendRequest checks to see whether we have an API token in static memory, and if we do not, it calls the Logon method on the API service. (The `ApiService` class contains code that presents an infinite loop condition.) If a logon token does exist, the method is called directly.

This approach requires a little jiggery-pokery because we need to hold a copy of the original parameters in memory in case we have to divert off and authenticate the API first. All of these calls are chained together in a set of asynchronous calls. Here's the SendRequest method:

```
// Method in RestServiceBase class…
    internal void SendRequest(RestRequestArgs args, Action<XElement> success, Failed
failed)
    {
        if (args == null)
            throw new ArgumentNullException("args");
        if (success == null)
            throw new ArgumentNullException("success");
        if (failed == null)
```

```
            throw new ArgumentNullException("failed");

        // create a request state...
        RequestState state = new RequestState()
        {
            Owner = this,
            Args = args,
            Success = success,
            Failed = failed
        };

        // are we authenticated?  if we're not, we need to call that first...
        if (!(IsAuthenticated))
        {
            // call the authenticate routine, and ask it to call the state we just set up
            // if authentication works...
            ApiService.Authenticate(new Action(state.DoRequest), failed);
        }
        else
        {
            // call the method directly...
            state.DoRequest();
        }
    }
```

The protocol definition states that on the RESTful services we will receive an XML document back containing values. (Figure 8-2 illustrates.)

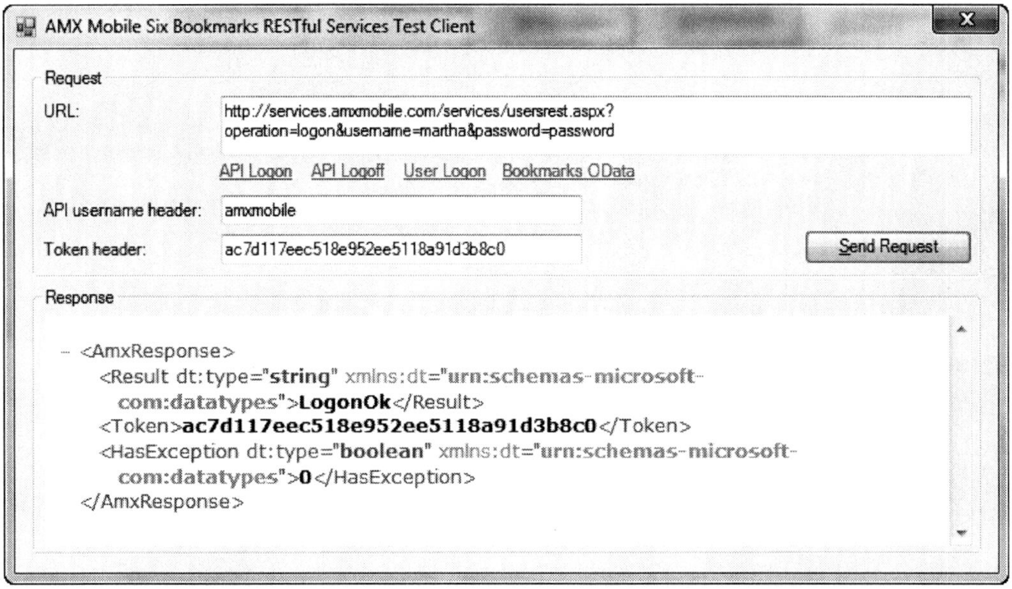

Figure 8-2. An example of a response from a successful request to the Users service

This document has to have a root element with the name AmxResponse. Further, if this document contains true within its HasException, we know that the server raised an exception that has to be visible on the client. If this document does not represent an exception, the success callback is called and the AmxResponse element is passed through to the caller.

```
// Private class within RestRequestProxy class…
        private class RequestState
        {
            internal RestServiceProxy Owner { get; set; }
            internal RestRequestArgs Args { get; set; }
            internal Action<XElement> Success { get; set; }
            internal Failed Failed { get; set; }

            internal void DoRequest()
            {
                // get a url...
                string url = this.Owner.ResolvedServiceUrl;
                url = HttpHelper.BuildUrl(url, this.Args);

                // call download.  this is an async method, so we need to block...
                XDocument doc = null;
                HttpHelper.Download(url, this.Owner.GetDownloadSettings(), delegate(string
result)
                {
                    // we'll have some content - initialize XDocument and parse it...
                    using (TextReader reader = new StringReader(result))
                    {
                        doc = XDocument.Load(reader);
                        if (doc == null)
                            throw new InvalidOperationException("'doc' is null.");
                    }

                    // look for the response element...
                    var responseElements = new List<XElement>(doc.Descendants("AmxResponse"));
                    if (responseElements.Count == 0)
                        throw new InvalidOperationException("An AmxResponse element was not
returned.");

                    // select out "HasException"...
                    XElement responseElement = responseElements[0];
                    bool hasException = XmlHelper.GetElementBoolean(responseElement,
"HasException", true);
                    if (!(hasException))
                        this.Success(responseElement);
                    else
                    {
                        // get the error...
                        string message = XmlHelper.GetElementString(responseElement, "Error",
true);
                        throw new InvalidOperationException(string.Format("The server returned
an error: {0}.", message));
                    }
```

```
            }, this.Failed);
        }
    }
```

In terms of how we're handling the XML, we have two options. Because I copied this code from Windows Phone, I've used the System.Xml.Linq namespace and XDocument class. It's likely that if you have old Windows Mobile code, you are using the System.Xml.XmlDocument class, which has been available in the .NET Compact Framework since version 1.

■ **Note** If you're migrating to Windows Phone, the "classic" version is no longer supported, and hence you will have to migrate the XML calls to the LINQ version.

File Access

The Windows Phone client uses the file system in two ways—it uses the data box to store entities, but it also uses the file system to store a small configuration file for the "remember me" functionality.

On Windows Phone, we use isolated storage. At the time, I discussed how isolated storage was originally added to .NET to help with Windows Forms controls exposes, as ActiveX controls sandbox their file store. Oddly, in Windows Mobile, we don't have isolated storage (which speaks volumes about what the world looked like when Windows Mobile was invented). More to the point, in terms of migration to Windows Phone, it's not possible to write files anywhere you like on the device's disk—you *have* to use isolated storage.

Luckily this one isn't that hard—the way that you use file streams and paths hasn't really changed. The only problem that you will run into is if your application requires file access outside of isolated storage for some reason, which essentially is not allowed.

■ **Note** If you're migrating to Windows Phone, the "isolated storage" file model is the only one that you have. All file access has to be reworked to use isolated storage.

Synchronization 1: Downloading Bookmarks

OData is a very new protocol, and I wanted to use it in the book because I felt it would become an important protocol over the next few years. Although it started life within Microsoft, it is now an open standard. (More importantly, knowing that the RESTful services were proprietary, I wanted to give the applications the capability of talking to an open protocol.)

If you followed along during the iOS and Android chapters, you'll know that we had to build an OData client ourselves. Over the next few years, it's likely that libraries will become available for iOS and Android that will make communicating with OData sources easier. That said, it's not particularly likely that anyone will build a Windows Mobile library for OData communications.

The Six Bookmarks application therefore has a roll-your-own OData client based, as mentioned before, on the roll-your-own Android implementation discussed previously.

In this section, we'll look at the code that downloads the bookmarks from the OData source and look at the stub within the synchronization routine that does the downloading. In a later section, we'll send changes back up.

The roll-your-own implementation essentially has to create an XML document of the appropriate form and send it to the appropriate URL. The server—obviously—will do the hard work in getting it into the underlying store.

■ **Note** When migrating from Windows Mobile to Windows Phone, if you happen to have rolled your own OData proxy, this will still work on Windows Phone, and hence the choice to migrate it over to the Windows Phone library/Visual Studio–generated proxy is up to you. (That said, if your OData service proxy makes calls in a synchronous fashion, you'll need to modify this so that calls can be made asynchronously.)

Object-Relational Mapping

I'm not going to talk about the object-relational mapping subsystem that is used in the Windows Mobile application. It's identical to the one for Windows Phone. More details can be found in Chapter 6.

Retrieving Entities

By default, when you address the OData source with an HTTP GET operation on the appropriate URL, you will receive a list of the entities. The URL that we request is this one:

```
http://services.multimobiledevelopment.com/services/Bookmarks.svc/Bookmark
```

When this request completes, our "success" callback will be called with an XDocument instance. Here's the code that initiates the request:

```
// Method within ODataServiceProxy class…
        public void GetAll<T>(Action<List<T>> callback, Failed failed)
            where T : Entity
        {
            EntityType et = EntityType.GetEntityType(typeof(T));

            // create a state object...
            ODataFetchState<T> state = new ODataFetchState<T>();
            state.Callback = callback;
            state.Failed = failed;

            // run...
            String url = GetServiceUrl(et);
            HttpHelper.DownloadXml(url, GetDownloadSettings(), new
Action<XDocument>(state.ReceiveXml), failed);
        }
```

The XML that we receive over this interface will look something like this:

```xml
<?xml version="1.0" encoding="iso-8859-1" standalone="yes"?>
<feed xml:base="http://services. multimobiledevelopment.com/services/Bookmarks.svc/"
xmlns:d="http://schemas.microsoft.com/ado/2007/08/dataservices"
xmlns:m="http://schemas.microsoft.com/ado/2007/08/dataservices/metadata"
xmlns="http://www.w3.org/2005/Atom">
  <title type="text">Bookmark</title>
  <id>http://services. multimobiledevelopment.com/services/bookmarks.svc/Bookmark</id>
  <updated>2010-04-18T10:54:32Z</updated>
  <link rel="self" title="Bookmark" href="Bookmark" />
  <entry>
    <id>http://services. multimobiledevelopment.com/services/Bookmarks.svc/Bookmark(1002)</id>
    <title type="text"></title>
    <updated>2010-04-18T10:54:32Z</updated>
    <author>
      <name />
    </author>
    <link rel="edit" title="Bookmark" href="Bookmark(1002)" />
    <category term="AmxMobile.Services.Bookmark"
scheme="http://schemas.microsoft.com/ado/2007/08/dataservices/scheme" />
    <content type="application/xml">
      <m:properties>
        <d:BookmarkId m:type="Edm.Int32">1002</d:BookmarkId>
        <d:UserId m:type="Edm.Int32">1001</d:UserId>
        <d:Name>.NET 247</d:Name>
        <d:Url>http://www.dotnet247.com/</d:Url>
        <d:Ordinal m:type="Edm.Int32">1</d:Ordinal>
      </m:properties>
    </content>
  </entry>
  <entry>
    <id>http://services. multimobiledevelopment.com/services/Bookmarks.svc/Bookmark(1001)</id>
    <title type="text"></title>
    <updated>2010-04-18T10:54:32Z</updated>
    <author>
      <name />
    </author>
    <link rel="edit" title="Bookmark" href="Bookmark(1001)" />
    <category term="AmxMobile.Services.Bookmark"
scheme="http://schemas.microsoft.com/ado/2007/08/dataservices/scheme" />
    <content type="application/xml">
      <m:properties>
        <d:BookmarkId m:type="Edm.Int32">1001</d:BookmarkId>
        <d:UserId m:type="Edm.Int32">1001</d:UserId>
        <d:Name>Google</d:Name>
        <d:Url>http://www.google.co.uk/</d:Url>
        <d:Ordinal m:type="Edm.Int32">0</d:Ordinal>
      </m:properties>
    </content>
  </entry>
  <entry>
```

```
    <id>http://services.multimobiledevelopment.com/services/Bookmarks.svc/Bookmark(1003)</id>
    <title type="text"></title>
    <updated>2010-04-18T10:54:32Z</updated>
    <author>
      <name />
    </author>
    <link rel="edit" title="Bookmark" href="Bookmark(1003)" />
    <category term="AmxMobile.Services.Bookmark"
scheme="http://schemas.microsoft.com/ado/2007/08/dataservices/scheme" />
    <content type="application/xml">
      <m:properties>
        <d:BookmarkId m:type="Edm.Int32">1003</d:BookmarkId>
        <d:UserId m:type="Edm.Int32">1001</d:UserId>
        <d:Name>Topaz Filer</d:Name>
        <d:Url>http://www.topazfiler.com/</d:Url>
        <d:Ordinal m:type="Edm.Int32">2</d:Ordinal>
      </m:properties>
    </content>
  </entry>
</feed>
```

To turn that XML back into entities, all we have to do is walk the feed/entry elements in the ATOM namespace. We can use the entity type to create instances of single entities and collections, and we can also use the entity type as a source of information as to what fields are defined on the entity. As we walk through the fields, we can retrieve the appropriate values from the XML and populate the entity. Here's some of the code involved that walks through the XML:

```
// LoadEntities method in the nested ODataFetchState class within ODataServiceProxy…
        protected List<T> LoadEntities(XDocument doc, EntityType et)
            {
                // feed...
                XElement feed = doc.Element(XName.Get("feed", AtomNamespace));
                if (feed == null)
                    throw new InvalidOperationException("'feedElement' is null.");

                // walk...
                List<T> results = et.CreateCollectionInstance<T>();
                var entries = feed.Elements(XName.Get("entry", AtomNamespace));
                foreach (XElement entry in entries)
                {
                    // get the content item...
                    XElement content = entry.Element(XName.Get("content", AtomNamespace));
                    if (content == null)
                        throw new InvalidOperationException("'content' is null.");

                    // then get the properties element...
                    XElement properties = content.Element(XName.Get("properties",
MsMetadataNamespace));
                    if (properties == null)
                        throw new InvalidOperationException("'properties' is null.");

                    // create an item...
```

```
            T item = (T)et.CreateInstance();
            if (item == null)
                throw new InvalidOperationException("'item' is null.");

            // then get the fields...
            Dictionary<string, object> values = new Dictionary<string, object>();
            foreach (XElement fieldElement in properties.Elements())
            {
                if (fieldElement.Name.Namespace == MsDataNamespace)
                {
                    // do we have that field?
                    EntityField field = et.GetField(fieldElement.Name.LocalName,
false);

                    if (field != null)
                    {
                        // get the value...
                        object value = this.GetValue(fieldElement);
                        item.SetValue(field, value, SetReason.UserSet);
                    }
                }
            }

            // add...
            results.Add(item);
        }

        // return...
        return results;
    }
```

Fetching Latest with the Sync Class

The operation of the Sync class is twofold. In the first instance, it has to be able to fetch a definitive set of bookmarks from the server and store them in the local database (more on the local database later). In the second instance, it has to be able to push local changes back. (This will be covered in a later section.)

Until we talk about the database activity, we'll assume that we can save a Bookmark instance by calling the SaveChanges method on the base Entity class. Here's the code that receives the bookmarks from the server and saves them locally. The wrinkle in this code is that the bookmarks from the server have the server's local/native ID in them. In order to insert them into our database, we need to exclude this server-side ID, and hence we clone the bookmark entities prior to calling SaveChanges. (We'll learn more about how the database is updated in response to a SaveChanges call in a later section.)

```
// GetLatestMethod within Sync class…
        private void GetLatest()
        {
            Debug.WriteLine("Getting latest...");

            BookmarksService service = new BookmarksService();
            service.GetAll((Action<List<Bookmark>>)delegate(List<Bookmark> bookmarks)
            {
                // ensure...
```

```
            SqlCeHelper db = new SqlCeHelper();
            db.EnsureTableExists(EntityType.GetEntityType(typeof(Bookmark)));

            // delete first...
            Bookmark.DeleteAll();

            // go through and save them...
            foreach (Bookmark fromServer in bookmarks)
            {
                // we need to clone it as the ones that come from the server will have an
ID set. we
                // need to junk this ID...
                Bookmark newBookmark = new Bookmark();
                newBookmark.Ordinal = fromServer.Ordinal;
                newBookmark.Name = fromServer.Name;
                newBookmark.Url = fromServer.Url;

                // set the local only stuff...
                newBookmark.IsLocalModified = false;
                newBookmark.IsLocalDeleted = false;

                // save...
                newBookmark.SaveChanges();
            }

            // signal that we've finished...
            this.Callback();

        }, this.Failed);
    }
```

Using SQL CE

As of the time of writing, we do not have access to a relational database on Windows Phone; however, we have had SQL CE available to us on Windows Mobile since the Windows CE days. Therefore using SQL CE seems like a natural choice. As I alluded to earlier, Microsoft is likely to enable SQL CE on Windows Phone, and, as such, the work in this section should drop straight in. (As I also alluded to earlier, SQLite would be nice to have on Windows Phone as well.)

All of the database functionality on the Windows Mobile application is done through a class called SqlCeHelper. This uses the .NET Compact Framework System.Data.SqlServerCe namespace to communicate with the SQL CE instance on the device.

SQL CE is file-based, much like SQLite, so all we have to do is nominate a file path to use and pass that over to SQL CE via a connection string. Unlike SQLite, SQL CE will fail to connect if the database does not exist, and, as such, we need to check for file existence and call a method on a management class called System.Data.SqlServerCe.SqlCeEngine to create a database if one does not exist.

As expected, the SqlServerCe namespace operates using the standards laid out in ADO.NET; therefore, if you're familiar with using ADO.NET with something like full-blown SQL Server or Oracle, there should not be too many surprises.

To start with, let's have a look at our CreateConnection method. The purpose of this method is to return back to us a configured SqlCeConnection instance. Here's the code:

```
// CreateConnection method within SqlCeHelper…
        private SqlCeConnection CreateConnection()
        {
            // conn string...
            string filePath = Path.Combine(SixBookmarksRuntime.Current.ApplicationFolderPath,
SixBookmarksRuntime.Current.DatabaseFilename);
            string connString = string.Format("Data Source={0};Persist Security Info=False",
filePath);

            // if the file does not exist, create it...
            if (!(File.Exists(filePath)))
            {
                SqlCeEngine engine = new SqlCeEngine(connString);
                engine.CreateDatabase();
            }

            // return...
            return new SqlCeConnection(connString);
        }
```

If you've been reading along during the Android chapter, you'll know that my preferred way to build data access layers (DAL) is to create a class that represents a SQL statement. This class can be used to build a proper, database-specific command at some point during the process. In addition, I also like to build an interface that describes the source of a SQL statement and continue that by making the DAL accept this interface as its base currency of execution instruction. The interface, I think, is particularly neat because it means you can create a class that is a concrete representation of a statement, but you can also create a class that is able to turn itself into a statement near the time of execution. Here's the interface:

```
using System;

namespace AmxMobile.WinMo.SixBookmarks
{
    public interface ISqlStatementSource
    {
        SqlStatement GetStatement();
    }
}
```

Here's the implementation of SqlStatement. This class holds not only the command text to execute but also a list of parameters that will be used with the statement. (Unlike SQLite, SQL CE uses named parameters.)

```
using System;

namespace AmxMobile.WinMo.SixBookmarks
{
    public class SqlStatement : ISqlStatementSource
    {
        public string CommandText { get; set; }
        public List<SqlStatementParameter> Parameters {get; private set; }
```

```csharp
public SqlStatement()
{
    this.Parameters = new List<SqlStatementParameter>();
}

public SqlStatement(string commandText)
    : this()
{
    this.CommandText = commandText;
}

public SqlStatement(string commandText, params object[] paramValues)
    : this(commandText)
{
    for (int index = 0; index < paramValues.Length; index++)
        this.AddParameter("p" + index.ToString(), paramValues[index]);
}

public SqlStatement GetStatement()
{
    return this;
}

private string GetNextUniqueName()
{
    int index = 0;
    while (true)
    {
        // check...
        string name = "z" + index.ToString();
        SqlStatementParameter existing = GetParameter(name);
        if (existing == null)
            return name;

        // next...
        index++;
    }
}

private SqlStatementParameter GetParameter(string name)
{
    foreach (SqlStatementParameter param in this.Parameters)
    {
        if (string.Compare(param.Name, name, true) == 0)
            return param;
    }

    // nope...
    return null;
}
```

```
        internal SqlStatementParameter AddParameter(object value)
        {
            return AddParameter(GetNextUniqueName(), value);
        }

        internal SqlStatementParameter AddParameter(string name, object value)
        {
            SqlStatementParameter param = new SqlStatementParameter(name, value);
            this.Parameters.Add(param);

            // return...
            return param;
        }
    }
}
```

One final thing to discuss on this implementation is that if you add a parameter without a name, it will allocate a name for you. (This comes in handy when building dynamic SQL with database engines that use named parameters. We'll see this later.)

Initially we need two basic methods—one that runs a statement and doesn't return a value (ExecuteNonQuery), and another that returns the first value from the first returned row (ExecuteScalar). Both of these methods establish a connection and defer to a method we'll see shortly, called CreateCommand, which turns the ISqlStatementSource instance into a SqlCeCommand instance. Here's the code:

```
// Methods in SqlCeHelper…
        internal void ExecuteNonQuery(ISqlStatementSource sql)
        {
            using (SqlCeConnection conn = CreateConnection())
            {
                SqlCeCommand command = CreateCommand(conn, sql);

                // execute...
                try
                {
                    command.ExecuteNonQuery();
                }
                catch (Exception ex)
                {
                    throw HandleException(command, ex);
                }
            }
        }

        internal object ExecuteScalar(ISqlStatementSource sql)
        {
            using (SqlCeConnection conn = CreateConnection())
            {
                SqlCeCommand command = CreateCommand(conn, sql);
```

```
        // execute...
        try
        {
            return command.ExecuteScalar();
        }
        catch (Exception ex)
        {
            throw HandleException(command, ex);
        }
    }
}
```

The operation CreateCommand is to take the supplied ISqlStatementSource instance and call the GetStatement method to get a real statement. (If the provided statement happens to be a SqlStatement instance already, the GetStatement method will return a reference to this.)

CreateCommand, as well as creating the basic command and setting the command text, will also set the parameters on the command. The final operation is to open the connection, if it's not already open. Here's the code:

```
// CreateCommand method within SqlCeHelper...
    private SqlCeCommand CreateCommand(SqlCeConnection conn, ISqlStatementSource sql)
    {
        SqlStatement real = sql.GetStatement();

        // create...
        SqlCeCommand command = conn.CreateCommand();
        command.CommandText = real.CommandText;

        // params...
        foreach (SqlStatementParameter param in real.Parameters)
            command.Parameters.Add(param.Name, param.Value);

        // open...
        if (conn.State != System.Data.ConnectionState.Open)
            conn.Open();

        // return...
        return command;
    }
```

The final method to look at during this stage is the HandleException method. When errors are thrown by SQL CE, the message text does not include the statement that failed. This makes troubleshooting very difficult—HandleException wraps the SQL CE exception in another exception that contains information on the failing query. (I haven't included parameter information, to keep the code simple in the book, but dumping the parameter values is very helpful in this sort of method.)

```
// HandleException method within SqlCeHelper...
    private Exception HandleException(SqlCeCommand command, Exception ex)
    {
```

```
        return new InvalidOperationException(string.Format("SQL statement execution
failed.  SQL: {0}", command.CommandText), ex);
    }
```

That covers the basics of how we can undertake basic database operations. Next we'll look at how we can ensure that the database tables that we want to work with exist.

Ensuring Tables Exist

If you've followed along during the iOS or Android chapters, you'll know that we need to be able to determine if the table to support a given entity exists. If the table does not exist, we need to create it.

To save cycles from us having to check again and again whether a table exists, we'll create a static property on SqlCeHelper that stores a list of the entity types that have been checked. When a call to EnsureTableExists is made, this property will be checked. If it's the first time we have seen a call for the given entity type, we'll go ahead and check if the table is there—if not, we'll create it. If it has been seen before, we'll short-circuit and return immediately.

In SQLite we have a directive (IF NOT EXISTS) that we can tack onto a CREATE TABLE statement that means an error is not raised if a given table exists. On SQL CE, we have to physically check the schema. This is done by querying the ANSI standard INFORMATION_SCHEMA.TABLES view that is exposed by SQL CE. As stated earlier, if we find that the table is not there, we'll create it. Here's the code:

```
// Static property, static constructor and EnsureTableExists method within SqlCeHelper...
        private static List<EntityType> CheckedTables { get; set; }

        static SqlCeHelper()
        {
            CheckedTables = new List<EntityType>();
        }

        internal void EnsureTableExists(EntityType et)
        {
            // have we already checked it?
            if (CheckedTables.Contains(et))
                return;

            // check it...
            SqlStatement sql = new SqlStatement("select table_name from
information_schema.tables where table_name=@p0", et.NativeName);
            object result = this.ExecuteScalar(sql);
            try
            {
                if(!(result is string))
                    CreateTable(et);
            }
            finally
            {
                CheckedTables.Add(et);
            }
        }
```

The CreateTable method simply has to obtain a statement that can be used to build the table based on the definition contained within the entity type's metadata. In the implementation featured, we are going to support strings, 32-bit integers, and Boolean values. In a real-world implementation, you would likely need to support more; however, in order to keep the size of the code down in the book, I have deliberately limited the data type support.

SQL CE does not support the VARCHAR SQL data type and, as such, needs to declare string fields as the UNICODE-capable NVARCHAR type.

Here's the code that will create a table for the given entity type:

```
// Methods within SqlCeHelper…
    private void CreateTable(EntityType et)
    {
        SqlStatement create = GetCreateStatement(et);

        // run...
        ExecuteNonQuery(create);
    }

    private SqlStatement GetCreateStatement(EntityType et)
    {
        StringBuilder builder = new StringBuilder();
        builder.Append("create table ");
        builder.Append(et.NativeName);
        builder.Append(" (");
        bool first = true;
        foreach (EntityField field in et.Fields)
        {
            if (first)
                first = false;
            else
                builder.Append(", ");

            // append...
            AppendCreateSnippet(builder, field);
        }
        builder.Append(")");

        // return...
        return new SqlStatement(builder.ToString());
    }

    private void AppendCreateSnippet(StringBuilder builder, EntityField field)
    {
        builder.Append(field.NativeName);
        builder.Append(" ");
        if (field.Type == DataType.String)
        {
            builder.Append("nvarchar(");
            builder.Append(field.Size);
            builder.Append(")");
        }
        else if (field.Type == DataType.Int32)
```

```
        {
            builder.Append("int");

            // autonumber?
            if (field.IsKey)
                builder.Append(" identity not null primary key");
        }
        else if (field.Type == DataType.Boolean)
            builder.Append("bit");
        else
            throw new NotSupportedException(string.Format("Cannot handle '{0}'.",
field.Type));
}
```

Now that we can create tables to store entities in, let's look at how we can actually insert them.

Building EntityChangeProcessor

In the Windows Phone implementation, we built a class called DataBoxEntityChangeProcessor that was able to create, change, or delete files from disk based on what had happened to the entity. If you followed along during the iOS or Android discussions, you'll know that we did essentially the same thing by using SQLite.

The Entity class contains a stub method that creates a change processor and defers. Here's the code:

```
// SaveChanges method within Entity…
        public void SaveChanges()
        {
            EntityChangeProcessor processor = new EntityChangeProcessor(this.EntityType);
            processor.SaveChanges(this);
        }
```

From there, the SaveChanges method within EntityChangeProcessor can determine whether the entity is new, has changed, or needs to be deleted, or whether no change needs to be made. Here's the code:

```
// SaveChanges method within EntityChangeProcessor…
        internal void SaveChanges(Entity entity)
        {
            if (entity.IsNew)
                Insert(entity);
            else if (entity.IsModified())
                Update(entity);
            else if (entity.IsDeleted)
                Delete(entity);
        }
```

The operation of the Insert, Update, or Delete methods is therefore one where a specialized SQL query is constructed to perform the operation in question. We'll start off by looking at Insert.

As you know, an insert statement is structured thus:

```
INSERT INTO <table> (<columns>) VALUES (<values>)
```

Therefore all we have to do is build a statement of that form based on the metadata held in the entity type and based on the values of the entity.

The one wrinkle is that best practice dictates that we have to use parameters to provide the values into the query. In SQL CE, we have named parameters—e.g., @foo and @bar—whereas in SQLite, we have ODBC-style ordinal parameters—i.e., every parameter is designated with ?. When we built the SqlStatement class, we included an overload of AddParameter that would choose a unique name within the context of the statement. This allows us to add named parameters into the query without having to worry about naming collisions.

Here's the code for Insert:

```
// Insert method within EntityChangeProcessor…
    internal void Insert(Entity entity)
        {
            SqlStatement sql = new SqlStatement();

            // create...
            StringBuilder builder = new StringBuilder();
            builder.Append("insert into ");
            builder.Append(this.EntityType.NativeName);
            builder.Append(" (");
            bool first = true;
            foreach (EntityField field in this.EntityType.Fields)
            {
                if (entity.IsModified(field))
                {
                    if (first)
                        first = false;
                    else
                        builder.Append(", ");
                    builder.Append(field.NativeName);
                }
            }
            builder.Append(") values (");
            first = true;
            foreach (EntityField field in this.EntityType.Fields)
            {
                if (entity.IsModified(field))
                {
                    if (first)
                        first = false;
                    else
                        builder.Append(", ");

                    // param...
                    object value = entity.GetValue(field);
                    SqlStatementParameter param = sql.AddParameter(value);
                    builder.Append("@");
                    builder.Append(param.Name);
                }
            }
        }
```

```
        builder.Append(")");

        // run...
        sql.CommandText = builder.ToString();

        // run...
        SqlCeHelper db = new SqlCeHelper();
        db.EnsureTableExists(entity.EntityType);
        db.ExecuteNonQuery(sql);
    }
```

■ **Note** This method works by looking for field values that have been modified. Therefore, if you try to insert an entity, and a value for a given field has not been set, SQL CE will attempt to insert the default value for that column. This may break constraints that you have specified on the table.

The Update method works essentially in the same way. The only real difference is that we need to limit the UPDATE statement to update just the entity that we specify. To do this, there is a method called AppendSelectConstraint that, as the name implies, appends a constraint to the query based on the key value of the entity. Here's the code:

```
// Methods within EntityChangeProcessor…
        internal void Update(Entity entity)
        {
            SqlStatement sql = new SqlStatement();

            // create...
            StringBuilder builder = new StringBuilder();
            builder.Append("update ");
            builder.Append(this.EntityType.NativeName);
            builder.Append(" set ");
            bool first = true;
            foreach (EntityField field in this.EntityType.Fields)
            {
                if (entity.IsModified(field))
                {
                    if (first)
                        first = false;
                    else
                        builder.Append(", ");
                    builder.Append(field.NativeName);
                    builder.Append("=@");

                    // value...
                    object value = entity.GetValue(field);
                    builder.Append(sql.AddParameter(value).Name);
                }
            }
```

```
            builder.Append(" where ");
            this.AppendSelectConstraint(builder, sql, entity);

            // run...
            sql.CommandText = builder.ToString();

            // run...
            SqlCeHelper db = new SqlCeHelper();
            db.EnsureTableExists(entity.EntityType);
            db.ExecuteNonQuery(sql);
        }

        private void AppendSelectConstraint(StringBuilder builder, SqlStatement sql, Entity
    entity)
        {
            EntityField key = this.EntityType.GetKeyField();
            if (key == null)
                throw new InvalidOperationException("'key' is null.");
            builder.Append(key.NativeName);
            builder.Append("=@");
            builder.Append(sql.AddParameter(entity.GetValue(key)).Name);
        }
```

Finally, although we do not use it in the application, and hence it's here just for completeness, here's the Delete method:

```
// Delete method within EntityChangeProcessor…
        internal void Delete(Entity entity)
        {
            SqlStatement sql = new SqlStatement();

            // delete...
            StringBuilder builder = new StringBuilder();
            builder.Append("delete from ");
            builder.Append(this.EntityType.NativeName);
            builder.Append(" where ");
            AppendSelectConstraint(builder, sql, entity);

            // run...
            sql.CommandText = builder.ToString();

            // run...
            SqlCeHelper db = new SqlCeHelper();
            db.EnsureTableExists(entity.EntityType);
            db.ExecuteNonQuery(sql);
        }
```

Selecting Entities

To round off the work that we need to do with SQL CE, we'll look at how we can select out entities again.

Once more, if you've been following along during the Android and iOS development, you'll know that my preferred method for selecting entities is to create a "SQL filter." The idea of a filter is that you create one that is bound to a given type, and by default that filter will select out all entities of that type. You can add constraints to the filter to limit the data returned to just the set that you want. The main limitation of such a SQL filter is that it's not suitable (in this implementation at least) to executing joins or returning sets of data—it's geared to providing a list of entities.

Our SqlFilter class essentially just has to associate an entity type with a set of constraints, and be able to turn those two into a SELECT statement. (SqlFilter will implement ISqlStatementSource, meaning that we can pass a SqlFilter directly into DAL methods without having to de-reference a command first.) Each constraint will comprise a pair of values made up of an EntityField instance and some value. Here's the code for SqlConstraint:

```
using System;

namespace AmxMobile.WinMo.SixBookmarks
{
    public class SqlConstraint
    {
        internal EntityField Field { get; private set; }
        internal object Value { get; private set; }

        internal SqlConstraint(EntityField field, object value)
        {
            this.Field = field;
            this.Value = value;
        }
    }
}
```

■ **Note** In this implementation, I have not included operators, implying that constraints can be matched only on an "equal to" basis. More complete implementations would include all common operators, including "not equal to," "less than," "contains," etc.

After instantiating a SqlFilter instance and passing in an entity type, the caller can then invoke the AddConstraint method to add constraints in. I have provided two overloads here—one that takes a name and one that takes an EntityField instance. (Typically developers would work with the string names of fields, as this is easier.) Here's the code:

```
// Methods within SqlFilter...
        internal void AddConstraint(string name, object value)
        {
            EntityField field = this.EntityType.GetField(name, true);
            AddConstraint(field, value);
        }

        internal void AddConstraint(EntityField field, object value)
```

```
    {
        this.Constraints.Add(new SqlConstraint(field, value));
    }
```

The most important method on SqlFilter is GetStatement. This method does two things—it will check to make sure a table for the related entity type exists, and it will build a concrete SqlStatement instance based on the metadata for the entity type and the parameter values. Here's the code:

```
// GetStatement method within SqlFilter…
    public SqlStatement GetStatement()
    {
        // check that we have a table...
        SqlCeHelper helper = new SqlCeHelper();
        helper.EnsureTableExists(this.EntityType);

        // build it...
        SqlStatement sql = new SqlStatement();
        StringBuilder builder = new StringBuilder();
        builder.Append("select ");
        bool first = true;
        foreach (EntityField field in this.EntityType.Fields)
        {
            if (first)
                first = false;
            else
                builder.Append(", ");
            builder.Append(field.NativeName);
        }
        builder.Append(" from ");
        builder.Append(this.EntityType.NativeName);

        // constraints...
        if (Constraints.Count > 0)
        {
            builder.Append(" where ");

            // walk...
            first = true;
            foreach (SqlConstraint constraint in this.Constraints)
            {
                if (first)
                    first = false;
                else
                    builder.Append(" and ");

                // add...
                builder.Append(constraint.Field.NativeName);
                builder.Append("=@");
                builder.Append(sql.AddParameter(constraint.Value).Name);
            }
        }
```

```
    // return...
    sql.CommandText = builder.ToString();
    return sql;
}
```

▓ **Note** You'll also note that the constraints are always combined using AND. Again, a more sophisticated implementation would allow for OR operators and nested operations.

The purpose of a SqlFilter is to get back a collection of entities or a single entity. The real implementation of ExecuteEntityCollection will reside on SqlCeHelper, but for increased utility, there are sub-methods on SqlFilter itself. Here's the code:

```
// Methods within SqlFilter...
        internal List<T> ExecuteEntityCollection<T>()
            where T : Entity
        {
            SqlCeHelper db = new SqlCeHelper();
            return db.ExecuteEntityCollection<T>(this);
        }

        internal T ExecuteEntity<T>()
            where T : Entity
        {
            List<T> items = ExecuteEntityCollection<T>();
            if (items == null)
                throw new InvalidOperationException("'items' is null.");
            if (items.Count > 0)
                return items[0];
            else
                return null;
        }
```

The final thing to look at in terms of the database bits and pieces is the implementation of the real ExecuteEntityCollection method on SqlCeHelper.

ExecuteEntityCollection has to do two things. It has to execute a command on the SQL CE database that returns back a "firehose"-style data reader on the connection. It then has to walk the rows returned by the reader and create concrete entities based on the data within. The result collection and individual entities are created by the CreateCollectionInstance and CreateInstance methods on EntityType. The values are set using the SetValue method. Importantly, when the value is set, the "set reason" is specified as Load. What this does is mark the field within the entity as being loaded, but it does *not* mark it as having been modified. This is important for keeping track of the entity's state—after all, when an entity has just been loaded from the database, none of its fields nor the entity itself has been modified. Here's the code:

```csharp
// ExecuteEntityCollection  method within SqlCeHelper…
        internal List<T> ExecuteEntityCollection<T>(ISqlStatementSource sql)
            where T : Entity
    {
        using (SqlCeConnection conn = CreateConnection())
        {
            SqlStatement real = sql.GetStatement();

            // get...
            EntityType et = EntityType.GetEntityType(typeof(T));

            // command...
            SqlCeCommand command = CreateCommand(conn, real);
            try
            {
                // walk the reader...
                SqlCeDataReader reader = command.ExecuteReader();
                using (reader)
                {
                    // create...
                    List<T> results = et.CreateCollectionInstance<T>();
                    while (reader.Read())
                    {
                        // create...
                        T item = (T)et.CreateInstance();

                        // walk...
                        for (int index = 0; index < et.Fields.Count; index++)
                        {
                            EntityField field = et.Fields[index];

                            // value...
                            object value = reader.GetValue(index);
                            item.SetValue(field, value, SetReason.Load);
                        }

                        // add...
                        results.Add(item);
                    }

                    // return...
                    return results;
                }
            }
            catch (Exception ex)
            {
                throw HandleException(command, ex);
            }
        }
    }
```

You'll notice that we call HandleException at the end—again, I've included this to make troubleshooting easier.

That brings us to the end of the (more detailed) examination of how the SQL CE implementation works. Now we can look at the remainder of the application's functionality.

Navigator

Showing the navigator form is the first example of how we have to transition from one form to the next. This is done in a different fashion on Windows Mobile—in our case, each form is created as a modal dialog and shown on top of the form below. Specifically, here's the code to show the NavigatorForm class when logon has passed and the synchronization operation has succeeded:

```
// Snippet of code from LogonOk method on LogonForm...
            using(NavigatorForm form = new NavigatorForm())
                form.ShowDialog();
```

In Windows Phone, there is no notion of modal forms—i.e., in the foregoing example, processing will halt on LogonForm until the NavigatorForm is dismissed. It puts the application into a certain "mode," hence the name "modal." Instead you have to ask the Sliverlight runtime to navigate to a URI that points to a page within your application. (In fact, neither iOS nor Android supports modal forms at all, and Windows Phone is odd in that its message box implementation is modal, whereas the iOS and Android ones are not.)

Another place where this is a little nasty is that in Windows Mobile, if you want to pass information to a child dialog, you simply define and set properties on that dialog. In Windows Phone, you cannot do this—you either have to pass values in the query string of the URI or use shared memory as a "broker" between the two classes. Both approaches have their plusses and minuses.

Another thing to consider is that on Android and Windows Phone you have a back button that operates outside of your direct control. (For example, on Android after you have logged in and can see the navigator, you can click the back button and get back to the logon form.)

■ **Note** When moving from Windows Mobile to Windows Phone, you need to consider that you no longer have modal forms and that navigation is done by specifying the URI of a local form.

Navigator Form Design

Like the iOS, Android, and Windows Phone implementations, the navigator form is a set of six buttons (one for each possible bookmark) and one button each for the configure, logoff, and about options. Figure 8-3 shows the designer view.

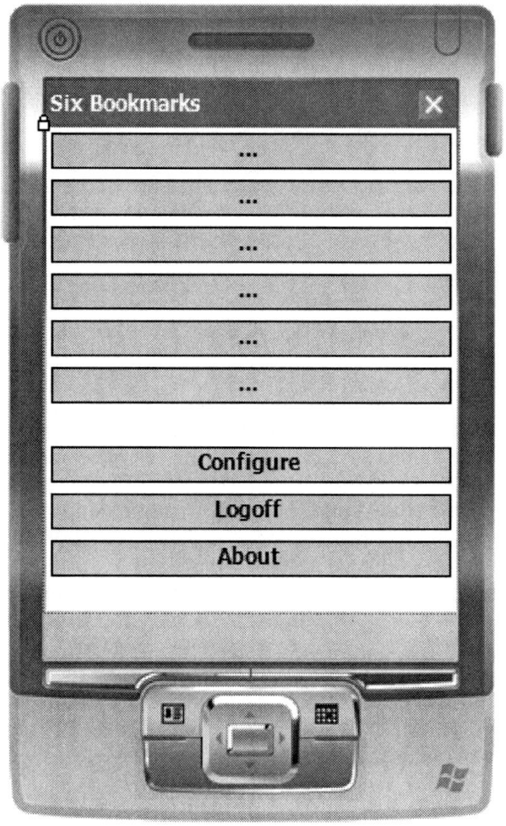

Figure 8-3. *The Navigator form*

The functionality of this view is to request a list of bookmarks for display, which is then used to configure the buttons.

The key difference between Windows Mobile and Windows Phone is how the device is instructed to show a web page. In Windows Mobile, this is done in the same way as it is in Windows Forms—you create a process targeted at the URL in question and let the operating system shell work out how to show it. (In this case, the Internet Explorer instance is started and instructed to show the URL.) Here's the Windows Mobile code:

```
// Navigate method within NavigatorForm…
        private void Navigate(string url)
        {
            System.Diagnostics.Process.Start(url, string.Empty);
        }
```

On Windows Phone, you give the full URL to Silverlight and let it work out whether it's supposed to show a form within the application or use Internet Explorer to go to the URL in question.

■ **Note** When moving from Windows Mobile to Windows Phone, any calls that show URLs have to be changed from starting a process bound to the URL to a call via the Silverlight `NavigationService` class.

Configuring Bookmarks

The configuration window highlights an important difference between the user interface approaches on iOS, Android, and Windows Phones.

All three of these devices have a user interface metaphor whereby an entire page is given over to a list. (This approach has been particularly well implemented on iOS, where it's extremely easy to build rich and functional lists.) It's extremely likely that any user of one of the new devices will expect to find list information presented in the vendor's preferred way, and hence a challenge to those migrating from Windows Forms lies in rebuilding list-based user interfaces.

Figure 8-4 shows the old-school approach used in Windows Mobile. In particular it has a standard Windows Forms `ListBox` control and two buttons.

Figure 8-4. *A design surface showing a* `ListBox`*, the intended target for bookmarks*

On the Windows Phone implementation, we implemented the list in the proper way, using a view model and a separate page for the singleton view. The dependencies in this approach mean that your current representation of data within your code is likely not to be compatible with the Silverlight way of doing things and, as such, migrating your list presentations from Windows Mobile to Windows Phone may not be trivial.

■ **Note** When moving from Windows Mobile to Windows Phone, old-school ways of presenting lists should be migrated to the new way of presenting lists, using view models, data templates, and the like.

The mechanics of the bookmark modification (i.e., the business logic) are no different between Windows Mobile and Windows Forms. A user interface is presented, and the values the user provided are patched into the entity when the changes are saved. Figure 8-5 shows the designer of the singleton edit.

Figure 8-5. *The singleton edit page*

As I've mentioned before, the actual logic of checking values and saving changes has not changed between the Windows Mobile and Windows Phone implementations. Let's look now at sending the changes back up to the server.

Synchronization 2: Uploading Changes

In this last section, we'll take a look at the other aspect of synchronization—pushing changes back up to the server.

The actual synchronization logic hasn't changed between the Windows Mobile and Windows Phone versions. The state of the bookmarks stored on the device is tracked via the IsLocalModified and IsLocalDeleted properties. When the "push changes" operation starts, it downloads the latest set of bookmarks from the server and combines the server and local set to create a delta between the two. This delta is then walked, pushing changes to the server as it progresses.

The difference between the two platforms is that on Windows Mobile we have had to roll our own OData client, whereas on Windows Phone we can use the Visual Studio-generated proxy. (As before, if you do happen to have coded up OData communication via a roll-your-own handler, it's up to you whether you want to migrate over to using the new Windows Phone approach. But remember that if your handler works synchronously, you will need to make it asynchronous.)

For completeness, I'll go through the implementation of the OData client in the Windows Mobile application.

OData Operations

There are three supported OData operations (excluding reading, which we have already covered). These are insert, update, and delete. Each of these methods uses a different HTTP request verb. Insert uses POST, update uses MERGE, and delete uses DELETE.

Making the request is simply a matter of building XML in the correct format. I won't go through the structure of the XML again here, as this has been covered in the iOS and Android chapters (plus the protocol can be found on the OData web site at www.odata.org/). The other wrinkle to handle is the URL.

For insert operations, the request is directed to the list URL, which in our case is this:
http://services.multimobiledevelopment.com/services/Bookmarks.svc/Bookmark.

For update and delete operations, the URL has to be specified as the specific URL for that specific item. This URL is actually provided for us when we request entities from the server; however, the protocol describes the URL as being the list URL plus the key of the entity in parentheses. For example, the following refers to the bookmark with an ID of 27:
http://services.multimobiledevelopment.com/services/Bookmarks.svc/Bookmark(27).

In our implementation, GetEntityUrlForPush takes an entity and returns back a derived URL for that entity. Here's the code:

```
// Methods within ODataServiceProxy…
    private string GetServiceUrl(EntityType et)
    {
        return HttpHelper.CombineUrlParts(this.ResolvedServiceUrl, et.NativeName);
    }

    private string GetEntityUrlForPush(Entity entity, int serverId)
    {
        return string.Format("{0}({1})", GetServiceUrl(entity.EntityType), serverId);
    }
```

The actual XML used for both update and insert is the same—only the verb and the URL change. For this reason, we have to build only one method and tweak its operation when dealing with the other. Here's the code for PushUpdate that builds the URL and also initializes a call to the server via ExecuteODataOperation (we'll see this in a moment), and PushInsert, which defers to PushUpdate.

```
// Methods within ODataServiceProxy...
        public void PushUpdate(Entity entity, int serverId, Action callback, Failed failed)
        {
            XDocument doc = new XDocument();

            // entry...
            XElement entryElement = new XElement(XName.Get("entry", AtomNamespace));
            doc.Add(entryElement);

            // content...
            XElement contentElement = new XElement(XName.Get("content", AtomNamespace));
            contentElement.Add(new XAttribute(XName.Get("type", string.Empty),
"application/xml"));
            entryElement.Add(contentElement);

            // properties...
            XElement propertiesElement = new XElement(XName.Get("properties",
MsMetadataNamespace));
            contentElement.Add(propertiesElement);

            // walk the fields...
            EntityType et = entity.EntityType;
            if (et == null)
                throw new InvalidOperationException("'et' is null.");
            foreach (EntityField field in et.Fields)
            {
                if (!(field.IsKey) && field.IsOnServer)
                {
                    // create...
                    XElement element = new XElement(XName.Get(field.Name, MsDataNamespace));
                    object value = entity.GetValue(field);
                    if (value != null)
                        element.Value = value.ToString();

                    // add...
                    propertiesElement.Add(element);
                }
            }

            // run...
            String url = null;
            ODataOperation op = ODataOperation.Update;
            String xmlAsString = doc.ToString();
            if (serverId != 0)
                url = GetEntityUrlForPush(entity, serverId);
            else
            {
```

```
            url = this.GetServiceUrl(et);
            op = ODataOperation.Insert;
        }

        // run...
        ExecuteODataOperation(op, url, xmlAsString, callback, failed);
    }

    public void PushInsert(Entity entity, Action callback, Failed failed)
    {
        // an insert is an update but with a different URL...
        PushUpdate(entity, 0, callback, failed);
    }
```

The delete operation does not require XML—all that we need to do is make a DELETE request against the entity's URL. Here's the code, which again defers to ExecuteODataOperation:

```
// PushDelete method within ODataServiceProxy...
        public void PushDelete(Entity entity, int serverId, Action callback, Failed failed)
        {
            string url = GetEntityUrlForPush(entity, serverId);
            ExecuteODataOperation(ODataOperation.Delete, url, null, callback, failed);
        }
```

Actually sending the request is just an issue of getting the headers right. We need to pass up our special headers defined on the Six Bookmarks protocol (x-amx-apiusername and x-amx-token), and we also need to tell the server that we're sending up application/atom-xml format data. Apart from that, it's just a matter of using the regular System.Net.HttpWebRequest class that's available on both Windows Mobile and Windows Phone. Here's the code:

```
// Methods within ODataServiceProxy...
        private void ExecuteODataOperation(ODataOperation opType, String url, String xml,
Action callback, Failed failed)
            {
            // create the request...
            HttpWebRequest request = (HttpWebRequest)WebRequest.Create(url);

            // set the method...
            if (opType == ODataOperation.Insert)
                request.Method = "POST";
            else if (opType == ODataOperation.Update)
                request.Method = "MERGE";
            else if (opType == ODataOperation.Delete)
                request.Method = "DELETE";
            else
                throw new NotSupportedException(string.Format("Cannot handle '{0}'.",
opType));

            // headers... (including our special tokens)...
            DownloadSettings settings = this.GetDownloadSettings();
            foreach (string name in settings.ExtraHeaders.Keys)
                request.Headers.Add(name, settings.ExtraHeaders[name]);
```

```csharp
        // do we have xml?
        if (!(string.IsNullOrEmpty(xml)))
        {
            byte[] bs = Encoding.UTF8.GetBytes(xml);
            request.ContentLength = bs.Length;
            request.ContentType = "application/atom+xml";
            using (Stream stream = request.GetRequestStream())
                stream.Write(bs, 0, bs.Length);
        }

        // create a state object...
        ODataRequestState state = new ODataRequestState();
        state.Request = request;
        state.Callback = callback;
        state.Failed = failed;

        // run...
        request.BeginGetResponse(new AsyncCallback(HandleODataOperationResponse), state);
    }

    private class ODataRequestState
    {
        internal HttpWebRequest Request;
        internal Action Callback;
        internal Failed Failed;
    }

    private void HandleODataOperationResponse(IAsyncResult result)
    {
        // state...
        ODataRequestState state = (ODataRequestState)result.AsyncState;

        // try...
        try
        {
            // unwrap...
            HttpWebResponse response =
(HttpWebResponse)state.Request.EndGetResponse(result);

            // dispose the response...
            response.Close();

            // ok...
            state.Callback();
        }
        catch (WebException ex)
        {
            StringBuilder builder = new StringBuilder();
            builder.Append("An error occurred when making an OData request.");
            if (ex.Response is HttpWebResponse)
            {
```

```
            using (Stream stream = ((HttpWebResponse)ex.Response).GetResponseStream())
            {
                StreamReader reader = new StreamReader(stream);
                builder.Append(reader.ReadToEnd());
            }
        }

        // throw...
        throw new InvalidOperationException(builder.ToString(), ex);
    }
    catch (Exception ex)
    {
        state.Failed(ex);
    }
}
```

One thing to consider in that code is that if an error does occur on the request, we're getting all of the content that comes back from the server and wrapping it in a new exception. This really helps with troubleshooting.

That's it! We've completed our whistle-stop tour of the Windows Mobile application.

Downloading Assemblies/Custom Bootstrappers

In this last section, I'd like to talk about a commonly done application feature that's not possible on Windows Phone, iOS, or Android.

In Windows Mobile, it's entirely possible to do a neat trick possible on desktops, whereby you create a bootstrapper application that downloads the latest version of the application from the Internet or an intranet. This makes managing applications easier, in that you have to touch a device only once in order to configure it and allow the device to automatically update as you go.

In the new order of the new phones, it's not possible to do this. This has been done as a security measure—all malware works by tricking the user into downloading and installing an application that he or she did not agree to. Thus, while it's possible to download a Windows Mobile assembly, late bind to it, and run it, you cannot do this on Windows Phone, Android, or iOS.

This can be a big problem (it has been for at least one of my customers). If you manage a fleet of devices and need to control exactly what version runs on those devices centrally and in a fashion that is not a burden on the users, you are effectively going to have to wait for the world to catch up with you again. For example, on Android Market, you can have only one version of the application published, and users will be prompted to upgrade as and when new versions become available. The same is true for the Apple App Store. Microsoft has said that on the Windows Phone Marketplace there will be the ability to define "beta groups" and do a more controlled rollout. However, when all is said and done, as a developer, you are essentially no longer allowed to download and run whatever code you fancy—the only practical way to get software onto the device is through the store.

Conclusion

In this chapter, I haven't shown you how to build the Windows Mobile application, but I have taken you through the code, which you can download from http://code.multimobiledevelopment.com/. With Microsoft deprecating the platform, it's unlikely any of you will be looking to start new development on Windows Mobile; however, it's very likely that a good number of you have Windows Mobile code that you need to migrate over. The main difference to look out for is a lack of synchronous calling capability on network requests—if you are doing any network communications, this will need to be changed. The second large difference is that the user interface is essentially not migratable—you're going to have to rebuild your user interface from scratch.

CHAPTER 9

■ ■ ■

BlackBerry: Installing the Toolset

In this chapter, we're going to look at installing the toolset for building native BlackBerry projects.

A Word About Versions

As of the time of writing, BlackBerry is working on bring the PlayBook to market—PlayBook being a competitor to the iPad. This does not work on the regular BlackBerry OS (currently version 6) but rather uses an embedded operating system called QNX. QNX was bought by RIM prior to the PlayBook. Strategically it looks like RIM has identified that native application development on BlackBerry OS is a bit of a dead end and has looked to diversify into using a different platform. (This is rather similar to Microsoft's approach with Windows Mobile and Windows Phone.) BlackBerry has also gone on the record saying that in the long term, QNX will be used as the OS of choice in the regular BlackBerry smartphones, as opposed to BlackBerry OS.

In this chapter and the next few, we're going to be developing on the regular BlackBerry OS version 6, as opposed to QNX.

Installing the Toolset

Development for BlackBerry is done within the Eclipse environment; hence, if you happened to go through the Android section in this book's sister book, you've got a bit of a head start. If you haven't, the first thing to do is install the Java SDK and the Eclipse IDE.

Installing the Java SDK

To find the Java SDK, Google "java sdk". The first few hits should take you to a page where you can download the Java JDK. The version that I have based the work in this book on is version 6u20.

Installing Eclipse

You can download Eclipse from `www.eclipse.org/`. In its Downloads section, it offers a number of what it calls "packages," which target different user sets. The package and version that I've used in this book is the Eclipse IDE for Java Developers, which is based on Eclipse 3.6 SR1.

The installer for Eclipse is straightforward—go through and use the options that seem the most sensible to you. As this process is straightforward and obvious, I'm not going to present any screenshots or steps in this section.

Installing the BlackBerry Plug-In

The BlackBerry development tools and project templates are presented within the Eclipse environment via a plug-in. Unlike most Eclipse plug-ins, which self-download and install from within Eclipse, you have to run a separate installer, downloadable from the RIM web site, to get started.

To find the plug-in, Google "blackberry eclipse plugin". The top hit should be a link to a page like this one: `http://us.blackberry.com/developers/javaappdev/javaplugin.jsp`.

Download the plug-in installer, and install the plug-in. You will need to tell the installer where Eclipse is installed—I'd advise caution on this because the installer implies that it has looked for where it is installed, and it actually has not!

Installing the BlackBerry Device Simulator

To test your applications, you can use the BlackBerry device simulator. You get a few of these by default when you install the plug-in.

The device that I'm using in these sections is the Storm2 9550 model, although you can, of course, use any model that you wish. One word of warning, though—it's far easier to work with the simulator if you use one that supports a touchscreen interface. This allows you to click directly on the screen, whereas if you do not have a simulated touchscreen, you have to drive the simulator by faking button clicks on the device.

To start the simulator, navigate to the location where the Eclipse plug-in was installed. This will be a path like `c:\Program Files (x86)\eclipse\plugins\net.rim.ejde.componentpack5.0.0_5.0.0.25\components\simulator`. You should find within that folder a batch file called `9550.bat`. Run this batch file, and the simulator will start. Figure 9-1 shows the running simulator.

Figure 9-1. The BlackBerry Storm2 9550 simulator running

As you would expect, you can use the simulator as if it were a regular BlackBerry device—although, at the moment, it doesn't have any Internet connection, which is something that we need to fix in the next section.

To prove that you do not have an Internet connection, open the Browser application and attempt to navigate to www.google.com/. The simulator will sit there for several minutes, and you won't get to see Google's home page.

Installing the BlackBerry Email and MDS Simulator

BlackBerry's heritage with regards to network connectivity is a bit odd because the OS predates the regular "TCP/IP over cellular network"–type stack that the other devices are based on. In addition, a lot of the functionality within a BlackBerry is tied to back-end/back-office systems (like BlackBerry Enterprise Server, or BES), and, as a result, the BlackBerry simulator requires some extra software to be running on your machine in order to give it access to the Internet. This comes in the guise of the BlackBerry Email and MDS Simulator.

To download the package, Google "blackberry email and mds simulator". The first hit should be the item that you require. By way of a gotcha, make sure that you download something called a "simulator package." You need to get hold of an executable or an MSI file. (It is possible to download a "runtime," which is the wrong thing.)

When you run the installer, it will check for prerequisites—specifically it will look for the Java JDK 1.5 or higher. (Figure 9-2 illustrates.)

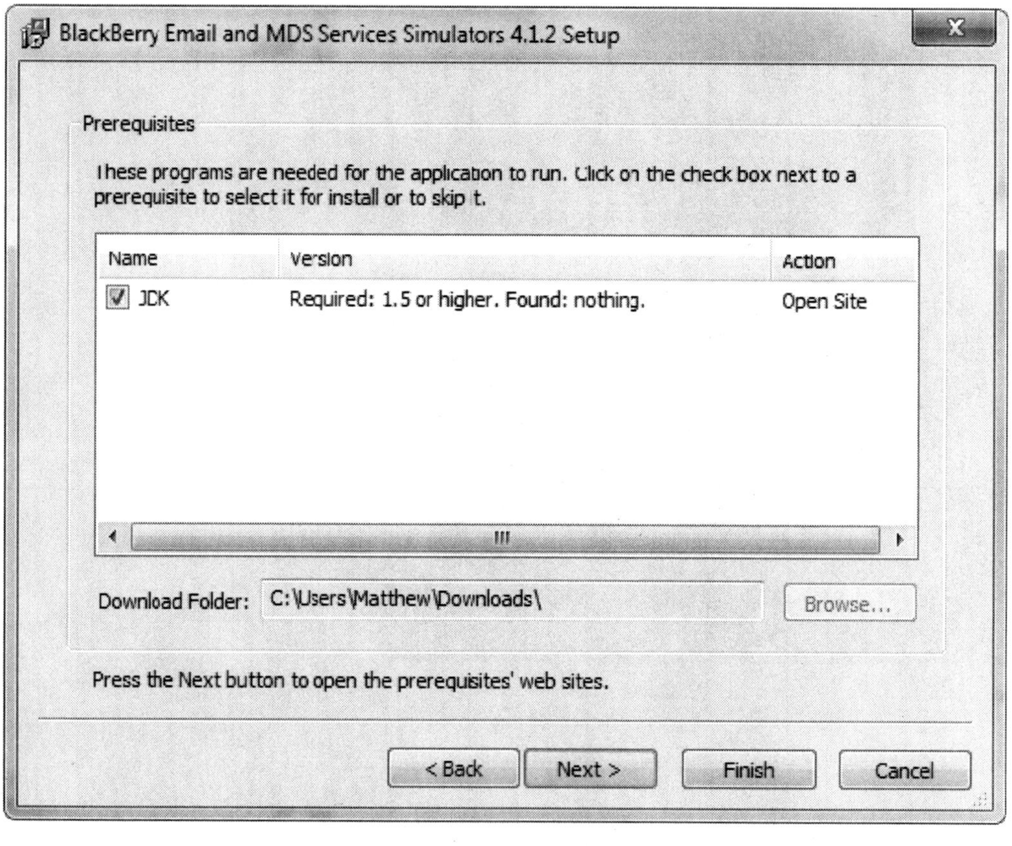

Figure 9-2. The prerequisites wizard asking for Java JDK 1.5

Your mileage may vary on this, but when I clicked Next and the wizard opened the web site to download the JDK package, I was met with a message saying that it had been deprecated. (The URL that it tries to go to as of the time of writing is http://java.sun.com/j2se/1.5.0/download.jsp.) I was able to make this work by downloading and installing the JDK 5.0 Update 22 package, although the prerequisites wizard failed to identify this on loading. Anyway, once this is done, you can progress through the installer and then try to run the MDS application.

To run the MDS application, open a command prompt and navigate to the directory where the MDS service was installed. (On my machine, this happened to be `C:\Program Files (x86)\Research In Motion\BlackBerry Email and MDS Services Simulators 4.1.2\MDS`.) From a command prompt (you cannot do this from Explorer—you *must* do this from a command prompt), run the `run.bat` file in that folder. This will start the service.

Now if you go back to the Browser application and try to go to Google again, you will see the home page. Figure 9-3 illustrates.

Figure 9-3. Google's home page in the BlackBerry simulator

We won't be building a network-aware application in this chapter, but we will need an Internet connection in the other BlackBerry chapters—hence the need to go through how to install and run the MDS simulator.

"Hello, World"

Now that we have the basic setup complete, we can turn our attention to the "Hello, World" application.

To start with, create a new Eclipse workspace and add a new BlackBerry project to it. Figure 9-4 shows the wizard. Provide the name HelloWorld for the project. The only other important thing on this page is to specify the Java Runtime Environment (JRE) that you wish to use. For this to work at all, you must specify a special "BlackBerry JRE." By default you are prompted to use the 5.0.0 version.

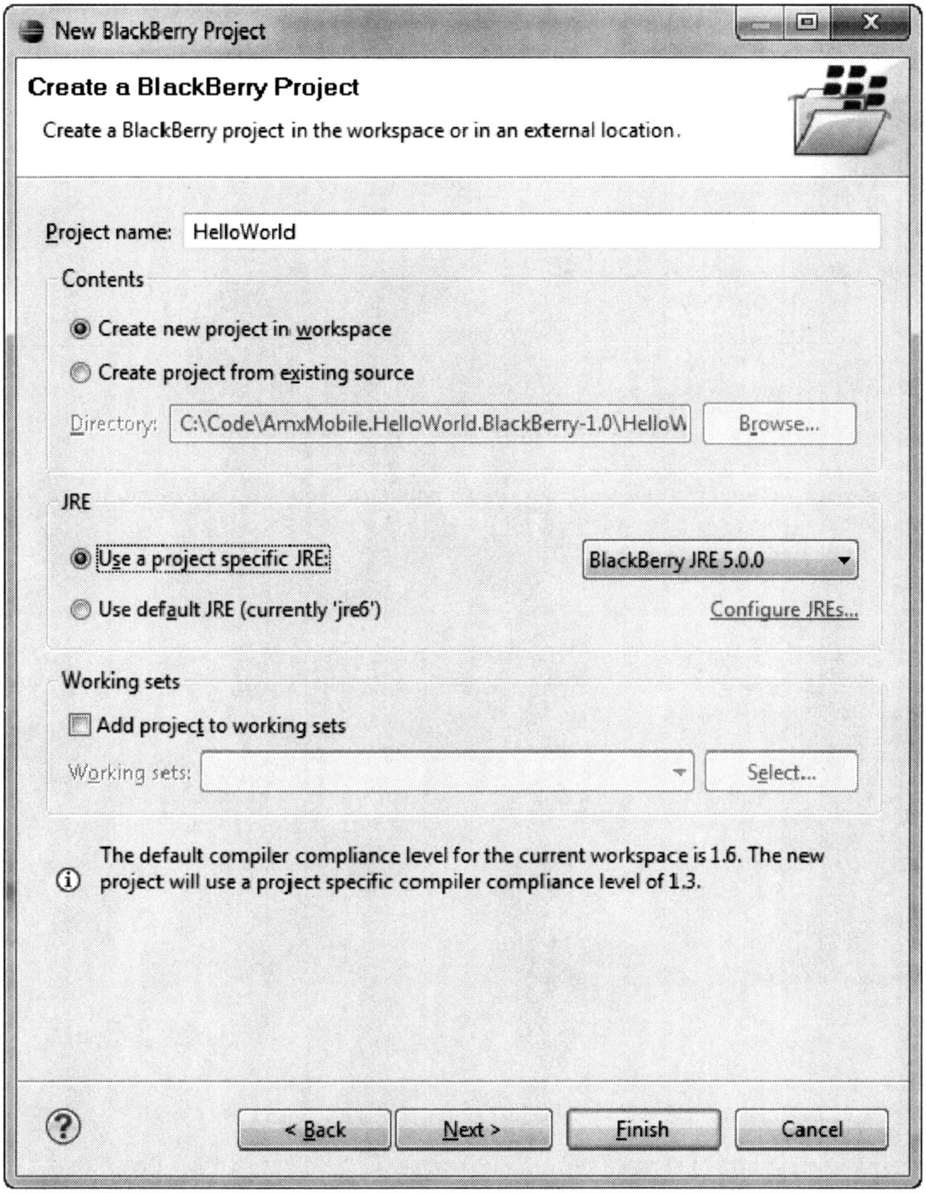

Figure 9-4. *The BlackBerry Project wizard*

You can click Finish on this page, as the remainder of the options are suitable for our needs.

When the project has been created, Eclipse's Package Explorer will show the project, but you don't have much created for you apart from a reference to the JAR file containing the BlackBerry libraries and a manifest file called BlackBerry_App_Descriptor.xml. Figure 9-5 illustrates.

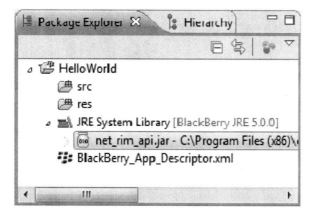

Figure 9-5. *The Package Explorer state on creating a new project*

For our project, we need to build two classes. One class will hold the regular Java main method that is used to boot the application. The other class will hold a form.

We'll start with the one that boots the application. Add a new class called AppMain, and add this code:

```
// AppMain class
import net.rim.device.api.ui.UiApplication;

public class AppMain extends UiApplication
{
        public static void main(String[] args)
        {
                AppMain instance = new AppMain();
        instance.enterEventDispatcher();
        }

    public AppMain()
    {
        pushScreen(new AppForm());
    }
}
```

The purpose of this code is to create a new instance of a type that extends the special UiApplication class. This, together with the call to enterEventDispatcher, effectively boots your application.

When building a user interface for a BlackBerry application, it's necessary to do it all programmatically by creating control instances and manually pushing them onto a presentation surface. There is no designer capability within the regular BlackBerry tools. (This fact, together with the crudeness of the BlackBerry user interface library, means it's very difficult to make swish-looking applications in comparison to the other dominant mobile platforms.)

Our AppForm class is actually very straightforward. We need to create a label for the form and add a button. Here's the code:

```
// AppForm class
import net.rim.device.api.ui.component.ButtonField;
import net.rim.device.api.ui.component.LabelField;
import net.rim.device.api.ui.container.MainScreen;

public class AppForm extends MainScreen
{
        public AppForm()
        {
        super();

        // title...
        LabelField applicationTitle = new LabelField("Hello, World");
        setTitle(applicationTitle);

        // button...
        ButtonField button = new ButtonField("Say 'Hello'", ButtonField.CONSUME_CLICK);
        this.add(button);
        }
}
```

To try this, run the application by launching the project with the debugger (Run – Debug). When the simulator starts, you will see the main screen, as per Figure 9-6.

Figure 9-6. The simulator showing the home screen

Oddly, the BlackBerry tools will not run the application for you, so you have to dig around and find it. If you click the wallpaper image, you can access the full menu, as per Figure 9-7.

Figure 9-7. The main menu

In the bottom right-hand corner, you will see the Downloads option. Your application should be in here. Figure 9-8 illustrates.

Note Your mileage may vary on this. If your application is not shown in the Downloads area, restart the debugger.

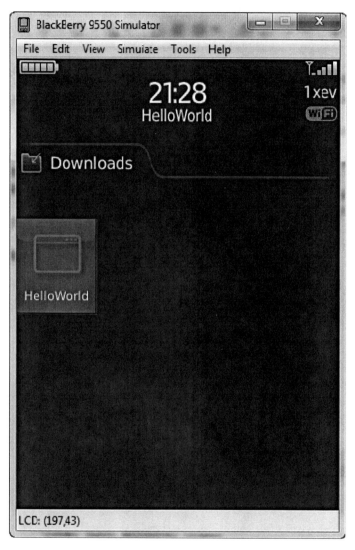

Figure 9-8. The "Hello, World" application in the Downloads area

If you click the application, it will show the user interface that we defined earlier. Figure 9-9 illustrates.

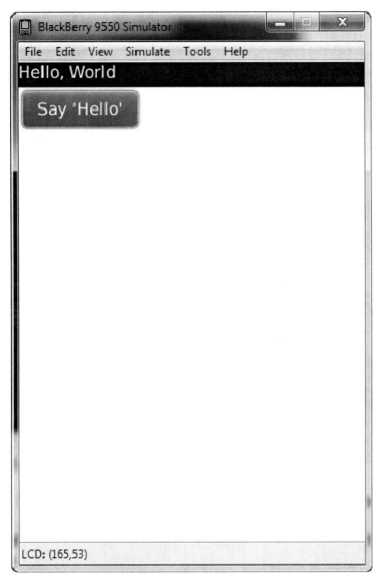

Figure 9-9. The "Hello, World" application

Handling the Button Click

To handle the button click, each control library class in the BlackBerry API will issue a `fieldChanged` event via an interface on (typically) the owner class. Therefore, to handle the button click in our application, all we have to do is set up this event and show a dialog. Helpfully within the BlackBerry API we do have a class that we can use to display ad hoc messages. This class is called `Dialog`.

Here is the revised code:

```
// Revised code for AppForm…
import net.rim.device.api.ui.Field;
import net.rim.device.api.ui.FieldChangeListener;
import net.rim.device.api.ui.component.ButtonField;
import net.rim.device.api.ui.component.Dialog;
import net.rim.device.api.ui.component.LabelField;
import net.rim.device.api.ui.container.MainScreen;

public class AppForm extends MainScreen implements FieldChangeListener
{
        public AppForm()
        {
        super();

        // title...
        LabelField applicationTitle = new LabelField("Hello, World");
        setTitle(applicationTitle);

        // button...
        ButtonField button = new ButtonField("Say 'Hello'", ButtonField.CONSUME_CLICK);
        button.setChangeListener(this);
        this.add(button);
        }

        public void fieldChanged(Field field, int context)
        {
                // show the message...
                Dialog.alert("Hello, world.");
        }
}
```

Now if you run the application, you can click the button and see a message, as per Figure 9-10.

Figure 9-10. The "Hello, world" message successfully displayed

Conclusion

That's it! Now that we know that we can build and run projects, we can start work on the Six Bookmarks application for BlackBerry.

BlackBerry: Building the Logon Form and Consuming REST Services

In this chapter, now that we have the toolset configured, we're going to start building our Six Bookmarks application for BlackBerry. This is going to involve starting a new project, creating the logon form layout, and then building the infrastructure to call up to our API and Users RESTful services at http://services.multimobiledevelopment.com/.

How This Project Was Built and Significant Issues with BlackBerry Development

As you know, this book has a companion title that covers the same Six Bookmarks application, but discusses iOS and Android rather than the platforms in this book. For those who do not have both books, Android is based on Java, just like BlackBerry is (albeit a different variant of Java, which I shall get to later). It also uses a similar approach to presenting its toolset—specifically a plug-in to Eclipse. So, in order to build the BlackBerry version of Six Bookmarks, I ported the code from the Android version using the stalwart technology that is "copy and paste." This is different from how the other software in the books was written, which was in every case a ground-up rewrite of each.

Why this is important is that it highlights problems alluded to in the last chapter with regards to BlackBerry development, or to put it another way, the challenges that are faced by those looking to develop native applications for BlackBerry that compete with those for iOS or Android, and, to an extent, Windows Phone 7.

Specifically this is all to do with bits that are missing. BlackBerry's Java runtime is based on a thing called J2ME, or "Java 2 Platform, Mobile Edition." J2ME was specifically written to support the *last* generation of feature phones and quasi-smartphones—think Nokia and Symbian here. This, in turn, is based on the Java Runtime Environment (JRE) v1.5. The v1.5 JRE is now quite old and doesn't have major language improvements such as generics and fast iterators (foreach statements). The library is also missing buckets of things that you will be used to if you are either a Java (Android or non-Android) or C# developer. There's no String.format method, for example. Quite unbelievably there is no sort function on dynamic arrays! And there are many more things missing that present the first layer of challenges.

The second layer of challenges comes from the fact that RIM has managed to get itself hugely behind the game in terms of building an API and toolset for developing the kinds of applications that are in vogue right now. For example, as mentioned in the last chapter, there is no WYSIWYG designer for building user interfaces. There are also other bits missing—e.g., it's hard to work with XML in any meaningful way, and there's a gaping hole in the library for HTTP communication, which means in the final BlackBerry chapter we're going to have to do a monumental hack to get things working (more later).

In summary, building native applications for BlackBerry is much more difficult than it is for any of the other featured platforms, but, with clever thinking and by picking your battles, it is possible to build applications that *do* the same things as are possible on the other platforms. It probably won't be that elegant, however.

Creating the Project

The first place to start is creating a new BlackBerry project for the Six Bookmarks application. To do this, you need to create a new workspace in Eclipse and then add a new project. If you're not running Eclipse, when it starts and you are prompted for a workspace folder path, create a new one. If you are running Eclipse, select File Switch Workspace Other, and then specify a new workspace folder path.

In either case, add a new BlackBerry project like you did in Chapter 9. Figure 10-1 illustrates my settings.

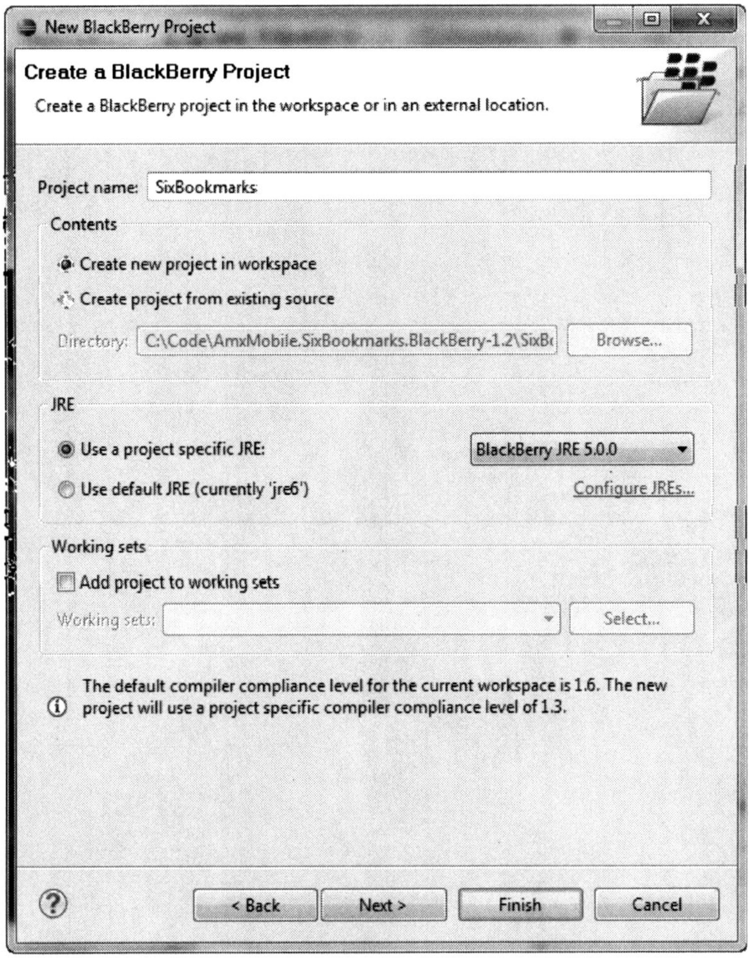

Figure 10-1. The New BlackBerry Project wizard

In the rest of this chapter, we will be looking at calling the services, and then we'll look at building a UI to call them by presenting the logon form to the user.

Conventions for Presenting Code

Each section in this book is going to have its own convention for presenting code, as each toolset presents its own challenges for presenting code in book form.

In the BlackBerry sections, in the code available on the download, I'm going to separate the code into distinct packages. I won't necessarily call out the package before presenting code; therefore look for package declarations in the code listing.

Another thing that I shall do with the code in these sections is where you're adding a method to an existing class, I'll add a comment at the top of the listing telling you which class to add the code to. If the actual class declaration is specified, I won't do this, and you should assume the name of the file matches the name of the class.

The final point is that in Java I'm not necessarily going to follow Java's code case conventions in terms of camel case method names, but I will typically use .NET's Pascal casing. There's an argument that when trying to maintain separate code bases with the same function, it's a little easier to keep the structure and coding conventions the same. .NET and Java are sufficiently flexible to accept each other's standards, and I've arbitrarily chosen .NET's.

Calling RESTful Services

In Chapter 5, we built some classes that acted as proxy objects that could communicate with the services at http://services.multimobiledevelopment.com/. In this chapter and the next, we're going to build the same objects again, but this time for BlackBerry.

If you recall, in Chapter 5, we built final classes called ApiService, UsersService, and BookmarksService. We also built base classes of ServiceProxy, RestServiceProxy, and ODataServiceProxy. Figure 10-2 illustrates.

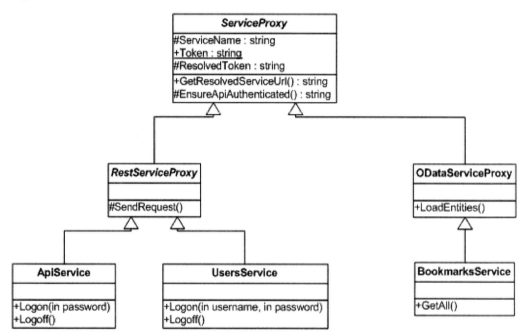

Figure 10-2. UML static structure sketch showing proxy class relationships

Let's now look at building these classes.

Issuing Web Requests

The first piece we need in place in order to use the API is the code that physically makes the requests to the server.

In Chapter 5, we used a class in BootFX called HttpHelper that internally used the .NET Framework's System.Net.HttpWebRequest and System.Net.HttpWebResponse classes to issue the requests and process the response. In this section, we're going to build a new version of HttpHelper for BlackBerry.

The classes available within BlackBerry to do this can be found in the javax.microedition.io namespace. This library is part of the J2ME library used by BlackBerry.

We're going to create two main methods and a number of helper methods. The first of the main methods (Download) will return a string that represents the response from the server. The second (DownloadXml) will take the result of Download and load it into an XML document that can be processed later.

The DownloadSettings Class

Recall that in Chapter 5, we passed up with the request special HTTP headers that told the server the username of the API account and the token for the requests. (These headers were called x-amx-apiusername and x-amx-token.) To make this happen, when the time comes, we need to provide to the Download and DownloadXml methods a list of such headers and their values. As such, we'll create a class called DownloadSettings that's designed to hold a collection of these settings in a regular Java Hashtable. (For those familiar with a more modern version of Java, we can't use generics here.)

Here's the listing:

```
package com.amxmobile.SixBookmarks.Runtime;

import java.util.Hashtable;

public class DownloadSettings
{
        private Hashtable _extraHeaders = new Hashtable();

        public DownloadSettings()
        {
        }

        public Hashtable getExtraHeaders()
        {
                return _extraHeaders;
        }

        public void AddHeader(String name, String value)
        {
                if(value == null)
                        value = "";

                getExtraHeaders().put(name, value);
        }
}
```

The Download and DownloadXml Methods

The Download method is not difficult, but it is a little bit fiddly, so we'll go through it step by step. What we're looking to do is, given a particular URL, use the J2RE HTTP API to call up to the server, wait for a response, and then process it either as an error, or as successful. In the case that it's successful, we want to read all of the data that the server wishes to give us and store it in a string. (Ultimately in its companion method we'll read that string into an object that represents an XML document.)

Before we do this, we need to create a new class to put this stuff into. Add a class HttpHelper to the project, like this:

```
package com.amxMobile.SixBookmarks.Runtime;

public class HttpHelper
{

}
```

We start off by creating a client instance and then asking it to issue an HTTP GET command to the given URL. Here's the code.

```
// Add to HttpHelper.java…
    public static String Download(String url, DownloadSettings settings) throws Exception
    {
        if(settings == null)
            settings  = new DownloadSettings();

    HttpConnection conn = null;
    InputStream stream = null;
    try
    {
        conn = (HttpConnection)Connector.open(url);
```

The next bit is specific to our project as we have to pass up these special headers. We'll walk through the ExtraHeaders property of the supplied DownloadSettings instance and configure the request object appropriately. Here's the code:

```
        // headers...
        Hashtable headers = settings.getExtraHeaders();
        Enumeration keys = headers.keys();
        while(keys.hasMoreElements())
        {
            String key = (String)keys.nextElement();
            conn.setRequestProperty(key, (String)headers.get(key));
        }
```

We're now ready to make the requests of the server. In the final part of the method, we'll copy the returned data into a string and clean up.

```
            // open...
        stream = conn.openInputStream();

        // walk...
        final int bufLen = 10240;
        byte[] buf = new byte[bufLen];
        StringBuffer raw = new StringBuffer();
```

```
        while(true)
        {
            int len = stream.read(buf, 0, bufLen);
            if(len == -1)
                    break;

            // append...
            raw.append(new String(buf, 0, len));
        }

        // return...
        String html = raw.toString();
        return html;
    }
    finally
    {
            if(stream != null)
                    stream.close();
            if(conn != null)
                    conn.close();

    }
}
```

That's all there is to the Download method. As mentioned before, DownloadXml will take the output of Download and load it into an object capable of representing an XML document. Specifically, this will be an org.w3c.dom.Document instance. It'll do this by deferring to a class called XmlHelper, which we'll build shortly. Here's the code:

```
// Add to HttpHelper.java...
                public static Document DownloadXml(String url, DownloadSettings settings)↵
throws Exception
        {
                // get the plain content...
                String xml = Download(url, settings);

                // turn that into some XML...
                Document doc = XmlHelper.LoadXml(xml);
                return doc;
        }
```

We'll stub out LoadXml on the new XmlHelper class now, so that the application continues to compile. Here's the stub code:

```
package com.amxMobile.SixBookmarks.Runtime;

public class XmlHelper
{
        public static Document LoadXml(String xml) throws Exception
        {
                throw new Exception("Not implemented.");
        }
}
```

Extra Methods on HttpHelper

There are two methods we will need on HttpHelper that help the caller build URLs that can be used with Download and DownloadXml.

When we come to make a request of our RESTful services, we're going to create a hashtable of name/value pairs that need to be built into the query string of the URL. We'll need methods called BuildUrl and BuildQueryString that will help us do this. Here's the code:

```java
public static String BuildQueryString(Hashtable<String, Object> values)
{
        StringBuilder builder = new StringBuilder();
        for(Object key : values.keySet())
        {
                if(builder.length() > 0)
                        builder.append("&");
                builder.append(key);
                builder.append("=");
                builder.append(values.get(key));
        }

        // return...
        String qs = builder.toString();
        return qs;
}

public static String BuildUrl(String url, Hashtable<String, Object> values)
{
        int index = url.indexOf("?");
        if(index != -1)
                url = url.substring(0, index);

        // add...
        url = url + "?" + BuildQueryString(values);
        return url;
}
```

Authenticating Our API Account

We've now got the pieces in place to start building the ServiceProxy, RestServiceProxy, and ApiService classes.

ServiceProxy is the base class that all of the service proxies will use. It has a number of functions:

- It will store as constant strings the username and password to your API account at http://services.multimobiledevelopment.com/. You will need to change this in order to use the project files if you download the code.

- It will store in static memory the token provided by the server that should be used with API requests. (Recall that within a session we make one request to tell the server we want a token, and then all other requests use that token.)

- It will store in instance memory the name of the service that the proxy relates to.

- It will provide a DownloadSettings instance that's configured with the special headers that we need to pass up, depending on the state of the stored token.

- It will manage the process of ensuring the API is authenticated.

Here's the code that does everything apart from ensuring that the API is authenticated, which we will do later. Add this new class to the project:

```
package com.amxmobile.SixBookmarks.Services;

import javax.microedition.global.Formatter;

public abstract class ServiceProxy
{
        private String _serviceName;
        private static String _token;

        private final String RootUrl = "http://services.multimobiledevelopment.com/services/";

        // YOU MUST CHANGE THESE VALUES IN ORDER TO USE THIS SAMPLE...
        protected final String ApiUsername = "amxmobile";
        private final String ApiPassword = "password";

        protected ServiceProxy(String serviceName)
        {
                _serviceName = serviceName;
        }

        public String getServiceName()
        {
                return _serviceName;
        }

        public String getResolvedServiceUrl()
        {
                return RootUrl + getServiceName();
        }

        protected static String getToken()
        {
                return _token;
        }

        protected void setToken(String token)
        {
```

```
            _token = token;
        }

    protected DownloadSettings GetDownloadSettings()
    {
        DownloadSettings settings = new DownloadSettings();
        settings.AddHeader("x-amx-apiusername", ApiUsername);
        settings.AddHeader("x-amx-token", getToken());

        // return...
        return settings;
    }
}
```

Here's something else we need to add to ServiceProxy—the EnsureApiAuthenticated method. We'll build this out later.

```
// Add to ServiceProxy.java
    protected void EnsureApiAuthenticated() throws Exception
    {
        throw new Exception("Not implemented.");
    }
```

The LogonResponse

Regardless of whether we're authenticating the API or the user, we'll need an object that describes the result of the call. We'll create a class called LogonResponse that holds this data together with a set of constants that represents the ultimate result. Here it is:

```
package com.amxmobile.SixBookmarks.Services;

import javax.microedition.global.Formatter;

public class LogonResponse
{
        public final static int RESULT_OK = 0;
        public final static int RESULT_INVALID_USERNAME = 1;
        public final static int RESULT_INVALID_PASSWORD = 2;
        public final static int RESULT_USER_INACTIVE = 3;

        private String _token;
        private String _message;
        private int _result;

        public LogonResponse(int result, String message, String token)
        {
                _result = result;
                _message = message;
                _token = token;
        }
```

```
public String getMessage()
{
        return _message;
}

public String getToken()
{
        return _token;
}

public int getResult()
{
        return _result;
}

public static int ParseLogonResult(String asString) throws Exception
{
        if(asString.compareTo("LogonOk") == 0)
                return RESULT_OK;
        else if(asString.compareTo("InvalidUsername") == 0)
                return RESULT_INVALID_USERNAME;
        else if(asString.compareTo("InvalidPassword") == 0)
                return RESULT_INVALID_PASSWORD;
        else if(asString.compareTo("AccountInactive") == 0)
                return RESULT_USER_INACTIVE;
        else
                throw new Exception(Formatter.formatMessage("Cannot handle '{0}'.",↵
new String[] { asString }));
        }
}
```

Building the XmlHelper Class

In Chapter 5, we used the BootFX HttpHelper class to smooth over the intricacies of making HTTP requests. We also used the BootFX class XmlHelper to make working with XML data easier.

BlackBerry uses the regular XML DOM manipulation API found in the com.w3c.dom namespace. Although extremely fiddly, this API provides a very powerful set of functions for reading and changing XML documents in a safe and ultimately maintainable fashion. (The full version of the API also allows you to create documents, but this creation functionality is not available on BlackBerry.)

■ **Note** For those who have not used the W3C implementation before but have used the .NET System.Xml namespace, the two are essentially the same.

For those who are coming at this completely cold, the principle is that a document is made up of "nodes." A node represents anything and everything in the document, e.g., elements, attributes, text values, type declarations, etc. When reading the document, you walk the nodes. When building or changing the document, you create nodes and insert them as children of other nodes.

The first two methods we'll add to XmlHelper will load a document from a string or from a stream. (Both use the regular Java I/O library.) Here's the code:

```
// Add to XmlHelper.java

public static Document LoadXml(String xml) throws Exception
{
        // create...
        ByteArrayInputStream stream = new ByteArrayInputStream(xml.getBytes());
        try
        {
                return LoadXml(stream);
        }
        finally
        {
                if(stream != null)
                        stream.close();
        }
}

private static Document LoadXml(InputStream stream) throws Exception
{
        DocumentBuilderFactory factory = DocumentBuilderFactory.newInstance();
        factory.setNamespaceAware(true);

        // builder...
        DocumentBuilder builder = factory.newDocumentBuilder();
        Document doc = builder.parse(stream);

        // return...
        return doc;
}
```

Personally, I'm a big fan of these object-model-style libraries for manipulating XML documents; however, the compromise that one has to make is that they're very fiddly to use. I tend to build helper libraries—like the one we're about to see—to make working with the documents easier.

▩ **Note** We're going to add the minimum number of functions here. Practically, you need a library that has far more variations of the types of data and the formats that can be returned. However, as always, review the version of the class in the project files at http://code.multimobiledevelopment.com/, as these will be developed further and have more functions.

It's worth mentioning, though, that some people do not like using these DOM-based libraries, as they are inefficient in terms of processor time and memory used. On mobile devices, this is a greater consideration than on a desktop or server; however, my personal philosophy is to follow a pragmatic, "balancing ease of building and ease of maintenance" approach, and parsers are much harder to build and maintain.

Back to the subject of building helper libraries for reading XML—one common requirement of such a library is to extract element values from a parent element given the name of a child. For example, consider the following XML. It would be very helpful to be able to issue a single request against the Customer element to get FirstName and LastName values back:

```
<Customer>
        <FirstName>Andy</FirstName>
<LastName>Williams</LastName>
</Customer>
```

If we have a Customer element and we want to get values back from the child values, a good approach is to have one method that returns the child element and another that extracts the value from it. In this implementation, we're going to support three data types: string, Boolean, and 32-bit integer. In a more advanced language implementation, we would use an enumeration here, but enumerations are not supported in the JRE supported on BlackBerry, and hence we'll have to use constants.

```
public class XmlHelper
{
        public final static int DATATYPE_STRING = 0;
        public final static int DATATYPE_INT32 = 1;
        public final static int DATATYPE_BOOLEAN = 2;

        // code omitted for brevity…
}
```

Within XmlHelper, we'll go ahead and create methods that return back strongly typed data and use a generic method that can fetch any type of data. Here's the code:

```
// Add to XmlHelper.java

        public static String GetElementString(Element element, String name, boolean↵
throwIfNotFound) throws Exception
        {
                return (String)GetElementValue(element, name, DATATYPE_STRING,↵
throwIfNotFound);
        }

        public static boolean GetElementBoolean(Element element, String name, boolean↵
throwIfNotFound) throws Exception
        {
                return ((Boolean)GetElementValue(element, name, DATATYPE_BOOLEAN,↵
throwIfNotFound)).booleanValue();
        }

        public static int GetElementInt32(Element element, String name, boolean↵
throwIfNotFound) throws Exception
        {
                return ((Integer)GetElementValue(element, name, DATATYPE_INT32,↵
```

```
throwIfNotFound)).intValue();
        }

        private static Object GetElementValue(Element element, String name, int dataType,↵
boolean throwIfNotFound) throws Exception
        {
                // find it...
                NodeList nodes = element.getElementsByTagName(name);
                if(nodes.getLength() == 1)
                {
                        if(dataType == DATATYPE_STRING)
                                return GetStringValue(nodes.item(0));
                        else if(dataType == DATATYPE_BOOLEAN)
                                return new Boolean(GetBooleanValue(nodes.item(0)));
                        else if(dataType == DATATYPE_INT32)
                                return new Integer(GetInt32Value(nodes.item(0)));
                        else
                                throw new Exception(Formatter.formatMessage("Cannot handle↵
'{0}'.", new String[] { new Integer(dataType).toString() }));
                }
                else if(nodes.getLength() == 0)
                {
                        if(throwIfNotFound)
                        {
                                throw new Exception(Formatter.formatMessage("An element↵
with name '{0}' was not found within an element with name '{1}'.",
                                                new String[] { name, element.getNodeName()↵
}));
                        }
                        else
                                return null;
                }
                else
                {
                        throw new Exception(Formatter.formatMessage("Too many ({0}) child↵
elements were found.",
                                                new String[] { new↵
Integer(nodes.getLength()).toString() } ));
                }
        }
```

Note that in the generic GetElementValue method, we're deferring to methods called GetStringValue, GetBooleanValue, and GetInt32Value. These methods will do the actual conversion for us. As the data in the XML file is formatted as text, the GetStringValue will be the "master" method, and the others will defer to that and convert the values. Here's the code:

```
// Add to XmlHelper.java

        public static String GetStringValue(Node item) throws Exception
        {
                if(item instanceof Element)
```

```
                {
                        Node node = item.getFirstChild();
                        if(node != null)
                                return node.getNodeValue();
                        else
                                return "";
                }
                else
                        throw new Exception(Formatter.formatMessage("Cannot handle '{0}'.",↵
new String[] { item.getClass().getName() }));
        }

        public static int GetInt32Value(Node item) throws Exception
        {
                String asString = GetStringValue(item);
                return Integer.parseInt(asString);
        }

        public static boolean GetBooleanValue(Node item) throws Exception
        {
                String asString = GetStringValue(item);
                if(asString.compareTo("0") == 0 || asString.toLowerCase().compareTo("false")↵
== 0)
                        return false;
                else if(asString.compareTo("1") == 0 ||↵
asString.toLowerCase().compareTo("true") == 0)
                        return true;
                else
                {
                        throw new Exception(Formatter.formatMessage("The value '{0}' could↵
not be recognised as valid Boolean value.",
                                        new String[] { asString }));
                }
        }
}
```

We can now go ahead and build the ApiService class and implement the Logon method.

Creating the Logon Method on the API Service

In Chapter 2, we looked at the protocol exposed by the service at
http://services.multimobiledevelopment.com/. By way of a reminder, here's what the XML from a
successful call to the Logon operation looks like on the service:

```
<AmxResponse>
  <Result dt:type="string" xmlns:dt="urn:schemas-microsoft-com:datatypes">LogonOk</Result>
  <Token>d8313229998afe2de52698934a51dfb6</Token>
  <HasException dt:type="boolean" xmlns:dt="urn:schemas-microsoft-com:datatypes">↵
0</HasException>
</AmxResponse>
```

And here's what a call that exposes an error looks like:

```
<AmxResponse>
  <Error>System.InvalidOperationException: Neither a logon token nor API key was provided↵
in the request.  Ensure a token was provided in the URL.
   at AmxMobile.Services.ServiceAuthenticator.GetApi(LogonToken&amp; token)
   at AmxMobile.Services.Web.RestBasePage.OnLoad(EventArgs e)</Error>
  <HasException dt:type="boolean" xmlns:dt="urn:schemas-microsoft-com:datatypes">↵
1</HasException>
</AmxResponse>
```

The reason I wanted to present these here is that we will need to write code that can detect when the server returned an exception and, if so, throw a Java exception instance based on the data in the XML.

Recall that in Chapter 5, we created a class called RestRequestArgs that would package up the values that we needed to send to the server. We'll do the same thing here by extending Hashtable and also forcing a value to be set representing the operation in the constructor. Here's the code:

```
package com.amxmobile.SixBookmarks.Services;

import java.util.Hashtable;

public class RestRequestArgs extends Hashtable
{
        public RestRequestArgs(String operation)
        {
                this.put("operation", operation);
        }
}
```

That's all we need to do with RestRequestArgs—the standard operation of Java's Hashtable class does the rest.

The job of RestServiceProxy will be to take a RestRequestArgs instance and combine it with the root URL and the service name to make the request. It will also detect whether an exception occurred on the server and throw a Java exception if it did. The method will also return the root AmxResponse element back to the caller. Here's the code for the new class RestServiceProxy:

```
package com.amxmobile.SixBookmarks.Services;

import javax.microedition.global.Formatter;

import org.w3c.dom.Document;
import org.w3c.dom.Element;

import com.amxmobile.SixBookmarks.Runtime.HttpHelper;
import com.amxmobile.SixBookmarks.Runtime.XmlHelper;

public class RestServiceProxy extends ServiceProxy
{
    protected RestServiceProxy(String serviceName)
    {
```

```
            super(serviceName);
    }

    protected Element SendRequest(RestRequestArgs args) throws Exception
{
    // ensure that we have an authenticated API...
    this.EnsureApiAuthenticated();

    // get the URL...
    String url = this.getResolvedServiceUrl();
    url = HttpHelper.BuildUrl(url, args);

    // download...
    Document doc = HttpHelper.DownloadXml(url, GetDownloadSettings());
            try
            {
                    // find the response...
                    Element root = doc.getDocumentElement();
                    if(root.getNodeName().compareTo("AmxResponse") != 0)
                            throw new Exception(Formatter.formatMessage("The root↵
element had an invalid name of '%s'.", new String[] { root.getNodeName() }));

                    // get...
                    boolean hasException = XmlHelper.GetElementBoolean(root, ↵
"HasException", true);
                    if(!(hasException))
                            return root;
                    else
                    {
                            // get the error...
                            String error = XmlHelper.GetElementString(root, "Error", ↵
true);
                            throw new Exception(Formatter.formatMessage("The server↵
returned an error: {0}", new String[] { error }));
                    }
            }
            catch(Exception ex)
            {
                    throw new Exception(Formatter.formatMessage("An error occurred↵
when processing a response returned from a REST request.\nURL: {0}\r\nInner: {1}",
                                    new String[] { url, ex.toString() }));
            }
    }
}
```

Note how the first thing this method does is call EnsureApiAuthenticated. We're going to build that in the next section (recall that we added it before and forced it to throw an exception).

Building the ApiService class should now be easy, as we have everything in place. Here's the code:

```
package com.amxmobile.SixBookmarks.Services;

import org.w3c.dom.Element;

import com.amxmobile.SixBookmarks.Runtime.XmlHelper;

public class ApiService extends RestServiceProxy
{
        public ApiService()
        {
                super("apirest.aspx");
        }

        public LogonResponse Logon(String password) throws Exception
        {
        // create the request...
        RestRequestArgs args = new RestRequestArgs("logon");
        args.put("password", password);

        // send the request...
        Element element = SendRequest(args);

        // what happened?
        String asString = XmlHelper.GetElementString(element, "Result", true);
        int result = LogonResponse.ParseLogonResult(asString);

        // message...
        String message = XmlHelper.GetElementString(element, "Message", false);

        // then what?
        if(result == LogonResponse.RESULT_OK)
        {
                String token = XmlHelper.GetElementString(element, "Token", true);
                return new LogonResponse(result, message, token);
        }
        else
                return new LogonResponse(result, message, "");
        }

        protected void EnsureApiAuthenticated()
    {
        // no-op...
    }
}
```

Now that we have a method that can call the Logon operation on the live service, let's wire it up so that it actually happens!

Wiring Up EnsureApiAuthenticated

The flow of the protocol defined by the service is that the RESTful and OData services require a server-provided token to validate the call. The "chicken and egg" situation is that we need to call the server to get a token; hence we need a special first step to do so.

EnsureApiAuthenticated is called in RestServiceProxy as part of the method that physically directs the request to the server. The operation of this method looks to see if a token is defined in global (static) memory, and, if not, it creates an instance of the ApiService proxy class and calls the Logon operation that we have just rigged up. To prevent a stack overflow situation, the ApiService class overrides the operation of EnsureApiAuthenticated to turn it into a "no-operation." Here's the implementation of EnsureApiAuthenticated that needs to be added to the base ServiceProxy class:

```
// Add to ServiceProxy.java - replace the existing stub method...

    protected void EnsureApiAuthenticated() throws Exception
    {
        // check that we've authenticated...
        String asString = getToken();
        if (asString == null || asString.length() == 0)
        {
            // call up to the API service...
            ApiService service = new ApiService();
            LogonResponse response = service.Logon(ApiPassword);
            if (response == null)
                throw new Exception("'response' is null.");

            // can we?
            if (response.getResult() == LogonResponse.RESULT_OK)
                this.setToken(response.getToken());
            else
            {
                throw new Exception(Formatter.formatMessage("The server request failed with↵
the error '{0}'.  Ensure that you have set the values of the ApiUsername and ApiPassword↵
constants to the credentials of your Six Bookmarks service account at {1}.",
                    new String[] { new Integer(response.getResult()).toString(), RootUrl }));
            }
        }
    }
```

You won't see much output from this flow, but it's absolutely required in order to make the protocol work the way that it needs to in order to communicate with the server.

We won't be calling this method for a while, but first let's press on and build the UsersService class.

Authenticating the User via UsersService

The Logon method on UserServices is very easy to implement. We've worked sufficiently hard on our base classes and supporting code that making the call is just a few lines. Here it is:

```
package com.amxmobile.SixBookmarks.Services;

import org.w3c.dom.Element;
```

```
import com.amxmobile.SixBookmarks.Runtime.XmlHelper;

public class UsersService extends RestServiceProxy
{
        public UsersService()
        {
                super("usersrest.aspx");
        }

    public LogonResponse Logon(String username, String password) throws Exception
    {
        // create the request...
        RestRequestArgs args = new RestRequestArgs("logon");

        // add the username and password...
        args.put("username", username);
        args.put("password", password);

        // send the request...
        Element element = SendRequest(args);

        String asString = XmlHelper.GetElementString(element, "Result", true);
        int result = LogonResponse.ParseLogonResult(asString);

        // message...
        String message = XmlHelper.GetElementString(element, "Message", false);

        // return...
        return new LogonResponse(result, message, "");
    }
}
```

And that's it! In the next sections, we'll build the logon form user interface and actually call the method (and, of course, the whole chain of operations that makes it possible).

Creating the Logon Form

Now that we have the business logic more or less done, we can build the user interface. As discussed in the last chapter, building the user interface on BlackBerry is done manually by programmatically adding controls to a presentation surface.

In the BlackBerry API, presentation surfaces are extended from Screen, although we'll be extending from MainScreen, which is the correct class to use to present a full-screen view to the user. Again, within the API, all of the control classes extend Field, and in this example we'll be seeing EditField, PasswordEditField, CheckBoxField, and ButtonField.

When building BlackBerry forms, convention dictates that we add a field to the form that displays a title. This is done using the setTitle method of MainScreen. Here's the code for a new LogonForm class that sets up the basic presentation interface as we require.

```
package com.amxmobile.SixBookmarks;

import net.rim.device.api.ui.*;
```

```
import net.rim.device.api.ui.component.*;
import net.rim.device.api.ui.container.*;

public class LogonForm extends MainScreen
{
        private EditField _usernameTextBox;
        private PasswordEditField _passwordTextBox;
        private CheckboxField _rememberMeCheckBox;
        private ButtonField _logonButton;

        public LogonForm()
        {
                super();

                // start...
                SixBookmarksRuntime.Start();

                // title...
                setTitle(new LabelField("Welcome to Six Bookmarks"));

                // controls...
                this.add(new LabelField("Username"));
                _usernameTextBox = new EditField();
                this.add(_usernameTextBox);

                this.add(new LabelField("Password"));
                _passwordTextBox = new PasswordEditField();
                this.add(_passwordTextBox);

                _rememberMeCheckBox = new CheckboxField("Remember me", true);
                this.add(_rememberMeCheckBox);

                _logonButton = new ButtonField("Logon", ButtonField.CONSUME_CLICK);
                this.add(_logonButton);
        }
}
```

If you run the application now, you will see the form, although it obviously won't do anything yet.
Figure 10-3 illustrates.

Figure 10-3. The basic logon form

You may recall in the last chapter that the way we received notification of a button click was by implementing FieldChangeListener on the form and calling the setChangeListener method. We can do this again and call a method called HandleLogon, this being a method that we'll flesh out in more detail in the next section. Here's the revised code:

```
package com.amxmobile.SixBookmarks;

import net.rim.device.api.ui.*;
import net.rim.device.api.ui.component.*;
import net.rim.device.api.ui.container.*;

public class LogonForm extends MainScreen implements FieldChangeListener
{
        private EditField _usernameTextBox;
        private PasswordEditField _passwordTextBox;
        private CheckboxField _rememberMeCheckBox;
        private ButtonField _logonButton;

        public LogonForm()
        {
                super();

                // start...
                SixBookmarksRuntime.Start();

                // title...
                setTitle(new LabelField("Welcome to Six Bookmarks"));
```

```
        // controls...
        this.add(new LabelField("Username"));
        _usernameTextBox = new EditField();
        this.add(_usernameTextBox);

        this.add(new LabelField("Password"));
        _passwordTextBox = new PasswordEditField();
        this.add(_passwordTextBox);

        _rememberMeCheckBox = new CheckboxField("Remember me", true);
        this.add(_rememberMeCheckBox);

        _logonButton = new ButtonField("Logon", ButtonField.CONSUME_CLICK);
        _logonButton.setChangeListener(this);
        this.add(_logonButton);
    }

    public void fieldChanged(Field field, int context)
    {
        try
        {
            if(field == _logonButton)
                HandleLogon();
        }
        catch(Exception ex)
        {
            MessageBox.Show(ex);
        }
    }

    private void HandleLogon() throws Exception
    {
        throw new Exception("Not implemented.");
    }
}
```

If you run the code now, it won't do anything much different than what it did before. Let's now look at the logon functionality itself.

Logging On

Toward the bottom of the Logon class listing, you'll notice the button handler called HandleLogon on the controller. What we need to do here is validate the user input—if it's valid, run a logon operation, and if it's invalid, tell the user about the problem.

Recall in Chapter 5 that when we needed to validate the logon input, we created a class called ErrorBucket that held a simple list of strings. We need a similar thing here, and so we'll add this class:

```
package com.amxmobile.SixBookmarks.Runtime;

import java.util.Vector;
```

```java
public class ErrorBucket
{
        private Vector _errors = new Vector();

        public ErrorBucket()
        {
        }

        public void AddError(String error)
        {
                this._errors.addElement(error);
        }

        public boolean getHasErrors()
        {
                if(this._errors.size() > 0)
                        return true;
                else
                        return false;
        }

        public String GetAllErrors()
        {
                StringBuffer builder = new StringBuffer();
                for(int index = 0; index < _errors.size(); index++)
                {
                        if(builder.length() > 0)
                                builder.append("\n");
                        builder.append(_errors.elementAt(index));
                }

                // return...
                return builder.toString();
        }
}
```

You'll see that the structure of the code is basically the same as that given in Chapter 5. This is an important point. Because you essentially cannot share code easily between the different platforms, if you do need to manage an intellectual property stack that encompasses different platforms, you can get considerable benefit by doing things the same way on each. This makes it easier to maintain the application, as developers approach problems with a "pre-loaded" expectation about how something should work.

Back on the LogonForm class, here's the HandleLogon method. This defers to DoLogon, which actually calls the service proxy.

```java
// Add to LogonForm.java - replace existing method…

        private void HandleLogon() throws Exception
        {
                ErrorBucket bucket = new ErrorBucket();
                String username = _usernameTextBox.getText().trim();
                if(username == null || username.length() == 0)
```

```
                bucket.AddError("Username not specified");
        String password = _passwordTextBox.getText();
        if(password == null || password.length() == 0)
                bucket.AddError("Password not specified");

        // errors?
        if(!(bucket.getHasErrors()))
                DoLogon(username, password, _rememberMeCheckBox.getChecked());
        else
                MessageBox.Show(bucket.GetAllErrors());
    }

    private void DoLogon(String username, String password, boolean rememberMe)↵
throws Exception
    {
        UsersService users = new UsersService();
        LogonResponse response = users.Logon(username, password);

        // now what?
        if(response.getResult() == LogonResponse.RESULT_OK)
        {
                // in a while we'll add code here to show the bookmarks page...
                MessageBox.Show("Logon OK!");
        }
        else
        {
                MessageBox.Show(response.getMessage());
        }
    }
}
```

I hope you can see there the power of creating these nicely defined service proxy objects, as the actual code to manipulate the remote service is very easy.

There isn't much to show in this chapter, as most of the code is behind-the-scenes stuff. However, if you do run the project, you can at least try providing different values for the username and password and seeing the results. Figure 10-4 shows the result of a successful logon.

Figure 10-4. Success! We've logged on.

Conclusion

In this chapter, we've covered a lot of ground related to building our proper BlackBerry application and being able to call the hosted services at http://services.multimobiledevelopment.com. We built a set of support methods for working with web resources and XML, and the proxy objects needed to call up to the server. We then went on to build the user interface and ultimately called the server's Logon method to log on the user. In the next chapter, we'll see how to use the bookmarks OData service to bring back bookmarks and store them in a local SQL database.

CHAPTER 11

■ ■ ■

BlackBerry:
An ORM Layer on SQLite

In the last chapter, we built the foundation of our application and built a logon screen that connected up to the logon service over the Internet. In this chapter, we're going to look at downloading the bookmarks from the OData service, storing them in a local SQLite database, and displaying them in the screen. We'll look at capturing changes to the bookmarks and pushing them back up to the server in the next chapter.

SQLite on BlackBerry

This will be the first time that we meet the SQLite database engine in this book. SQLite is used and mentioned heavily in this book and this book's sister book, which covers the Microsoft mobile technologies, BlackBerry and HTML5.

SQLite is an open source in-memory database engine that is long-established and is published under an unusual license, in that it is placed in the public domain with no licensing restrictions. It is baked into BlackBerry, iOS, and Android, plus HTML5 web browsers that wish to support HTML5 local storage also use SQLite. In fact, the only place where it is not supported natively by the device vendor is on Windows Phone 7 and Windows Mobile, although community efforts exist to make the platform available there as well.

It is an ANSI-92–compatible database; thus if you already know how to develop software that uses a relational database, you already know how to use SQLite.

Entities

In Chapter 3, we went through the principle of building an object-relational mapping layer that could be "repurposed" for use in the Android, iPhone, BlackBerry and Windows Mobile applications. (This layer will work on Windows Phone 7, just as soon as it has a database management system available!) Chapter 3 discusses the theory of how you build such a thing. This chapter is going to look at how you actually do it.

As discussed in Chapter 3, the most important thing about an ORM layer is to imbue it with decent metadata. It's only through this metadata that you can code in a decent level of "magic" to make working with the ORM entities easier than working with the native data directly. Without good metadata, you'll spend half your life fighting the ORM tool.

In this section, we're going to look at building the metadata to support the entities and the entity class itself. In the next section, we'll look at physically calling the database and obtaining a list of entities.

■ **Note** The ORM layer that we build here is going to be pretty basic and missing support for various data types and other functions. This is done to make the book easier to comprehend. However, keep an eye on the documentation at www.multimobiledevelopment.com/, as it's my fervent hope that this author continues to develop and enhance such functionality for all of the platforms going forward.

EntityType

In Chapter 3, I discussed the idea of an EntityType class. This class does two things. In the first instance, there exists exactly one instance of an entity type for every database table in the system. In the second instance, static members of the entity type maintain a register of all of the available entity types. The upshot of this is that from anywhere in the application, you access a list of all of the tables that exist, and from there, all of the fields that exist on any table.

In more sophisticated implementations of this sort of metadata system that you might see, the entity types are loaded from attributes (C#) or annotations (Java) embedded within the code. However, in the simple implementations we'll see in this book, we're going to programmatically set up the entity types.

In Chapter 3, we discussed that we need an EntityItem class, EntityField class, and EntityType class. EntityItem is used to provide every piece of metadata in the system with both a "programmatic name" and a "native name." The "native name" is the name of the item in the underlying store, and the "programmatic name" is the name that we would prefer to use. This abstraction is helpful for situations where you have a table called—for example—TBL_CUST and would prefer your related class to be called Customer. (In our actual implementation, both the native name and programmatic name will generally be the same.)

Without further ado, here's a listing that contains the code for EntityItem. Add this to the project in the usual way.

```
package com.amxmobile.SixBookmarks.Entities;

public abstract class EntityItem
{
        private String _name;
        private String _lowerName;
        private String _nativeName;

        protected EntityItem(String name, String nativeName)
        {
                _name = name;
                _lowerName = name.toLowerCase();

                if(nativeName != null)
                        _nativeName = nativeName;
                else
                        _nativeName = name;
        }

        public String getName()
        {
```

```
                return _name;
        }

        public String getLowerName()
        {
                return _lowerName;
        }

        public String getNativeName()
        {
                return _nativeName;
        }
}
```

Now we can look at the fields.

A single field has a number of attributes, mainly the following:

- A native name and a (programmatic) name

- A data type

- A size

- Flags indicating special functionality (In this chapter, we're going to have only one, which indicates whether the field is a key field. In a full-on implementation, another example of a flag would be indicating whether the field could be nullable.)

In this example, we're going to support just two data types—in a more full-on implementation, we'd obviously need to support all of the data types that the underlying database supports. (If we implement all of them now, half the book will be taken up with methods exposing out all of the data types.) Our server-side service used only strings and 32-bit integers, so these are the two that we will use.

▓ **Note** We will use Boolean data types on the entity, but we'll store them as integers in the SQLite database. SQLite's data type support is a little strange—you can store any value in any column in SQLite regardless of the definition, and it just tries to "work it out" when it retrieves data. For this and other reasons, we're going to handle Boolean data in our data access layer rather than natively in SQLite.

We can now build `EntityField`. As well as supporting native name (defined in the base), name (also defined in the base), data type, size, and an indication as to whether the field is a key, we'll have another property holding the ordinal of the field within the type. In addition, we need some constants that define the supported data types. (I'll explain more about this ordinal value later.) Here's the listing:

```
public class EntityField extends EntityItem
{
        public final static int DATATYPE_STRING = 0;
        public final static int DATATYPE_INT32 = 1;
```

```
        private int _type;
        private int _size;
        private boolean _isKey;
        private int _ordinal;
        private boolean _isOnServer = true;

        public EntityField(String name, String nativeName, int type, int size,int ordinal)
        {
                super(name, nativeName);

                // set...
                _type = type;
                _size = size;
                _ordinal = ordinal;
        }

        public int getOrdinal()
        {
                return _ordinal;
        }

        public int getDataType()
        {
                return _type;
        }

        public int getSize()
        {
                return _size;
        }

        public boolean getIsKey()
        {
                return _isKey;
        }

        public void setIsKey(boolean value)
        {
                _isKey = value;
        }
}
```

Next, we'll look at the EntityType class. This has a number of different functions. I won't go through them all here; rather, I will concentrate on the basics for keeping a register of the available entity types and the fields against each one.

So that we can effectively work with entities, we need EntityType to be able to instantiate instances of individual entities and collections of entities. In this example, we're going to have only one entity— Bookmark. In any real-world application, you're likely to have many entity types. We'll hold references to the relevant Java types so that we can create the object instances that we want programmatically. (A Java type is synonymous to a .NET type. Both provide runtime access to the type metadata system.) Our motivation for this arrangement is so that we can say to framework code "give me a list of bookmarks," and the framework code itself will be able to create an appropriate collection type and individual entities.

In addition, we're going to add a method to `EntityType` called `AddField`. This will be used to programmatically define the fields available on an entity type. This `AddField` method will look at the size of the fields collection and use this size as the ordinal for the field. Thus, when we add fields, the first will have ordinal 0, the second ordinal 1, and so on. Having field ordinals will come in handy when getting or setting in-memory values against the entity.

Here's the listing for `EntityType` that looks after storing the instance and collection types, and storing the list of fields. It, too, extends `EntityItem`—note that when we create an instance, we'll call the base class and set the programmatic name to the name of the Java class, and the native name to whatever the user specifies.

```
package com.amxmobile.SixBookmarks.Entities;

import java.util.Enumeration;
import java.util.Hashtable;
import java.util.Vector;

import javax.microedition.global.Formatter;

public class EntityType extends EntityItem
{
        private static Hashtable _entityTypes = new Hashtable();

        private Vector _fields = new Vector();
        private Class _instanceType = null;
        private Class _collectionType = null;

        public EntityType(Class instanceType, Class collectionType, String nativeName)
        {
                super(instanceType.getName(), nativeName);
                _instanceType = instanceType;
                _collectionType = collectionType;
        }

        public Vector getFields()
        {
                return _fields;
        }

        public EntityField AddField(String name, String nativeName, int type, int size)
        {
                EntityField field = new EntityField(name, nativeName, type, size,↵
 _fields.size());
                _fields.addElement(field);

                // return...
                return field;
        }
```

```java
        public Class getInstanceType()
        {
                return _instanceType;
        }

        public Class getCollectionType()
        {
                return _collectionType;
        }

        public Entity CreateInstance() throws Exception
        {
                return (Entity)getInstanceType().newInstance();
        }

        public Vector CreateCollectionInstance() throws Exception
        {
                return (Vector)getCollectionType().newInstance();
        }
}
```

We've assumed that entities will always have a base class of Entity (which we'll build shortly) and also be of type Vector. (For the uninitiated, a Vector is a dynamic array, *a la* ArrayList in more modern Java implementations. Entity is going to hold an instance of a row in a table in the database.)

Also on an entity type, we're going to need to be able to find a field with a specific name, find the key fields, or determine whether a field with a specified name actually exists. (This latter one is used for populating entities from data received over XML where the XML may reference fields that we don't know about.) Here are the three methods that also need to be added to EntityType:

```java
// Add to EntityType.java

        public EntityField GetField(String name, boolean throwIfNotFound) throws Exception
        {
                name = name.toLowerCase();
                for(int index = 0; index < _fields.size(); index++)
                {
                        EntityField field = (EntityField)_fields.elementAt(index);
                        if(field.getLowerName().compareTo(name) == 0)
                                return field;
                }

                // throw...
                if(throwIfNotFound)
                        throw new Exception(Formatter.formatMessage("Failed to find a field↵
with name '{0}'.", new String[] { name }));
                else
                        return null;
        }

        public EntityField GetKeyField() throws Exception
        {
                for(int index = 0; index < _fields.size(); index++)
```

```
        {
                EntityField field = (EntityField)_fields.elementAt(index);
                if(field.getIsKey())
                        return field;
        }

        // throw...
        throw new Exception("Failed to find a key field.");
    }

    public boolean IsField(String name) throws Exception
    {
        EntityField field = this.GetField(name, false);
        if(field != null)
                return true;
        else
                return false;
    }
```

Another method that we'll need on `EntityType` is one that returns the short name of a class. The getName method on a regular Java `Class` type returns a fully qualified name, including the package, e.g., `com.AmxMobile.SixBookmarks.Database.Bookmark`. This method—which needs to be added to `EntityType`—returns just the last part:

```
// Add to EntityType.java

    public String getShortName()
    {
        String name = getName();
        int index = name.lastIndexOf((char)'.');
        return name.substring(index + 1);
    }
```

Next, recall that the other function `EntityType` needs is the ability to hold a register of the available entity types. We'll do this by creating a static hashtable on `EntityType` and methods called `RegisterEntityType` and `GetEntityType`.

Here's the code to hold and query the register:

```
public class EntityType extends EntityItem
{
        private static Hashtable _entityTypes = new Hashtable();

        // code omitted for brevity…

        public static void RegisterEntityType(EntityType entityType)
        {
                _entityTypes.put(entityType.getInstanceType().getName(), entityType);
        }

        public static EntityType GetEntityType(Class type) throws Exception
        {
```

```
        String name = type.getName();
        Enumeration keys = _entityTypes.keys();
        while(keys.hasMoreElements())
        {
                String key = (String)keys.nextElement();
                if(key.compareTo(name) == 0)
                        return (EntityType)_entityTypes.get(key);
        }

        // throw...
        throw new Exception(Formatter.formatMessage("Failed to get entity type for↩
  '{0}'.", new String[] { type.getName() }));
    }

    // code omitted for brevity…
}
```

Creating the Basic Entity Class

We need a way of programmatically registering the entity type for the bookmark entity. One way to do this is to create a global "runtime" class that is used to boot up and tear down the application. We'll add one of these to our project, called SixBookmarksRuntime; however, we won't build this until a little later.

Before we do that, we need to create our Bookmark and BookmarkCollection objects.

BookmarkCollection is the easy one, as all we're going to do with this is create a new class that inherits from Vector. Here's the listing:

```
package com.amxmobile.SixBookmarks.Database;

import java.util.Vector;

public class BookmarkCollection extends Vector
{
}
```

Bookmark is a little more complicated, as we need to have an Entity class to inherit from. Entity is quite a lengthy class, and we're going to add to this as we go. For now we'll stub the basics.

The basic functionality of an entity is to store a dynamic list of data that represents the columns in the underlying database table. An entity will be created manually either by the developer or by framework code that retrieves the data from some source. At some point during the entity's life, the data stored within will either be read for display on a screen, or be used to make some sort of change request to the underlying store.

In our entity, we are going to hold three sets of values. Firstly, we're going to store a reference to our related EntityType instance. Secondly, we're going to store an array of values that map 1:1 with the columns defined as being in the underlying store. (The entity type is going to tell us which columns are defined.) Thirdly and finally, we're going to store a bunch of flags and other fields that will help the entity keep track of its internal state.

Storage of data within the entity will be done in "slots." You will notice that on our EntityField instance we have a property called Ordinal and that we calculated this ordinal in the AddField method on EntityType. This ordinal value is the index of the slot in the entity. Thus, if we have five fields, we'll have five slots numbered from zero to four inclusive.

■ **Note** Recall that in Chapter 3 we spoke about the BootFX application framework and its ORM functionality. Internally within BootFX, this functionality is known as "storage."

Here's the listing for this basic "storage" functionality in Entity:

```
package com.amxMobile.SixBookmarks.Entities;

import java.util.*;
import com.amxMobile.SixBookmarks.Runtime.*;

package com.amxmobile.SixBookmarks.Entities;

import java.util.Enumeration;
import java.util.Hashtable;

import javax.microedition.global.Formatter;

public abstract class Entity
{
        private EntityType _entityType;

        private Object[] _values;
        private int[] _flags;

        private static final int FIELDFLAGS_NOTLOADED = 0;
        private static final int FIELDFLAGS_LOADED = 1;
        private static final int FIELDFLAGS_MODIFIED = 2;

        protected Entity() throws Exception
        {
                _entityType = EntityType.GetEntityType(this.getClass());

                // slots...
                int count = _entityType.getFields().size();
                _values = new Object[count];
                _flags = new int[count];
        }

        public EntityType getEntityType()
        {
                return _entityType;
        }
}
```

Note in that listing that within the constructor, we ask EntityType to provide an entity type instance back to us that represents the entity itself via the GetEntityType static method. Caching this within the class allows us quick access to the entity's metadata directly from within the class. Also worthy of note is the fact that we define the size of the _values and _flags arrays to be equal to the number of available fields.

Being able to store data isn't much use without a set of methods that can retrieve and set the values in them. We'll start by looking at the methods that set values.

Setting Values in an Entity

Whenever we set a value within an entity, we'll be doing one of two things—we'll be plugging in a value that either the user has provided through some form of input, or we have retrieved from a database or service. It's important that we can distinguish between these two operations—if the user has done something to invoke the change (e.g., keyed a value into a form), we probably need to update the underlying store with that value. Conversely, if the user has not changed something, we do not want to be issuing unnecessary update requests back to the underlying store.

In the last section, we added constants to indicate the state of the field's storage slot, specifically FIELDFLAGS_NOTLOADED, FIELDFLAGS_LOADED, and FIELDFLAGS_MODIFIED. In addition, we need some constants that will be used to tell the entity what sort of set operation has occurred. Here are the SETREASON_LOAD and SETREASON_USER constants in place within the Entity class:

```
public abstract class Entity
{
        private EntityType _entityType;

        private Object[] _values;
        private int[] _flags;

        private static final int FIELDFLAGS_NOTLOADED = 0;
        private static final int FIELDFLAGS_LOADED = 1;
        private static final int FIELDFLAGS_MODIFIED = 2;

        public static final int SETREASON_LOAD = 0;
        public static final int SETREASON_USER = 1;

        // code omitted for brevity...
}
```

As we add methods to the entity, we'll find that oftentimes we need to add overloads for each of the methods that take either the name of a field as a string or an actual instance of an EntityField. This is going to create additional code, but there is a substantially higher level of utility in not requiring the caller to dig out an EntityField instance every time he or she wishes to access field data. Whenever one of the string-based "name" overloads is used, we'll defer to the entity type instance for the field name. Here's additional code for the Entity class that will allow values to be set within the slots.

```
// Add to Entity.java

        protected void SetValue(String name, Object value, int setReason) throws Exception
        {
                EntityField field = getEntityType().GetField(name, true);
                SetValue(field, value, setReason);
        }

        public void SetValue(EntityField field, Object value, int setReason) throws Exception
```

```
{
        int ordinal = field.getOrdinal();
        SetValue(ordinal, value, setReason);
}

private void SetValue(int ordinal, Object value, int setReason) throws Exception
{
        _values[ordinal] = value;

        // if...
        SetFlag(ordinal, FIELDFLAGS_LOADED);
        if(setReason == SETREASON_USER)
                SetFlag(ordinal, FIELDFLAGS_MODIFIED);
}

private void SetFlag(int ordinal, int flag)
{
        _flags[ordinal] = _flags[ordinal] | flag;
}
```

You'll also see that there is a third, private overload that takes the ordinal of the field. This isn't strictly required here, but this pattern of a private overload that takes the ordinal makes for easier work when getting values out.

Also note the if statement toward the end of the third overload. This will set a flag to indicate that a value is available, and if the reason for calling the method was that the user asked us to (e.g., by keying in a new value into a text box), we'll also indicate that the field is modified by deferring to the SetFlag method.

Retrieving the values is—perhaps oddly—a little trickier, as we have to deal with the different data types. In the first instance, we need to be able to behave differently depending on the state of the data. For example, if we're trying to retrieve the value for a field, and we have not loaded it, we need to throw an error indicating that the value is not available. (Some implementations, including BootFX, will demand load data in this situation. However, for simplicity, we're not doing this here.)

Here are some helper methods to be placed into the Entity class that let us understand the state of field slots in the entity:

```
// Add to Entity.java

public boolean getIsLoaded(EntityField field)
{
        return getIsLoaded(field.getOrdinal());
}

private boolean getIsLoaded(int index)
{
        return IsFlagSet(index, FIELDFLAGS_LOADED);
}

public boolean getIsModified(EntityField field)
{
        return getIsModified(field.getOrdinal());
}
```

```
private boolean getIsModified(int index)
{
        return IsFlagSet(index, FIELDFLAGS_MODIFIED);
}

private boolean IsFlagSet(int index, int flag)
{
        if((_flags[index] & flag) == flag)
                return true;
        else
                return false;
}
```

These work on individual fields, and you can see how we've tried to keep it neat. The public modifier on the getIsLoaded and getIsModified overloads is required, as later on we'll need to access these from another class.

Now that we can do that, we can add methods to tell whether the entity is new, or whether it has been modified. The rules here are as follows:

- *In order to tell if the entity is **new**:* If we do not have a key value defined, then it's new.

- *In order to tell if the entity is **modified**:* If we walk the fields and discovered that at least one is modified, then the entity is modified.

- *In order to tell if the entity is **deleted**:* We'll maintain a flag, but we won't implement this now.

Here's the code:

```
// Add to Entity.java

public boolean getIsNew() throws Exception
{
        EntityField key = getEntityType().GetKeyField();

        // state...
        if(!(getIsLoaded(key)) && !(getIsModified(key)))
                return true;
        else
                return false;
}

public boolean getIsDeleted()
{
        return false;
}

public boolean getIsModified()
{
        for(int index = 0; index < _flags.length; index++)
        {
```

```
                        if(getIsModified(index))
                                return true;
                }

                // nope...
                return false;
        }
```

Those methods lay the groundwork for the GetValue methods that we implied must exist when we created our SetValue methods earlier. The only difference in the rule is that if we ask for a value, if we're not new and we don't have it, we have to throw an error, as we can't demand-load the value. Here's the code:

```
// Add to Entity.java

        public Object GetValue(String name) throws Exception
        {
                EntityField field = getEntityType().GetField(name, true);
                return GetValue(field.getOrdinal());
        }

        public Object GetValue(EntityField field) throws Exception
        {
                return GetValue(field.getOrdinal());
        }

        private Object GetValue(int index) throws Exception
        {
                // do we need to demand load?
                if(!(getIsLoaded(index)) && !(getIsNew()))
                        throw new Exception("Demand loading is not implemented.");

                // return...
                return _values[index];
        }
```

Recall that before, I said that we were going to have limited support for data types in this implementation. Here's why: in order to give the entity a higher level of utility, we need to create versions of GetValue that are strongly typed. These will deal with the mucking around with trying to get data out of the entity coerced into the type of data that the caller is expecting (especially tricky with the JRE 1.5, as we have to do all of the boxing of value-types manually). Here's the implementation of GetValue equivalents that provide for strongly typed string and integer values:

```
// Add to Entity.java

        public String GetStringValue(String name) throws Exception
        {
                EntityField field = getEntityType().GetField(name, true);
                return GetStringValue(field);
        }
```

```
public String GetStringValue(EntityField field) throws Exception
{
        Object value = GetValue(field);
        if(value != null)
                return value.toString();
        else
                return null;
}

public int GetInt32Value(String name) throws Exception
{
        EntityField field = getEntityType().GetField(name, true);
        return GetInt32Value(field);
}

public int GetInt32Value(EntityField field) throws Exception
{
        Object value = GetValue(field);
        if(value == null)
                return 0;
        else if(value instanceof Integer)
                return ((Integer)value).intValue();
        else if(value instanceof Long)
                return (int)((Long)value).longValue();
        else
                throw new Exception(Formatter.formatMessage("Cannot handle '{0}'.",⏎
new String[] { value.getClass().getName() }));
}

public boolean GetBooleanValue(String name) throws Exception
{
        EntityField field = getEntityType().GetField(name, true);
        return GetBooleanValue(field);
}

public boolean GetBooleanValue(EntityField field) throws Exception
{
        Object value = GetValue(field);
        if(value == null)
                return false;
        else if(value instanceof Integer)
        {
                int asInt = ((Integer)value).intValue();
                if(asInt == 0)
                        return false;
                else
                        return true;
        }
        else
                throw new Exception(Formatter.formatMessage("Cannot handle '{0}'.",⏎
new String[] { value.getClass().getName() }));
}
```

Now that we can get data into and out of our base entity, let's look at creating a strongly typed Bookmark class.

Building Bookmark

The point of ORM is that you're looking to get the entity layer to do most of the hard work of managing the data for you—the principle being that it is easier to call a property called Name and know you're getting a string value back than it is to request an item with the name "name" out of a bucket of values returned over a SQL interface. Thus, we need to add a bunch of properties to Bookmark that abstract calls to GetValue and SetValue.

The fields that we're going to store locally, as a minimum, are a local unique ID, the ordinal, the name, and the URL.

However, there's one thing to consider. In order for our database to support the synchronization functionality that we'll build in the next chapter, we also need to store flags to indicate whether the item has been modified or deleted *locally*. We'll add two additional columns called LocalModified and LocalDeleted to achieve this.

Here's the code for the new Bookmark class that extends entities and provides getters and setters for our six columns.

```
package com.amxmobile.SixBookmarks.Database;

import java.util.*;

import com.amxmobile.SixBookmarks.Entities.*;

public class Bookmark extends Entity
{
        public final static String BookmarkIdKey = "BookmarkId";
        public final static String OrdinalKey = "Ordinal";
        public final static String NameKey = "Name";
        public final static String UrlKey = "Url";
        public final static String LocalModifiedKey = "LocalModified";
        public final static String LocalDeletedKey = "LocalDeleted";

        public Bookmark() throws Exception
        {
        }

        public Bookmark(Hashtable values) throws Exception
        {
                super(values);
        }

        public int getBookmarkId() throws Exception
        {
                return GetInt32Value(BookmarkIdKey);
        }

        public void setBookmarkId(int value) throws Exception
        {
```

```
                SetValue(BookmarkIdKey, new Integer(value), Entity.SETREASON_USER);
        }

        public int getOrdinal() throws Exception
        {
                return GetInt32Value(OrdinalKey);
        }

        public void setOrdinal(int value) throws Exception
        {
                SetValue(OrdinalKey, new Integer(value), Entity.SETREASON_USER);
        }

        public String getName() throws Exception
        {
                return GetStringValue(NameKey);
        }

        public void setName(String value) throws Exception
        {
                SetValue(NameKey, value, Entity.SETREASON_USER);
        }

        public String getUrl() throws Exception
        {
                return GetStringValue(UrlKey);
        }

        public void setUrl(String value) throws Exception
        {
                SetValue(UrlKey, value, Entity.SETREASON_USER);
        }

        public boolean getLocalModified() throws Exception
        {
                return GetBooleanValue(LocalModifiedKey);
        }

        public void setLocalModified(boolean value) throws Exception
        {
                SetValue(LocalModifiedKey, new Boolean(value), Entity.SETREASON_USER);
        }

        public boolean getLocalDeleted() throws Exception
        {
                return GetBooleanValue(LocalDeletedKey);
        }

        public void setLocalDeleted(boolean b) throws Exception
        {
```

```
                    SetValue(LocalDeletedKey, new Boolean(b), Entity.SETREASON_USER);
        }
}
```

You can see there that I have created a set of constants at the top of the class that define the names of the fields. This approach makes working with the data much easier and stops errors resulting from typos.

■ **Note** ORM layers usually have code generation so that you do not have to scaffold up all of these classes manually—which is good, because, frankly, setting them up manually is a pain.

Registering the EntityType

Now that we have a functional Bookmark class defined, we can build the SixBookmarksRuntime class that we mentioned earlier. This class's sole function will be to boot up the application, a key aspect of which is defining the entity type for the Bookmark entity. (If we had more than one entity, we'd obviously initialize types for the other types here also.)

This operation is reasonably straightforward—we need to create an entity type that knows about Bookmark and BookmarkCollection, add fields to it (remembering to set the BookmarkId field to be the key), and then register the entity type in the static memory managed by EntityType. Here's the code:

```
package com.amxmobile.SixBookmarks.Runtime;

import net.rim.blackberry.api.browser.*;

import com.amxmobile.SixBookmarks.Database.*;
import com.amxmobile.SixBookmarks.Entities.*;

public class SixBookmarksRuntime
{
        public static void Start()
        {
                // create the entity type...
                EntityType bookmark = new EntityType(Bookmark.class,↵
BookmarkCollection.class, "Bookmarks");
                bookmark.AddField(Bookmark.BookmarkIdKey, Bookmark.BookmarkIdKey,↵
EntityField.DATATYPE_INT32, -1).setIsKey(true);
                bookmark.AddField(Bookmark.OrdinalKey, Bookmark.OrdinalKey,↵
EntityField.DATATYPE_INT32, -1);
                bookmark.AddField(Bookmark.NameKey, Bookmark.NameKey,↵
EntityField.DATATYPE_STRING, 128);
                bookmark.AddField(Bookmark.UrlKey, Bookmark.UrlKey,↵
EntityField.DATATYPE_STRING, 256);
                bookmark.AddField(Bookmark.LocalModifiedKey, Bookmark.LocalModifiedKey,↵
EntityField.DATATYPE_INT32, -1).setIsOnServer(false);
                bookmark.AddField(Bookmark.LocalDeletedKey, Bookmark.LocalDeletedKey,↵
EntityField.DATATYPE_INT32, -1).setIsOnServer(false);
```

```
                // register it...
                EntityType.RegisterEntityType(bookmark);
        }

}
```

With the runtime class created, we can call the Start method. It doesn't really matter where this happens in the code, so long as it happens before we need to use the entities. An easy place to locate it in our code is within the constructor in the LogonForm class activity that we went through in the last chapter. Here's the modification to the LogonForm class (some code has been removed for brevity):

```
// Modify Logon class…
package com.amxMobile.SixBookmarks;

public class Logon extends Activity implements OnClickListener, ILogonView
{
// code removed for brevity…

        public LogonForm()
        {
                super();

                // start...
                SixBookmarksRuntime.Start();

                // title...
                setTitle(new LabelField("Welcome to Six Bookmarks"));

                // controls...
                this.add(new LabelField("Username"));
                _usernameTextBox = new EditField();
                this.add(_usernameTextBox);

                this.add(new LabelField("Password"));
                _passwordTextBox = new PasswordEditField();
                this.add(_passwordTextBox);

                _rememberMeCheckBox = new CheckboxField("Remember me", true);
                this.add(_rememberMeCheckBox);

                _logonButton = new ButtonField("Logon", ButtonField.CONSUME_CLICK);
                _logonButton.setChangeListener(this);
                this.add(_logonButton);
        }

// code removed for brevity…
}
```

Displaying Some Fake Bookmarks

We've still got a long way to go until we can get some data out of the database and onto the screen, so we'll take a little diversion here and display some fake bookmarks. This will involve us creating the form that will be used to show the bookmarks, and then we'll manually create some Bookmark objects to show on them. Later, we'll replace the fake bookmarks with ones that we've loaded from the SQLite database.

Creating the Form

We'll now turn our attention to building the form that will display the bookmarks. This form will be quite simple—it will display six buttons for each of the six available bookmarks, one button to open the configuration window, another button to log off, and a final button to show an About message. (For our application, the About message will open a web page.)

To get started, add a new class to the project called NavigatorForm. As you know by now, we have to programmatically define the form. This involves creating fields for each of the buttons and manually creating button controls. As we create new button controls, we'll wire up their ChangeListener event such that the form itself consumes and handles the event. For the "six bookmarks" buttons, we'll create and hold those in a dynamic array (a Vector instance). For the other buttons, we'll create fields. Here's the framework of the form:

```
package com.amxmobile.SixBookmarks;

import java.util.*;

import net.rim.device.api.ui.*;
import net.rim.device.api.ui.component.*;
import net.rim.device.api.ui.container.*;

import com.amxmobile.SixBookmarks.Database.*;
import com.amxmobile.SixBookmarks.Runtime.*;

public class NavigatorForm extends MainScreen implements FieldChangeListener
{
        private BookmarkCollection _bookmarks = null;
        private Vector _buttons = new Vector();
        private ButtonField _configureButton;
        private ButtonField _logoffButton;
        private ButtonField _aboutButton;

        public NavigatorForm()
        {
                super();

                // title...
                setTitle(new LabelField("Six Bookmarks"));

                // buttons...
                for(int index = 0; index < 6; index++)
                        AddButton(index);
```

```
                // configure button...
                _configureButton = new ButtonField("Configure", ButtonField.CONSUME_CLICK);
                _configureButton.setChangeListener(this);
                this.add(_configureButton);

                // about button...
                _aboutButton = new ButtonField("About", ButtonField.CONSUME_CLICK);
                _aboutButton.setChangeListener(this);
                this.add(_aboutButton);

                // about button...
                _logoffButton = new ButtonField("Logoff", ButtonField.CONSUME_CLICK);
                _logoffButton.setChangeListener(this);
                this.add(_logoffButton);

                // init...
                try
                {
                        Initialize();
                }
                catch(Exception ex)
                {
                        MessageBox.Show(ex);
                }
        }

        private void Initialize() throws Exception
        {
                // we'll do this later...
        }

        private void AddButton(int index)
        {
                ButtonField button = new ButtonField("...", ButtonField.CONSUME_CLICK);
                button.setChangeListener(this);
                _buttons.addElement(button);
                this.add(button);
        }

        public void fieldChanged(Field field, int context)
        {
                try
                {
                        // we'll do this later...
                }
                catch(Exception ex)
                {
                        MessageBox.Show(ex);
                }
        }
}
```

You'll notice in that code that to make our lives a little easier we have created an AddButton helper function. This removes at least some of the code duplication in this method. You'll also notice that we have not wired up the Initialize or the fieldChanged methods.

To get from the logon form to this form, we need go back and edit LogonForm. Previously we had this show a message box. We now need to make it create and show NavigatorForm instead. Modify the code in LogonForm as follows:

```
// Modify existing method in LogonForm...
        private void DoLogon(String username, String password, boolean rememberMe) throws
Exception
        {
                UsersService users = new UsersService();
                LogonResponse response = users.Logon(username, password);

                // now what?
                if(response.getResult() == LogonResponse.RESULT_OK)
                {
                        // open...
                        UiApplication.getUiApplication().pushScreen(new NavigatorForm());
                }
                else
                {
                        MessageBox.Show(response.getMessage());
                }
        }
```

If you run this code now and log on, you'll see something like Figure 11-1.

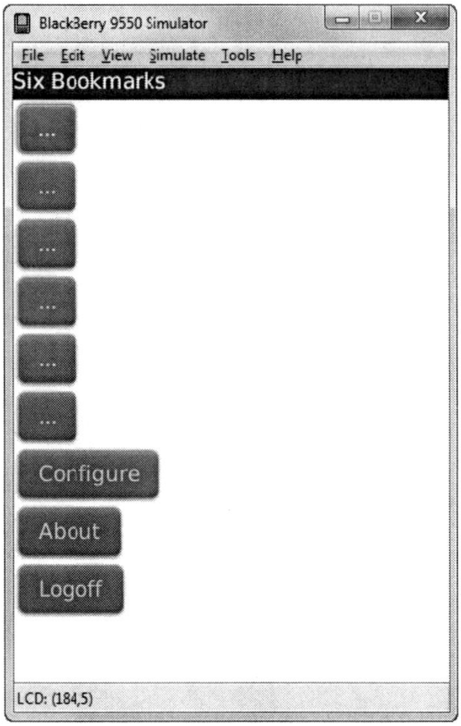

Figure 11-1. The Navigator form waiting for bookmark display to be implemented

Showing a Web Page

Central to the operation of this application is the ability to show a web page. We can implement this now and have the device show this book's home page at www.multimobiledevelopment.com/ by way of an About message. Luckily for us, asking BlackBerry OS to show a web page is very easy. Here's a static helper method to add to SixBookmarksRuntime:

```
// Add method to SixBookmarksRuntime...
        public static void OpenUrl(String url)
        {
                BrowserSession browser = Browser.getDefaultSession();
                browser.displayPage(url);
        }
```

Back in NavigatorForm, wiring up the About button is simply a matter of adding handling code within the fieldChanged method defined on FieldChangeListener. Here's the code:

```
// Modify code in NavigatorForm...
        public void fieldChanged(Field field, int context)
        {
                try
                {
                        if(field == _aboutButton)
                                HandleAbout();
```

```
        }
        catch(Exception ex)
        {
                MessageBox.Show(ex);
        }
}

private void HandleAbout()
{
SixBookmarksRuntime.OpenUrl("http://www.multimobiledevelopment.com/");
}
```

If you run the project now and click the About button, you'll see the web page as per Figure 11-2.

Figure 11-2. The About screen

Creating Fake Bookmarks

Now that we know that we can display the page and navigator to a web page, we can quickly add in some fake bookmarks and see what happens.

The first thing we need to do is change the behavior of the Initialize method to create some fake bookmarks and then rattle those bookmarks through code that will update the buttons. Ultimately we'll change the collection of fake bookmarks to be real ones drawn from the local SQLite database. (These, of course, will be populated from the cloud-based service.)

Here's the code that is needed to create the fake bookmarks and show them on the screen:

```
// Modify Initialize method within and add methods to NavigatorForm...
private void Initialize() throws Exception
        {
                // show some fake bookmarks...
                _bookmarks = new BookmarkCollection();

                // one...
                Bookmark bookmark = new Bookmark();
                bookmark.setName(".NET 247");
                bookmark.setUrl("http://www.dotnet247.com/");
                bookmark.setOrdinal(0);
                _bookmarks.addElement(bookmark);

                // two...
                bookmark = new Bookmark();
                bookmark.setName("Apress");
                bookmark.setUrl("http://www.apress.com/");
                bookmark.setOrdinal(1);
                _bookmarks.addElement(bookmark);

                // walk the bookmarks and show them.  (we'll keep this code
                // even though we'll replace the code that obtain the list of
                // bookmarks...)
                for(int index = 0; index < _bookmarks.size(); index++)
                        Initialize((Bookmark)_bookmarks.elementAt(index));
        }

        private void Initialize(Bookmark bookmark) throws Exception
        {
                ButtonField button = GetBookmarkButton(bookmark.getOrdinal());
                button.setLabel(bookmark.getName());
        }

        private ButtonField GetBookmarkButton(int ordinal)
        {
                return (ButtonField)_buttons.elementAt(ordinal);
        }
```

As alluded to, the Initialize(Bookmark bookmark) and GetBookmarkButton methods will stay even when we're getting real bookmarks. The GetBookmarkButton method loads the button reference from the array that we set up in the constructor. The Initialize method will find a button and set the name.

The ultimate purpose here is to show the URL related to the bookmark. This is why we keep the bookmarks around in the _bookmarks field—when a button click is received, we need to de-reference the Bookmark instance, find the URL, and show it using the OpenUrl method that we built previously. Here's the code:

```
// Modify fieldChanged method within and add methods to NavigatorForm...
        public void fieldChanged(Field field, int context)
        {
                try
```

```
        {
                if(field == _configureButton)
                        HandleConfigure();
                else if(field == _aboutButton)
                        HandleAbout();
                else
                        HandleNavigationClick(field);
        }
        catch(Exception ex)
        {
                MessageBox.Show(ex);
        }
}

private void HandleNavigationClick(Field field) throws Exception
{
        int index = GetButtonIndex((ButtonField)field);

        // show...
        Bookmark bookmark = _bookmarks.GetByOrdinal(index);
        if(bookmark != null)
                SixBookmarksRuntime.OpenUrl(bookmark.getUrl());
        else
                HandleConfigure();
}

private void HandleConfigure()
{
        // we'll implement this later...
        MessageBox.Show("TBD");
}
```

The operation of the button is that if there isn't a bookmark wired to it, we'll show the configuration form. We haven't built this yet—and in fact will not do so until the next chapter—so we'll add a stub method.

If you run this code now, you'll see two fake bookmarks, plus you'll be able to click them. Figure 11-3 and Figure 11-4 illustrate.

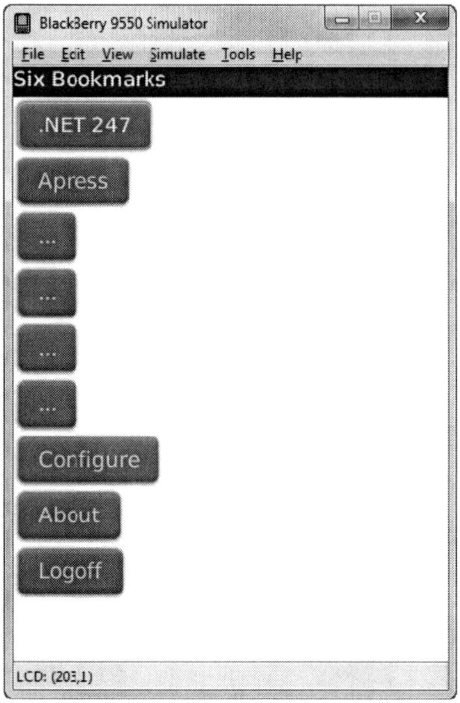

Figure 11-3. Two fake bookmarks displayed on the Navigator form

Figure 11-4. *The result of pressing the Apress button*

Building the Sync Class

At this point, we've covered a lot of ground. We have the foundation of an ORM system in place, we can create bookmark entities, and we can display them on the screen. In the remainder of this chapter, we're going to see how we can download bookmarks from the online service, store them in a local SQLite database, and then read them back from the SQLite database for display on the screen. In the next chapter, we're going to look at how the bookmarks can be modified and how changes can be pushed back up to the server.

Calling the Server's Bookmarks OData Service

In the last chapter, we created a few classes, including ServiceProxy, ApiService, and LogonService, to communicate with the restful services at http://services.multimobiledevelopment.com/. In this section, we're going to look at building BookmarksService, which is able to communicate with the Bookmarks OData service. We'll also build the base ODataServiceProxy class to support the operations of BookmarksService.

As we know, the OData service returns XML, and by default, this XML is formatted using the ATOM standard. All we have to do, then, is issue requests to the service and interpret the results. We can take the ATOM-formatted list of bookmarks and turn them into Bookmark entities for later use.

The HTTP request is the easy part—we need to issue a request to the following URL, passing up the special x-amx-apiusername and x-amx-token HTTP headers. We'll be using this URL:

```
http://services.multimobiledevelopment.com/services/bookmarks.svc/Bookmark
```

To begin, familiarize yourself with the format of data to be returned by using the test tool presented in Chapter 2. Here's a sample XML response containing a single bookmark:

```
<feed xml:base="http://services.amxmobile.com/services/Bookmarks.svc/"↵
 xmlns:d="http://schemas.microsoft.com/ado/2007/08/dataservices"↵
 xmlns:m="http://schemas.microsoft.com/ado/2007/08/dataservices/metadata"↵
 xmlns="http://www.w3.org/2005/Atom">
  <title type="text">Bookmark</title>
  <id>http://services.amxmobile.com/services/bookmarks.svc/Bookmark</id>
  <updated>2010-05-15T06:22:09Z</updated>
  <link rel="self" title="Bookmark" href="Bookmark" />
  <entry>
    <id>http://services.amxmobile.com/services/Bookmarks.svc/Bookmark(1002)</id>
    <title type="text">
    </title>
    <updated>2010-05-15T06:22:09Z</updated>
    <author>
      <name />
    </author>
    <link rel="edit" title="Bookmark" href="Bookmark(1002)" />
    <category term="AmxMobile.Services.Bookmark"↵
 scheme="http://schemas.microsoft.com/ado/2007/08/dataservices/scheme" />
    <content type="application/xml">
      <m:properties>
        <d:BookmarkId m:type="Edm.Int32">1002</d:BookmarkId>
        <d:UserId m:type="Edm.Int32">1001</d:UserId>
        <d:Name>.NET 247</d:Name>
        <d:Url>http://www.dotnet247.com/</d:Url>
        <d:Ordinal m:type="Edm.Int32">1</d:Ordinal>
      </m:properties>
    </content>
  </entry>
</feed>
```

The thing that I like about XML is that with a bit of common sense—providing the developer has not created horrendously bad XML—it's normally easy to understand what you need to do. There, we can clearly see that the entry element contains the bookmark data and that the content/m:properties element contains the fields we want. All we have to do now is walk the document, creating new Bookmark instances for each entry that we discover.

Namespaces

If you haven't done much XML before, you may not know how to work with XML namespaces, and seeing as the foregoing document is littered with them, you're going to need to know how!

Namespaces provide a way of managing naming collisions within XML. Imagine I am trying to create a document that combines standards from two different protocols. If both standards call for me to add an element called Name, I'm going to run into a problem—for example:

```
<MyDocument>
        <Name>I'm a value from Standard XYZ</Name>
        <Name>I'm a value from Standard ABC</Name>
</MyDocument>
```

The consumer is going to struggle with this document because there is no way of knowing which Name element maps to which standard/protocol.

If the people defining the protocol insist that a namespace is used, the problem is easily solved.

Namespaces are (typically) defined within the root element of the document. They are in the form of a URI, but there is no rule that the URI has to actually point to anything that can be downloaded. (But those that define open standards often do work and redirect the caller to relevant information.)

Here's our previous XML file modified to include namespaces:

```
<MyDocument xmlns:a="http://www.foo.com/" xmlns:b="http://www.bar.com/">
        <a:Name>I'm a value from Standard XYZ (www.foo.com)</a:Name>
        <b:Name>I'm a value from Standard ABC (www.bar.com)</b:Name>
</MyDocument>
```

In this case, when encountering the name elements, the name prefix de-references a namespace URI, and you now know which is which.

The one final wrinkle with namespaces is that you can have a default namespace. This is defined within the document by applying an attribute to the root element with the name xmlns but without a suffix—for example:

```
<MyDocument xmlns="http://www.foo.com/" xmlns:b="http://www.bar.com/">
        <Name>I'm a value from Standard XYZ (www.foo.com)</Name>
        <b:Name>I'm a value from Standard ABC (www.bar.com)</b:Name>
</MyDocument>
```

Where this catches newcomers out is that *both* MyDocument and Name no longer can be accessed without specifying the default namespace of http://www.foo.com/ as part of any requests to query against the XML. This is important, as our ATOM-formatted OData response has a default namespace of http://www.w3.org/2005/Atom, which you can see defined in the root feed element.

We'll go through how to query the document and handle namespaces in the next section.

Adding Functionality to XmlHelper

XmlHelper needs some methods added to help parse the document that we'll get back. Specifically, we need to be able to query a given element for a sub-element with a given qualified name. By qualified, I mean "we'll need to provide the namespace." Here's the method in question that needs to be added to XmlHelper:

```
// Add to XmlHelper.java
        public static Element GetElement(Element root, String namespaceUri, String name, ↵
boolean throwIfNotFound) throws Exception
        {
                NodeList nodes = root.getElementsByTagNameNS(namespaceUri, name);
                if(nodes.getLength() > 0)
                        return (Element)nodes.item(0);
                else
```

```
                    {
                              if(throwIfNotFound)
                              {
                                        throw new Exception(Formatter.formatMessage("A node with↵
      name '{0}' in namespace '{1}' was not found.",
                                                      new String[] { name, namespaceUri }));
                              }
                              else
                                        return null;
                    }
          }
```

Querying the Feed

Let's look now at parsing the XML we got back from the server.

First of all, let's stub our ODataServiceProxy class. This is going to extend ServiceProxy and will implement some generic support of OData-based data. Although we work with only one OData service, it's not unusual to work with several in a production application, and therefore it's worth breaking out functionality into a base class by way of illustration. Here's ODataServiceProxy. Core to this part is the definition of constants for the various namespaces that we'll be using, and forward-definition of constants that define the kind of OData operation that we ultimately need to support (i.e., inserting, updating, and deleting rows). These change operations are covered in the next chapter.

```
package com.amxMobile.SixBookmarks.Services;

import java.util.*;
import org.w3c.dom.*;
import com.amxMobile.SixBookmarks.Database.*;
import com.amxMobile.SixBookmarks.Entities.*;
import com.amxMobile.SixBookmarks.Runtime.*;

public class ODataServiceProxy extends ServiceProxy
{
        private final String AtomNamespace = "http://www.w3.org/2005/Atom";
        private final String MsMetadataNamespace =↵
  "http://schemas.microsoft.com/ado/2007/08/dataservices/metadata";
        private final String MsDataNamespace =↵
  "http://schemas.microsoft.com/ado/2007/08/dataservices";

        private final int ODATAOPERATION_INSERT = 0;
        private final int ODATAOPERATION_UPDATE = 1;
        private final int ODATAOPERATION_DELETE = 2;

        public ODataServiceProxy(String serviceName)
        {
                super(serviceName);
        }
}
```

This class is going to need a couple of methods to help build URLs for the requests. We need only one now, which is the one that selects all entities for a given type. An example is http://services.multimobiledevelopment.com/services/Bookmarks.svc/Bookmark. Here's the method to add to ODataServiceProxy:

```java
// Add to ODataServiceProxy.java
    public String GetServiceUrl(EntityType et)
    {
            return getResolvedServiceUrl() + "/" + et.getShortName();
    }
```

We can then add our BookmarksService class, including a GetAll method whose (obvious) function is to retrieve all of the bookmarks from the server. This method will to get the URL that returns all the bookmarks, and then defer to a method called LoadEntities that we will build into the base ODataServiceProxy class in a moment. Here's the code:

```java
package com.amxmobile.SixBookmarks.Services;

import org.w3c.dom.*;

import com.amxmobile.SixBookmarks.Database.*;
import com.amxmobile.SixBookmarks.Entities.*;
import com.amxmobile.SixBookmarks.Runtime.*;

public class BookmarksService extends ODataServiceProxy
{
    public BookmarksService()
    {
            super("Bookmarks.svc");
    }

    public BookmarkCollection GetAll() throws Exception
    {
            EntityType et = EntityType.GetEntityType(Bookmark.class);

            // run...
            String url = GetServiceUrl(et);
    Document doc = HttpHelper.DownloadXml(url, GetDownloadSettings());

            // load...
            return (BookmarkCollection)LoadEntities(doc, et);
    }
}
```

As you can see, the GetAll method will call up to the server to get some XML and then defer to a method we'll build now, called LoadEntities, to turn the entry elements within the XML into real Bookmark instances.

Let's look at LoadEntities now. I'll present this listing in chunks and comment as we go, as it's quite long.

The first job is to get back a list of feed elements, determine we have one, and then work with the first one we get.

```java
// Add to ODataServiceProxy.java…
```

```
protected Vector LoadEntities(Document doc, EntityType et) throws Exception
{
// parse...
NodeList feedElements = doc.getElementsByTagNameNS(AtomNamespace, "feed");
if(feedElements.getLength() == 0)
        throw new Exception("A 'feed' element was not found.");

// feed...
Element feed = (Element)feedElements.item(0);
NodeList entryElements = feed.getElementsByTagNameNS(AtomNamespace, "entry");
```

Note that in the code, we're using the getElementsByTagNameNS method on the XML Document DOM class. This method allows us to pass in a namespace name to use so that we can do this strong matching against a specific namespace.

Next, we'll ask the entity type to create a collection instance for us, and then we'll walk the elements contained within the entryElements node list.

```
// walk...
Vector results = et.CreateCollectionInstance();
for(int i = 0; i < entryElements.getLength(); i++)
{
        Element entry = (Element)entryElements.item(i);
```

The fields we want are contained within a sub-element of entry called content/m:properties. content is accessed through the default namespace, but properties requires a separate namespace. This second namespace is defined in the MsMetadataNamespace constant defined at the top of the class.

```
// get the content item...
Element content = XmlHelper.GetElement(entry, AtomNamespace, ↵
"content", false);
        if(content == null)
                throw new Exception(Formatter.formatMessage("A content↵
element not found on item '{0}'.", new String[] { new Integer(i).toString() }));

// then get the properties element...
Element properties = XmlHelper.GetElement(content, ↵
MsMetadataNamespace, "properties", false);
        if(properties == null)
                throw new Exception(Formatter.formatMessage("A properties
element not found on item '{0}'.", new String[] { new Integer(i).toString() }));
```

The m:properties element then contains the field values we want prefixed with d:, which, in this case, maps to another namespace defined in the MsDataNamespace constant.

We need to walk each of these child elements and see whether the name maps to a field on the entity type related to the Bookmark class. In order to be less brittle, we want to allow the service (of which we may not have any direct control in the case of consuming third-party data) to pass through data that we are not interested in. Hence, for each field we encounter, we see if it is a field, and if so, we add it to a bucket of values.

Also in this code snippet, you'll see a reference to GetValue. We'll build this shortly.

```
// then get the fields...
```

```
                    NodeList fields = properties.getElementsByTagName("*");
                    Hashtable values = new Hashtable();
                    for(int j = 0; j < fields.getLength(); j++)
                    {
                            Element field = (Element)fields.item(j);

                            // value...
                            Object value = GetValue(field);

                            // is it a field?
                            if(et.IsField(field.getLocalName()))
                                    values.put(field.getLocalName(), value);
                    }
```

We're almost there at this point. We have a collection of name/value items that we can use to populate the initial data for an entity. Here's the code that calls a constructor on Bookmark that does not exist yet – we'll add the new constructor in a moment.

```
                    // create...
                    Bookmark bookmark = new Bookmark(values);
                    results.addElement(bookmark);
            }
```

At this point, we're finished. We can close the loop that walks the entry element and return our collection back to the caller.

```
                    // return...
                    return results;
            }
```

Actually, though, we're not quite finished because we need to implement the GetValue method. This value will take an element instance and extract from it the value. It will use the type attribute of the element to determine the type and convert the represented-as-a-string-in-XML value back to the caller as a value of the correct type. Here's the code:

```
// Add to ODataServiceProxy.java…
        private Object GetValue(Element field) throws Exception
        {
                // fields are provided with a data element, like this....
                // <d:BookmarkId m:type="Edm.Int32">1002</d:BookmarkId>
                String asString = field.getAttribute("m:type");

                // nothing?
                if(asString == null || asString.length() == 0)
                        return XmlHelper.GetStringValue(field);
                else if(asString.compareTo("Edm.Int32") == 0)
                        return new Integer(XmlHelper.GetInt32Value(field));
                else
                        throw new Exception(Formatter.formatMessage("Cannot handle '{0}'.", ↵
new String[] { asString }));
        }
```

Creating Entities from Name/Value Collections

At the moment, we don't have a way of creating an entity from a collection of name/value items (and we've made a class within LoadEntities that assumes that we do), so we need to add this to Bookmark and to Entity. To Bookmark we need to add this additional constructor:

```java
// Add to Bookmark.java…
    public Bookmark() throws Exception
    {
    }

    public Bookmark(Hashtable values) throws Exception
    {
        super(values);
    }
```

That method defers to a constructor on the base Entity class that we also need to add. Here's the listing for that:

```java
// Add to Entity.java…
protected Entity() throws Exception
{
    _entityType = EntityType.GetEntityType(this.getClass());

    // slots...
    int count = _entityType.getFields().size();
    _values = new Object[count];
    _flags = new int[count];
}

protected Entity(Hashtable values) throws Exception
{
    // make sure the original initialization code runs - v. important to call↵
the base constructor…
    this();

    // set...
    Enumeration keys = values.keys();
    while(keys.hasMoreElements())
    {
        String key = (String)keys.nextElement();
        EntityField field = getEntityType().GetField(key, true);
        SetValue(field, values.get(key), SETREASON_LOAD);
    }
}
```

Note that when we call SetValue, we are specifying the SetReason.Load. This tells the entity that it has a value for a given field but does not update the internal state to mark the item as modified.

That's it as far as calling the service is concerned; however, we won't physically call the service until quite a bit later in this chapter.

Managing the Database

BlackBerry OS, like all of the smartphone implementations apart from Windows Phone, comes with the open source SQLite database baked in. We're going to use this database for storing the bookmarks locally, which we will do via a new class called DatabaseHelper that extends SQLiteOpenHelper. Whenever we need to access the database, we'll create an instance of DatabaseHelper.

The database that we use requires a name. What we want to do with the database name is give it the same name as the logged-on user. The reason we do this is that if User A logs on and changes some bookmarks, these will be saved in the local database. If User B logs on, his bookmarks will be downloaded and overwrite User A's. This is, on a mobile device, very unlikely, but it is an obvious logic problem, and thus it's better to fix it rather than leave in what most would classify as a bug.

To solve this problem, we'll set the database name when the user logs in. In LogonForm, modify DoLogon so that it will set the database name in the shortly-to-be-built DatabaseHelper class:

```
// Modify method in LogonForm.java
        private void DoLogon(String username, String password, boolean rememberMe) ↵
  throws Exception
        {
                UsersService users = new UsersService();
                LogonResponse response = users.Logon(username, password);

                // now what?
                if(response.getResult() == LogonResponse.RESULT_OK)
                {
                        // store the credentials?
                        if(rememberMe)
                                StoreCredentials(username, password);
                        else
                                ClearCredentials();

                        // set the user...
                        DatabaseHelper.setUser(username);

                        // open...
                        UiApplication.getUiApplication().pushScreen(new NavigatorForm());
                }
                else
                {
                        MessageBox.Show(response.getMessage());
                }
        }
```

We can now build DatabaseHelper. Here's the listing:

```
package com.amxmobile.SixBookmarks.Database;

import java.util.*;
import javax.microedition.global.*;
import net.rim.device.api.database.*;
import com.amxmobile.SixBookmarks.Entities.*;

public class DatabaseHelper
{
        private static Vector _loadMap = new Vector();

        private static String DatabaseName = null;

        public DatabaseHelper()
        {
        }

        public static void setUser(String username)
        {
                DatabaseName = "SixBookmarks-" + username;
        }
}
```

That doesn't get us very far through the process of writing to the database! However, now whenever we need access anywhere in the application to a database, all we have to do is create an instance of DatabaseHelper and call methods that we're about to build.

The SqlStatement Class and ISqlStatementSource Interface

When building an ORM layer, the thing I have found most helpful is adding a metadata system as we've described previously in the book. A close second to this is making sure that any statements you wish to issue to the database are wrapped up in an object instance that you control. This gives you more control and flexibility as to how statements are passed over to the base data access layer within the ORM framework. (Most newcomers to the field when building data access layers pass around strings that are either dynamic SQL statements or names of stored procedures. This approach tends to be very brittle.)

To that end, we're going to create a class called SqlStatement. This will hold the command text that's to be sent to the database engine and a list of parameter values. SQLite does not support named parameters, and so we're going to just keep a simple list.

In addition to SqlStatement, we're also going to create an ISqlStatementSource interface. This adds another layer of flexibility to the data access layer (DAL) by allowing us to pass objects directly into the DAL that are not necessarily fully formed SQL statements but do have the capability to turn into them. (We're going to see this later when we build a class called SqlFilter, which will create a SqlStatement instance immediately before the point of execution.)

Here's ISqlStatementSource—it has only a single method:

```
package com.amxMobile.SixBookmarks.Runtime;

public interface ISqlStatementSource
{
        SqlStatement GetSqlStatement();
}
```

When we implement ISqlStatementSource on SqlStatement, we're just going to return a reference to this, as we don't have to do any additional processing to build the query string once we have a SqlStatement instance.

Here's the implementation of SqlStatement:

```
package com.amxmobile.SixBookmarks.Database;

import java.util.*;

public class SqlStatement implements ISqlStatementSource
{
        private String _commandText;
        private Vector _parameterValues = new Vector();

        public SqlStatement()
        {
        }

        public SqlStatement(String commandText)
        {
                _commandText = commandText;
        }

        public String getCommandText()
        {
                return _commandText;
        }

        public void setCommandText(String commandText)
        {
                _commandText = commandText;
        }

        public SqlStatement GetSqlStatement()
        {
                return this;
        }

        public void AddParameterValue(Object value)
        {
                _parameterValues.addElement(value);
        }

        public Object[] getParameterValues()
        {
                Object[] results = new Object[_parameterValues.size()];
                for(int index = 0; index < _parameterValues.size(); index++)
                        results[index] = _parameterValues.elementAt(index);

                // return...
                return results;
```

```
        }
}
```

That's the base classes done. Let's have a look now at creating concrete instances of statements that have some function.

Creating Tables

Job one with regards to our new database is to create new tables to store data in. We're going to do this by examining at runtime the structure of the entity that we need to create a table for, and we'll do this by walking the fields defined against the entity type. This is where the power of a good metadata system starts to shine through—this relatively complex operation of dynamically creating a SQL table is a doddle to do.

As we know, SQLite uses a regular ANSI-92 SQL syntax; therefore we want to issue a statement that looks something like this:

```
CREATE TABLE IF NOT EXISTS Bookmarks
        (BookmarkId integer primary key autoincrement,
        Ordinal integer,
        Name varchar(128),
        Url varchar(256))
```

We're going to add two methods to DatabaseHelper. One is called GetCreateScript, and this method will be responsible for returning a script like the previous one. This will defer during processing to a method called AppendCreateSnippet. This second method's job will be to write into the SQL string the snippet that defines the field, e.g., Ordinal integer or Name varchar(128). Here's the code:

```
// Add to DatabaseHelper.java…
        private SqlStatement GetCreateScript(EntityType et) throws Exception
        {
                StringBuffer builder = new StringBuffer();
                builder.append("CREATE TABLE IF NOT EXISTS ");
                builder.append(et.getNativeName());      // now the columns...
                builder.append(" (");
                Vector fields = et.getFields();
                for(int index = 0; index < fields.size(); index++)
                {
                        if(index > 0)
                                builder.append(", ");

                        // defer...
                        AppendCreateSnippet(builder, (EntityField)fields.elementAt(index));
                }
                builder.append(")");

                // return...
                return new SqlStatement(builder.toString());
        }

        private void AppendCreateSnippet(StringBuffer builder, EntityField field) throws⏎
    Exception
```

```
        {
                builder.append(field.getNativeName());
                builder.append(" ");

                // switch...
                int type = field.getDataType();
                if(type == EntityField.DATATYPE_STRING)
                {
                        builder.append("varchar(");
                        builder.append(field.getSize());
                        builder.append(")");
                }
                else if(type == EntityField.DATATYPE_INT32)
                {
                        builder.append("integer");

                        // key?
                        if(field.getIsKey())
                                builder.append(" primary key autoincrement");
                }
                else
                        throw new Exception(Formatter.formatMessage("Cannot handle '{0}'.",↵
new String[] { new Integer(field.getDataType()).toString() }));
        }
```

■ **Note** Recall that we support only two data types in this implementation—strings and 32-bit integers. Here's another reason I've chosen that for this book—the AppendCreateSnippet method would be huge if we supported all available data types.

We obviously need to call that method somehow. One way to do this is to create a method that ensures the table for a given entity type exists prior to use. In fact, this is exactly what we'll do by adding a method called EnsureTableExists to the DatabaseHelper class. We'll also then rig our code so that EnsureTableExists is called at relevant points during the statement execution cycle.

You'll notice in our create script that we're using the special SQLite IF TABLE EXISTS directive to tell SQLite to ignore the create call if the table is already there. It would be acceptable, therefore, to issue a call to create the table every time we received a call into EnsureTableExists. However, for efficiency—especially important as we're on a low-horsepower device—we'll make EnsureTableExists keep track of whether a create call has been called in the running session. We'll do this by adding a static field to the DatabaseHelper class that keeps a list of the names of the entities that have been "ensured." If we get asked to ensure the table for an entity that we think we've already done, we'll quit the method early and save processor cycles. Here's the code:

```
public class DatabaseHelper extends SQLiteOpenHelper
{
        private static Vector _loadMap = new Vector();
```

```
        // code removed for brevity...

        public void EnsureTableExists(EntityType et) throws Exception
        {
                // have we already called it?
                String name = et.getName();
                if(_loadMap.contains(name))
                        return;

                // create...
                SqlStatement sql = GetCreateScript(et);
                ExecuteNonQuery(sql);

                // add...
                _loadMap.addElement(name);
        }
}
```

You'll note that EnsureTableExists calls ExecuteNonQuery. This is the first of the data access methods that execute SQL statements against the SQLite database. Note that GetCreateScript returns a SqlStatement instance, and also recall that we said that our data access methods were going to work with ISqlStatementSource instances. Our ExecuteNonQuery method is going to take an ISqlStatementSource and use the GetStatement method defined on it to de-reference an actual statement to execute. (In fact, though, when passing in a concrete SqlStatement instance, the call on the interface will result in a reference to the concrete SqlStatement being returned.)

Here's the implementation of ExecuteNonQuery:

```
// Add to DatabaseHelper.java
        public void ExecuteNonQuery(ISqlStatementSource sql) throws Exception
        {
                // open...
                Database db = GetDatabase();
                Statement statement = null;
                try
                {
                        statement = GetRealSqlStatement(db, sql);
                        statement.execute();
                }
                finally
                {
                        if(statement != null)
                                statement.close();
                        if(db != null)
                                db.close();
                }
        }
```

Of note in that listing is that we use a try…finally construct to close the database, regardless of whether execution succeeded or failed. This is (obviously) to keep resource usage to a minimum.

Examining the Database with Sqliteman

At this point, we can take an entity type and create a database for it. We might as well do this now, as we have quite a long way to go before we can get some real data into it!

We haven't yet built the Sync class, but we can start to do this now. We'll start it off by asking it to ensure the database exists, but we won't add the logic to do anything other than that.

Here's the code:

```
package com.amxmobile.SixBookmarks.Database;

import java.util.*;

import com.amxmobile.SixBookmarks.Entities.*;
import com.amxmobile.SixBookmarks.Services.*;

public class Sync
{
        private DatabaseHelper _database;
        private EntityType _entityType;

        public void DoSync() throws Exception
        {
                _database = new DatabaseHelper();

                // make sure we have a table...
                _entityType = EntityType.GetEntityType(Bookmark.class);
                _database.EnsureTableExists(_entityType);

                // we'll add more code here later...
        }

        private EntityType getEntityType()
        {
                return _entityType;
        }

        private DatabaseHelper getDatabase()
        {
                return _database;
        }
}
```

Recall the code that we added to the LogonForm to start the navigator activity. We're going to change the DoLogon method *again* to call the sync code prior to launching the navigator. Here's the listing:

```
// Modify code in LogonForm.java…
        private boolean DoLogon(String username, String password, boolean rememberMe)↵
  throws Exception
        {
                UsersService users = new UsersService();
                LogonResponse response = users.Logon(username, password);
```

```
            // now what?
            if(response.getResult() == LogonResult.LogonOk)
            {
                    // store the credentials?
                    if(rememberMe)
                            StoreCredentials(username, password);
                    else
                            ClearCredentials();

                    // set the user...
                    DatabaseHelper.setUser(username);

                    // do a sync...
                    Sync sync = new Sync();
                    sync.DoSync(this);

                    // open...
                    UiApplication.getUiApplication().pushScreen(new NavigatorForm());
            }
            else
            {
                    MessageBox.Show(this, response.getMessage());
                    return false;
            }
    }
```

One wrinkle when working with SQLite and the BlackBerry emulator is that you need to nominate a folder on the host machine's disk as a fake SD card. This is done via the Simulate–Change SD Card option on the emulator application. Figure 11-5 shows my D:\Temp\BBSD folder mapped as a fake SD card.

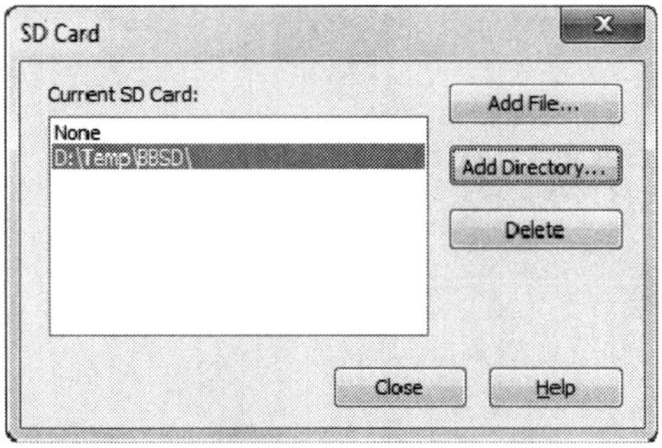

Figure 11-5. The BlackBerry emulator's SD card "mount" screen

Now if you run the application and log on, a Sync instance will be created and DoSync will be called. The database and table will (one hopes) have been created. However, being engineers, we probably need to see it to believe it.

If you navigate into the folder you used as your fake SD card, you can drill in and find a database file called SixBookmarks-<username>. You can then use a utility called Sqliteman (http://sqliteman.com) to examine the database. Figure 11-6 shows the Bookmarks table in situ, although obviously we have not added any data to it yet.

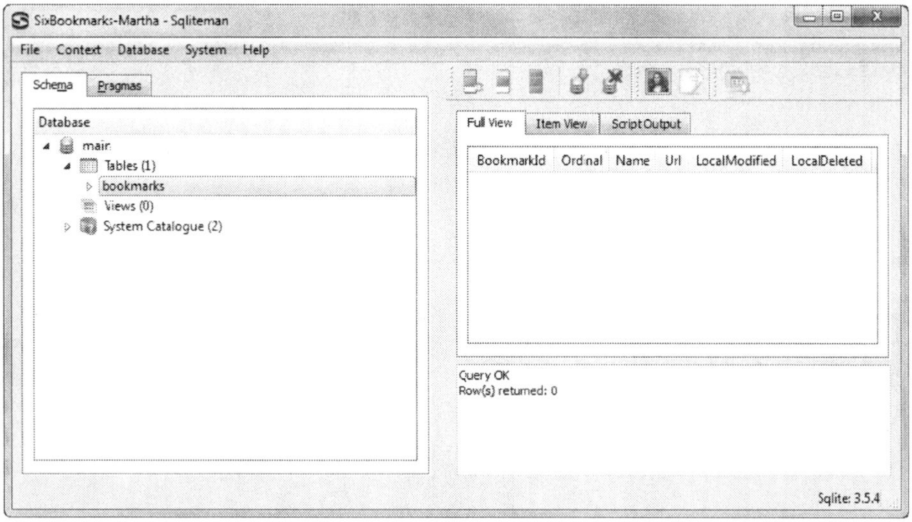

Figure 11-6. Sqliteman showing the "bookmarks" table

Let's look in the next section at how we can write bookmarks to the database.

Writing Bookmarks to the Database

What we'll do in this section is start developing the synchronization routine. In this chapter, we'll look at downloading the server bookmarks and storing them locally. In the next chapter, we'll look at passing the changes back up to the server.

Earlier in this section, we built the BookmarksService class. We defined a method on this called GetAll, which returned a set of bookmarks from the server. We're going to use this to get the list of bookmarks to insert.

When using an ORM layer, what we want to be able to do is ask the entity itself to commit in-memory changes to the database. Further, we want to be able to use the metadata system to build the query that we wish to use. We're going to use a "unit of work" pattern to do this by implementing a class called EntityChangeProcessor, passing this an entity, and having the processor work out whether it's to do nothing with it or whether it needs to issue an insert, update, or delete operation to the database.

On the Entity class, we have already defined methods called IsNew, IsModified, and IsDeleted. IsNew and IsModified have been implemented to work in this chapter, whereas IsDeleted is a stub implementation that just returns false. In this chapter, we're going to make the processor understand insert operations *only* and look at update and delete in the next chapter.

Building the Change Processor

First off, let's add a SaveChanges method to Entity. This is very easy—it's going to create a "change processor" passing in the entity type related to the entity.

```
// Add to Entity.java…
        public void SaveChanges() throws Exception
        {
                EntityChangeProcessor processor = new↵
EntityChangeProcessor(this.getEntityType());
                processor.SaveChanges(this);
        }
```

The basics of the EntityChangeProcessor include storing the entity type in an instance field and deciding whether to call an Insert, Update, or Delete method based on the change that has occurred. Here's the code:

```
package com.amxmobile.SixBookmarks.Entities;

import com.amxmobile.SixBookmarks.Database.*;

public class EntityChangeProcessor
{
        private EntityType _entityType;

        public EntityChangeProcessor(EntityType et)
        {
                _entityType = et;
        }

        public EntityType getEntityType()
        {
                return _entityType;
        }

        public void SaveChanges(Entity entity) throws Exception
        {
                //  do we need to do anything?
                if(entity.getIsNew())
                        this.Insert(entity);
                else if(entity.getIsModified())
                        throw new Exception("Not implemented.");
                else if(entity.getIsDeleted())
                        throw new Exception("Not implemented.");

                // nothing to do...
        }

        private void Delete(Entity entity) throws Exception
        {
                // get the statement...
                SqlStatement sql = this.GetDeleteStatement(entity);

                // run the statement...
                DatabaseHelper db = new DatabaseHelper();
                db.EnsureTableExists(getEntityType());
```

```
            db.ExecuteNonQuery(sql);
    }
```

As mentioned previously, in this chapter, we're going to look only at inserting entities, so let's look now at the Insert method.

Inserting Entities

The Insert method simply has to build a SQL statement that can insert the entity and then execute it against the database.

The SQL statement that we wish to issue looks like the one called out here. Note that in this statement we're not specifying a value for BookmarkId—this will be allocated for us by the database. Also, just a reminder that the ? characters in the statement are placeholders for parameters.

```
INSERT INTO Bookmarks (Ordinal, Name, Url) VALUES (?, ?, ?)
```

■ **Note** For simplicity, the implementation here does not select back from the database the ID that was allocated as part of the statement. If you need to do this, issuing the select last_insert_rowid() statement on the same connection will return back the ID. The version of the code available from the web site does include this functionality.

The GetInsertStatement will create a SqlStatement instance that can be used to insert the provided Entity instance. Here's the code:

```
// Add to EntityChangeProcessor.java…
        private SqlStatement GetInsertStatement(Entity entity) throws Exception
        {
                StringBuffer builder = new StringBuffer();
                SqlStatement sql = new SqlStatement();

                // et...
                EntityType et = getEntityType();

                // create...
                builder.append("INSERT INTO ");
                builder.append(et.getNativeName());
                builder.append(" (");
                boolean first = true;
                for(int index = 0; index < et.getFields().size(); index++)
                {
                        EntityField field = (EntityField)et.getFields().elementAt(index);
                        if(entity.getIsModified(field))
                        {
                                if(first)
                                        first = false;
```

287

```
                              else
                                      builder.append(", ");
                              builder.append(field.getNativeName());
                      }
              }
              builder.append(") VALUES (");
              first = true;
              for(int index = 0; index < et.getFields().size(); index++)
              {
                      EntityField field = (EntityField)et.getFields().elementAt(index);
                      if(entity.getIsModified(field))
                      {
                              if(first)
                                      first = false;
                              else
                                      builder.append(", ");
                              builder.append("?");

                              // add in the parameter....
                              sql.AddParameterValue(entity.GetValue(field));
                      }
              }
              builder.append(")");

              // return...
              sql.setCommandText(builder.toString());
              return sql;
      }
```

Once we have the statement, we can run it like so:

```
// Add to EntityChangeProcessor.java…
      protected void Insert(Entity entity) throws Exception
      {
              // get the statement...
              SqlStatement sql = this.GetInsertStatement(entity);

              // run the statement...
              DatabaseHelper db = new DatabaseHelper();
              db.EnsureTableExists(getEntityType());
              db.ExecuteNonQuery(sql);
      }
```

Now we just need to run it.

Our DoSync routine on the Sync class is stubbed out with some basic code, but it does not do anything yet. We need to make this call a method we'll build, called GetLatest. Here's the code:

```
// Modify DoSync method in Sync.java…
      public void DoSync(IContextSource source) throws Exception
      {
              _contextSource = source;
              _database = new DatabaseHelper(source);
```

```
        // make sure we have a table...
        _entityType = EntityType.GetEntityType(Bookmark.class);
        _database.EnsureTableExists(_entityType);

        // get the latest...
        GetLatest();
    }
```

We'll build GetLatest in the next section.

Downloading Bookmarks

The code we're about to look at is a little strange. I'll explain...

When we created the OData service proxy method to return all the bookmarks, we made this return Bookmark entities. I chose to do that because I felt it was unnecessarily complicated to have a separate set of classes representing bookmarks that go over the wire, compared to bookmarks that live in the local database. It's not unusual to have this separation, and in many cases, it is desirable. (Google "data transfer object" for more information.)

Where this gets a little strange is that the OData service returns back the entities with the BookmarkId property populated with values that represent the internal, private IDs in the *server's* database. Our change processor is configured to treat entities that do not have a loaded ID as new, and entities that do have a loaded ID as potentially modified and deleted. Thus, if we pass our change processor an entity that we have downloaded, it will look at it and assume it has been modified because the ID value is set. It will attempt to issue an UPDATE rather than an INSERT statement, and the process will create incorrect results.

What we, therefore, have to do is walk each downloaded bookmark and create a new Bookmark instance for each. We'll walk the fields described in the metadata and patch all of the fields that are not *key* fields into the new entity. We can then pass this entity over to the change processor—it will detect an unloaded ID value and assume it is to be inserted. Thus, the operation will work properly. Here's the code to go into the Sync class:

```
// Add to Sync.java...
        private void GetLatest() throws Exception
        {
            // clear the bookmarks table...
            getDatabase().ExecuteNonQuery(new SqlStatement("delete from bookmarks"));

            // get the bookmarks from the server...
            BookmarksService service = new BookmarksService();
            BookmarkCollection bookmarks = service.GetAll();
            for(int i = 0; i < bookmarks.size(); i++)
            {
                Bookmark bookmark = (Bookmark)bookmarks.elementAt(i);

                // the bookmarks we get from the server have server IDs populated. ↵
  we need to
                // remove the server ID and save locally by creating a new item...

                // create and copy all of the fields except the key field...
                Bookmark newBookmark = new Bookmark();
```

289

```
                      Vector fields = getEntityType().getFields();
                      for(int j = 0; j < fields.size(); j++)
                      {
                              EntityField field = (EntityField)fields.elementAt(j);
                              if(!(field.getIsKey()) && bookmark.getIsLoaded(field))
                                      newBookmark.SetValue(field, ↵
bookmark.GetValue(field), Entity.SETREASON_USER);
                      }

                      // set local modified and deleted...
                      newBookmark.setLocalModified(false);
                      newBookmark.setLocalDeleted(false);

                      // save...
                      newBookmark.SaveChanges();
              }
      }
```

■ **Note** This is another good example of how helpful a metadata system is. Should we add new fields to the entity, this code will automatically adapt its operation and continue to work without us having to remember to do it.

Now if we run the project, the sync routine will run and the local database will be populated. You won't see different results yet—we'll do that in the next section. However, if you open up the database in Sqliteman, you'll see the bookmarks downloaded from the server. Figure 11-7 illustrates.

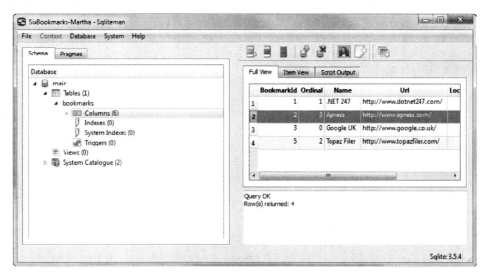

Figure 11-7. Sqliteman showing the data within the "bookmarks" table

Reading Bookmarks and Displaying Them on the Navigator

Now that we know we have bookmarks in our local database, we can replace the code that displays the mock bookmarks with code that retrieves the entities from the database. The code we've written to display the bookmarks on the screen remains unchanged—we need to modify only the retrieval code.

We already have a database method that will execute a query without expecting a result (ExecuteNonQuery). We now need to write a method that will return a collection of entities— ExecuteEntityCollection. To do this, we're going to create a class called SqlFilter.

The purpose of SqlFilter is to retrieve values from the database based on the principle of constraining data down from the maximum possible set (all rows in a table) to the set that you want. It could be that the set you want is the maximum possible set ("get all"), a single row represented by a key value ("get by ID"), or any other set that you fancy.

Recall that we created ISqlStatementSource earlier, and also recall that we created our ExecuteNonQuery method to accept an ISqlStatementSource and then ultimately de-reference a real SqlStatement instance to run. We'll do the same thing with our ExecuteEntityCollection, and we'll also make SqlFilter implement ISqlStatementSource, but this time the behavior will be to dynamically build a new SQL statement to execute.

The SQL statement that SqlFilter needs to generate is straightforward—it'll look something like this:

```
SELECT BookmarkId, Name, Value, Ordinal from Bookmarks
```

Here's the code, including a helper method also called ExecuteEntityCollection that will defer to a DatabaseHelper instance for execution:

```
package com.amxmobile.SixBookmarks.Database;

import java.util.*;
import com.amxmobile.SixBookmarks.Entities.*;

public class SqlFilter implements ISqlStatementSource
{
        public static final int OPERATOR_EQUALTO = 0;
        public static final int OPERATOR_NOTEQUALTO = 1;

        private EntityType _entityType;

        private Vector _constraints = new Vector();

        public SqlFilter(Class type) throws Exception
        {
                this(EntityType.GetEntityType(type));
        }

        public SqlFilter(EntityType et)
        {
                _entityType = et;
        }

        private EntityType getEntityType()
        {
```

```
                        return _entityType;
                }

        public SqlStatement GetSqlStatement() throws Exception
        {
                SqlStatement sql = new SqlStatement();
                StringBuffer builder = new StringBuffer();

                // et...
                EntityType et = getEntityType();

                // columns...
                builder.append("SELECT ");
                Vector fields = et.getFields();
                for(int index = 0; index < fields.size(); index++)
                {
                        if(index > 0)
                                builder.append(", ");
                        builder.append(((EntityField)fields.elementAt(index))↵
.getNativeName());
                }

                // from...
                builder.append(" FROM ");
                builder.append(et.getNativeName());

                // where...
                Vector constraints = getConstraints();
                if(constraints.size() > 0)
                {
                        builder.append(" WHERE ");
                        for(int index = 0; index < constraints.size(); index++)
                        {
                                if(index > 0)
                                        builder.append(" AND ");
                                ((SqlConstraint)constraints.elementAt(index))↵
.Append(sql, builder);
                        }
                }

                // return...
                sql.setCommandText(builder.toString());
                return sql;
        }

        public Vector ExecuteEntityCollection() throws Exception
        {
                // shortcut method - defer to the helper...
                DatabaseHelper db = new DatabaseHelper();
                return db.ExecuteEntityCollection(this, getEntityType());
        }
}
```

Executing the Entity Collection

Now that we have a statement to run, we need to connect to the database and execute it. This will return back a forward-only cursor that we can iterate through creating entities as we go.

Here's the base ExecuteEntityCollection method that needs to be on DatabaseHelper:

```java
// Add to DatabaseHelper.java
public Vector ExecuteEntityCollection(ISqlStatementSource sql, EntityType et) throws Exception
        {
                EnsureTableExists(et);

                // get...
                Database db = GetDatabase();
                Statement statement = null;
                Cursor cursor = null;
                try
                {
                        // set...
                        statement = GetRealSqlStatement(db, sql);
                        cursor = statement.getCursor();

                        // execute a cursor...
                        Vector results = et.CreateCollectionInstance();

                        // cursor...
                        while(cursor.next())
                        {
                                // load...
                                Entity entity = LoadEntity(cursor, et);
                                results.addElement(entity);
                        }

                        // return...
                        return results;
                }
                finally
                {
                        if(cursor != null)
                                cursor.close();
                        if(statement != null)
                                statement.close();
                        if(db != null)
                                db.close();
                }
        }
```

You can see there how this gets a real statement from the source object and opens a connection to the database. We can ask the entity type to return a collection instance, and once we have that, we can run the statement and return a cursor. Each iteration of the loop defers to LoadEntity, which we'll build now.

LoadEntity has to create an entity instance and then populate it with values from the database. There is an assumption here that the columns defined in the filter's statement include every field available on the entity type. On a more sophisticated ORM implementation, this may not be the case, but in our case it is. Thus, we need to walk the entity type fields, retrieve the value from the row, and set the value on the entity. When we do this, we need to mark the call as having SetReason.Load. This flag tells the entity that the value has been loaded but *not* modified. If we were to call SaveChanges, nothing would happen—the ID field would be loaded, and hence it would not be new, no column would be modified, and hence the whole entity would be unchanged. (The entity has obviously not been deleted either, but we have not implemented that check yet.)

Here's the code for LoadEntity:

```java
// Add to DatabaseHelper.java…
    private Entity LoadEntity(Cursor c, EntityType et) throws Exception
    {
        // create a new instance...
        Entity entity = et.CreateInstance();

        // row...
        Row row = c.getRow();

        // load data...
        for(int index = 0; index < et.getFields().size(); index++)
        {
            Object value = row.getObject(index);

            // field...
            EntityField field = (EntityField)et.getFields().elementAt(index);
            int type = field.getDataType();
            if(type == EntityField.DATATYPE_STRING)
                    entity.SetValue(field, (String)value, Entity.SETREASON_LOAD);
            else if(type == EntityField.DATATYPE_INT32)
            {
                if(value == null)
                        value = new Integer(0);

                // set...
                entity.SetValue(field, value, Entity.SETREASON_LOAD);
            }
            else
            {
                throw new Exception(Formatter.formatMessage("Cannot handle
'{0}'.",
                                            new String[] { new
Integer(field.getDataType()).toString() }));
            }
        }

        // return...
        return entity;
    }
```

Asking the Navigator Controller to Load the Real Bookmarks

All that remains now is to modify the Initialize method of the navigator form so that it loads the real bookmarks from the database rather than the fake ones we've been using up until now. Here's the code:

```
// Modify method in NavigatorForm.java…
        private void Initialize() throws Exception
        {
                SqlFilter filter = new SqlFilter(Bookmark.class);
                _bookmarks = (BookmarkCollection)filter.ExecuteEntityCollection();
                for(int index = 0; index < _bookmarks.size(); index++)
                        Initialize((Bookmark)_bookmarks.elementAt(index));
        }
```

If we run the project, we now go end to end, and we'll see the bookmarks get synchronized from the server and shown on the navigator. Figure 11-8 shows some sample results.

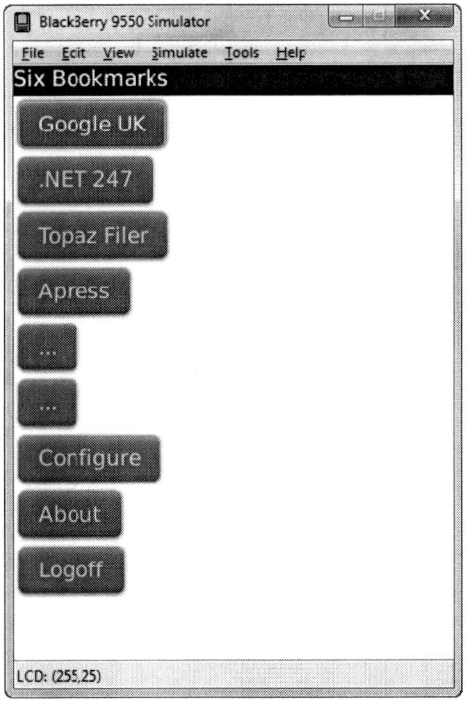

Figure 11-8. Success! The application shows the bookmarks selected from the database after downloading from the server.

■ **Note** The filter created in the `Load` method will return all bookmarks, even ones with the `LocalDeleted` value set to `true`. In the next chapter, we'll change this method to exclude ones that have been deleted via configuration.

Conclusion

In this chapter, we have covered considerable ground in that we can now join activities together, call up to the OData service, store entities in our local database, and read them back. We also built a fully functional (albeit slightly limited) object-relational mapping system complete with metadata subsystem. In the next chapter, we'll look to extend this by adding code to update entities locally when changed and pass the updates back to the server.

■ ■ ■

BlackBerry: Pushing Changes to the Server

This is the last of the BlackBerry chapters, and it's where we pull the functionality of the application together. As of this point, we have a synchronization class that will pull the latest version of the bookmarks from the server and an ORM layer that will put them in the database. We also have forms for logging on and showing the bookmarks implemented. What we're going to do in this chapter is create two new forms—one for asking the user which bookmark needs to be edited and one that actually edits the bookmark. We'll then complete the synchronization routine by making it send inserts, updates, or deletes back to the server. This is going to include modifying the `SqlFilter` functionality to allow it to constrain data and doing more work with classes that handle HTTP communications.

▓ **Note** In this chapter, although we have an entity type that relates only to bookmarks, the code has been designed to be generic enough to be easily adapted to work with multiple types of entities.

Capturing Local Changes

We'll start by creating the UI to capture the changes, and in the second part of this chapter, we will look at how those changes can be streamed up to the server. Firstly, we'll look at modifying our `SqlFilter` class to make it more sophisticated.

Constraining SQL Filters

When we built `SqlFilter` in the last chapter, we used it only to return all items. We're going to need more sophistication in this chapter, and so we'll add the ability to add constraints to the query.

In BootFX, the open source ORM tool that the database work in this book is based on, which we discussed in Chapter 3, there are two kinds of constraints, field constraints and free constraints. A field constraint is bound to a single field and is used to say things like "I want this field to be equal to this value." A free constraint allows you to patch in a snippet of SQL if you need more sophistication. The advantage of field constraints is that they're really easy to code up, but they are limited. The disadvantage of free constraints—when working with traditional database servers that run on server hardware—is that they are SQL dialect–specific, i.e., if you write one that works on SQL Server, you're not guaranteed it will run on MySQL, Oracle, etc. Here, just to illustrate the point and for consistency with BootFX, we're going to build a base class called `SqlConstraint` and a field constraint implementation in `SqlFieldConstraint`, but we will not build `SqlFreeConstraint`.

When we come to build our query (recall we do this in the `GetStatement` method on `SqlFilter`), we'll walk the list of constraints that we have and call a method on the constraint called `Append`, which will be responsible for actually modifying the query. `SqlConstraint` will be an abstract class with an abstract `Append` method, like so:

```
package com.amxMobile.SixBookmarks.Runtime;

package com.amxmobile.SixBookmarks.Database;

public abstract class SqlConstraint
{
        public SqlConstraint()
        {
        }

        public abstract void Append(SqlStatement sql, StringBuffer builder) throws Exception;
}
```

The field constraints will need to know three things: the field that they're binding to, the value to match, and the operator to use for the matching. In this book, I've created just two operators—equal to or not equal to. In a real-world implementation, you'd likely need more operators. We defined these constants when we built the `SqlFilter` class originally.

When we're building our SQL statement, the constraint just has to add the small portion of the `WHERE` clause that contains the expression to match. Here's a sample statement with the constraint's area of responsibility underlined:

```
SELECT * FROM BOOKMARKS WHERE LocalDeleted=0
```

In other words, it's just a small part of the statement that the constraint cares about.

Here's the implementation of `SqlFieldConstraint` that holds the field, the operator, and the value:

```
package com.amxmobile.SixBookmarks.Database;

import javax.microedition.global.*;

import com.amxmobile.SixBookmarks.Entities.*;

public class SqlFieldConstraint extends SqlConstraint
{
        private EntityField _field;
        private Object _value;
        private int _operator;

        public SqlFieldConstraint(EntityField field, Object value)
        {
                this(field, SqlFilter.OPERATOR_EQUALTO, value);
        }

        public SqlFieldConstraint(EntityField field, int op, Object value)
```

```
{
        _field = field;
        _value = value;
        _operator = op;
}

public EntityField getField()
{
        return _field;
}

public Object getValue()
{
        return _value;
}

public int getOperator()
{
        return _operator;
}

public void Append(SqlStatement sql, StringBuffer builder) throws Exception
{
        // add the snippet...
        EntityField field = getField();
        builder.append(field.getNativeName());

        // what operator?
        if(_operator == SqlFilter.OPERATOR_EQUALTO)
                builder.append("=");
        else if(_operator == SqlFilter.OPERATOR_NOTEQUALTO)
                builder.append(" <> ");
        else
                throw new Exception(Formatter.formatMessage("Cannot handle '{0}'.",
new String[] { new Integer(_operator).toString() }));

        // add the parameter and its value value...
        builder.append("?");
        sql.AddParameterValue(getValue());
}
}
```

All that remains is to make `SqlFilter` aware of the constraints.

I've found in the past that it's more practical to design these classes by hiding the physical `SqlConstraint` objects away from the caller and adding methods to `SqlFilter` that actually add the constraints in. I've also found that it's generally a good idea that when working with items that map down to the entity metadata subsystem, creating one method overload that takes the item's name and a second overload that takes the related `EntityField` instance itself is also a good idea. Thus, we create one method that takes a field name and another that takes an `EntityField` instance. In addition, we also need to optionally provide the operator, assuming "equal to" in situations where an operator is not provided. Here's the code:

```
// Add field and methods to SqlFilter…
package com.amxMobile.SixBookmarks.Runtime;

public class SqlFilter implements ISqlStatementSource
{
        private EntityType _entityType;
        private Vector _constraints = new Vector();

        // code omitted for brevity...
        private Vector getConstraints()
        {
                return _constraints;
        }

        public void AddConstraint(String name, int value) throws Exception
        {
                AddConstraint(name, new Integer(value));
        }

        public void AddConstraint(String name, boolean value) throws Exception
        {
                AddConstraint(name, new Boolean(value));
        }

        public void AddConstraint(String name, Object value) throws Exception
        {
                EntityField field = getEntityType().GetField(name, true);
                AddConstraint(field, value);
        }

        public void AddConstraint(EntityField field, Object value)
        {
                getConstraints().addElement(new SqlFieldConstraint(field, value));
        }

        public void AddConstraint(String name, int operator, Object value) throws Exception
        {
                EntityField field = getEntityType().GetField(name, true);
                AddConstraint(field, operator, value);
        }

        public void AddConstraint(EntityField field, int operator, Object value)
        {
                getConstraints().addElement(new SqlFieldConstraint(field, operator, value));
        }
}
```

Now that we can create and store constraints, we just need to modify the GetSqlStatement method to detect the existence of constraints and apply them. Here's the modified version of GetSqlStatement:

```
// Modify GetSqlStatement method within SqlFilter…          public SqlStatement GetSqlStatement()
throws Exception
        {
                SqlStatement sql = new SqlStatement();
                StringBuilder builder = new StringBuilder();

                // et...
                EntityType et = getEntityType();

                // columns...
                builder.append("SELECT ");
                ArrayList<EntityField> fields = et.getFields();
                for(int index = 0; index < fields.size(); index++)
                {
                        if(index > 0)
                                builder.append(", ");
                        builder.append(fields.get(index).getNativeName());
                }

                // from...
                builder.append(" FROM ");
                builder.append(et.getNativeName());

                // where...
                Vector constraints = getConstraints();
                if(constraints.size() > 0)
                {
                        builder.append(" WHERE ");
                        for(int index = 0; index < constraints.size(); index++)
                        {
                                if(index > 0)
                                        builder.append(" AND ");
                                ((SqlConstraint)constraints.elementAt(index)).Append(sql,
builder);
                        }
                }

                // return...
                sql.setCommandText(builder.toString());
                return sql;
        }
```

In the last chapter, when we created our GetRealSqlStatement method, we didn't have any constraints; hence we did not have any parameters to pass in. What we need to do now is revisit GetRealSqlStatement, and in the part where we set up the query to run, we need to package up and pass in the variables. (Slightly sinisterly, if we forget to do this and have a query string that defines parameters, but do not pass in any parameters, SQLite quietly accepts the query and assumes the parameter values are all null. It would be more defensive of it to throw an exception.)

Here are the modifications to GetRealSqlStatement:

```
private Statement GetRealSqlStatement(Database db, ISqlStatementSource sql) throws
Exception
{
        SqlStatement wrapped = sql.GetSqlStatement();
        return GetRealSqlStatement(db, wrapped);
}

private Statement GetRealSqlStatement(Database db, SqlStatement sql) throws Exception
{
        Statement real = db.createStatement(sql.getCommandText());

        // prep...
        real.prepare();

        // populate params...
        Object[] params = sql.getParameterValues();
        for(int index = 0; index < params.length; index++)
        {
                Object param = params[index];
                if(param instanceof String)
                        real.bind(index + 1, (String)param);
                else if(param instanceof Integer)
                        real.bind(index + 1, ((Integer)param).intValue());

                else if(param instanceof Long)
                        real.bind(index + 1, ((Long)param).longValue());

                else if(param instanceof Boolean)
                        real.bind(index + 1, ((Boolean)param).booleanValue());

                else
                        throw new Exception(Formatter.formatMessage("Cannot handle
'{0}'.", new String[] { param.getClass().getName() }));
        }

        // return..
        return real;
}
```

That's it! Now we can make our SQL queries more sophisticated.

Excluding Deleted Entities from the View

The reason I wanted to walk through adding the constraints to SqlFilter first was that we need to modify the code that gets the bookmarks from the local database to display in the navigator view. Specifically, we need to exclude deleted items.

We're about to start building our Configuration window. One of the things this will allow the user to do is delete bookmarks. However, we cannot delete bookmarks from our local database because if we do not have an item locally, we don't know that the server version is not in sync and needs to be deleted.

Thus, when we delete locally, we'll "soft delete" rather than "hard delete" the item. We'll do this by setting the `LocalDeleted` field of the bookmark to 1.

This, then, begs the question that for our user interface, we need to not show soft deleted bookmarks—hence the need for the changes to `SqlFilter` that ultimately allow for a `WHERE` clause to be added to our query.

We'll define a convention whereby we add business methods that return bookmarks back to us as static methods on the `Bookmark` class. We'll add `GetBookmarksForDisplay` now (which will bring back all bookmarks where `LocalDeleted` is 0), and we'll add some more methods later. Here's the listing:

```
// Add method to Bookmark...
    public static BookmarkCollection GetBookmarksForDisplay() throws Exception
    {
        // get those that are flagged as modified and deleted...
        SqlFilter filter = new SqlFilter(Bookmark.class);
        filter.AddConstraint("LocalDeleted", 0);

        // return...
        return (BookmarkCollection)filter.ExecuteEntityCollection();
    }
```

In the last chapter, we modified the `Initialize` method to the `NavigatorForm`, which looked like this:

```
// Existing HandleLoad method in NavigatorController...
    private void Initialize() throws Exception
    {
        SqlFilter filter = new SqlFilter(Bookmark.class);
        _bookmarks = (BookmarkCollection)filter.ExecuteEntityCollection();
        for(int index = 0; index < _bookmarks.size(); index++)
            Initialize((Bookmark)_bookmarks.elementAt(index));
    }
```

We can now change this to defer to `GetBookmarksForDisplay`, rather than creating a `SqlFilter` directly. Here's the code:

```
// Modify HandleLoad method in NavigatorController...
    private void Initialize() throws Exception
    {
        _bookmarks = Bookmark.GetBookmarksForDisplay();
        for(int index = 0; index < _bookmarks.size(); index++)
            Initialize((Bookmark)_bookmarks.elementAt(index));
    }
```

If you run the application now, you won't see any difference, but behind the scenes we are limiting the display items. Now that we've got that out of the way, we can build our configuration form.

Getting a Bookmark by Ordinal

Later on, we're going to need to retrieve a bookmark that has a specific ordinal. While we have our head into creating these filters, we'll add this now. Essentially, all we need is a filter that is configured to constrain by a specific ordinal value *and* to exclude items that have been deleted. Here's the method to add to `Bookmark`:

```
// Add method to Bookmark…
        public static Bookmark GetByOrdinal(int ordinal) throws Exception
        {
                SqlFilter filter = new SqlFilter(Bookmark.class);
                filter.AddConstraint("Ordinal", ordinal);
                filter.AddConstraint("LocalDeleted", 0);

                // return...
                return (Bookmark)filter.ExecuteEntity();
        }
```

This method uses `ExecuteEntity` on `SqlFilter`. We haven't built that yet, so let's add it now. Here's the code:

```
// Add method to SqlFilter…
        public Entity ExecuteEntity() throws Exception
        {
                Vector items = ExecuteEntityCollection();
                if(items.size() > 0)
                        return (Entity)items.elementAt(0);
                else
                        return null;
        }
```

Building the Configuration Form

We're going to build two forms for the configuration part of the application. One of the forms will display a list of bookmarks to configure. The second form will display the details of a single bookmark. This is a standard pattern of mobile applications. Figures 12-1 and 12-2 show a typical "list and singleton" from the iPhone's iPod application.

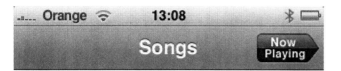

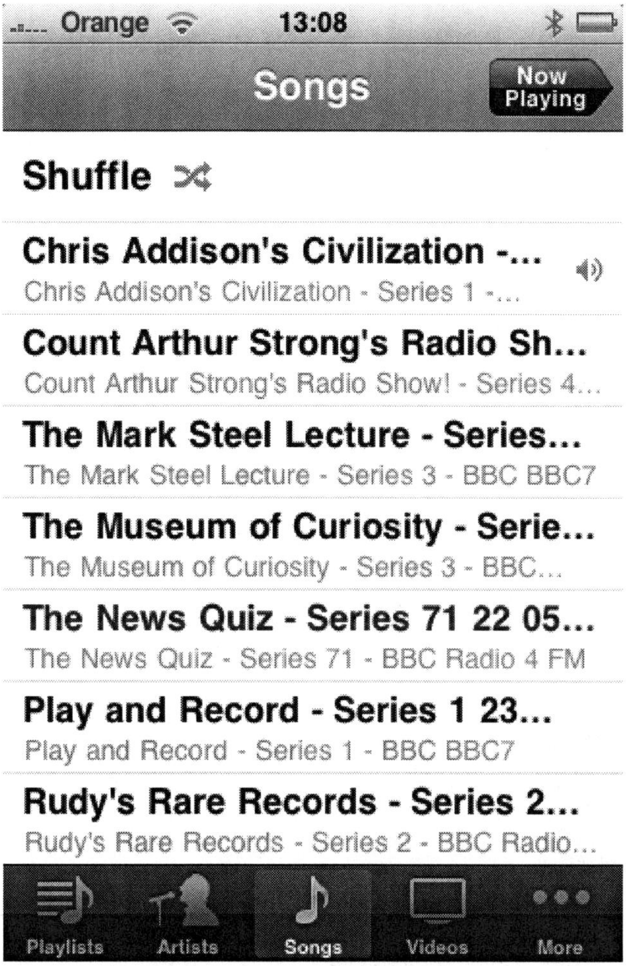

Orange
13:08
Songs
Now Playing
Shuffle
Chris Addison's Civilization -...
Chris Addison's Civilization - Series 1 -...
Count Arthur Strong's Radio Sh...
Count Arthur Strong's Radio Show! - Series 4...
The Mark Steel Lecture - Series...
The Mark Steel Lecture - Series 3 - BBC BBC7
The Museum of Curiosity - Serie...
The Museum of Curiosity - Series 3 - BBC...
The News Quiz - Series 71 22 05...
The News Quiz - Series 71 - BBC Radio 4 FM
Play and Record - Series 1 23...
Play and Record - Series 1 - BBC BBC7
Rudy's Rare Records - Series 2...
Rudy's Rare Records - Series 2 - BBC Radio...
Playlists
Artists
Songs
Videos
More

Figure 12-1. *A "list" view in the iPhone's iPod application*

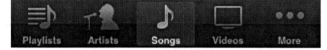

Figure 12-2. A "singleton" view of an item in the iPhone's iPod application

The modern device platforms (Android, iOS, and Windows Phone) have support for lists and singletons built in. BlackBerry does not have the same level of particular support that iOS and Windows Phone do, but the implementation is not going to be difficult.

As you know by now, building the user interface on BlackBerry is a matter of programmatically adding controls to the form. For our form, we're going to need a list and two buttons—one to add a new bookmark and one to edit the selected bookmark. We'll also use a `HorizontalFieldManager` control to give us more control over how the buttons are displayed—specifically we'll use this to lay them out side by side.

Here's the code for `ConfigureForm`.

```
package com.amxmobile.SixBookmarks;

import net.rim.device.api.ui.*;
import net.rim.device.api.ui.component.*;
import net.rim.device.api.ui.container.*;
```

```
import com.amxmobile.SixBookmarks.Database.*;
import com.amxmobile.SixBookmarks.Runtime.*;

public class ConfigureForm extends MainScreen implements FieldChangeListener
{
        private BookmarkCollection _bookmarks;
        private ObjectListField _list;
        private ButtonField _addButton;
        private ButtonField _backButton;

        public ConfigureForm()
        {
                super();

                // title...
                setTitle(new LabelField("Configure"));

                // list...
                _list = new ObjectListField() {
                        protected boolean navigationClick(int status, int time)
                        {
                                try
                                {
                                        HandleConfigure();
                                }
                                catch (Exception ex)
                                {
                                        MessageBox.Show(ex);
                                }
                                return true;
                        };
                };
                this.add(_list);

                // horizontal layout...
                HorizontalFieldManager horiz = new HorizontalFieldManager();
                this.add(horiz);

                // add...
                _addButton = new ButtonField("Add", ButtonField.CONSUME_CLICK);
                _addButton.setChangeListener(this);
                horiz.add(_addButton);

                // back...
                _backButton = new ButtonField("Back", ButtonField.CONSUME_CLICK);
                _backButton.setChangeListener(this);
                horiz.add(_backButton);

                // init...
                try
                {
                        Initialize();
```

```
        }
        catch(Exception ex)
        {
                MessageBox.Show(ex);
        }
    }
```

One aspect to call out there is the anonymous method related to the `avigationClick` event of the list. We'll build this later, but essentially what this is doing is opening up the configuration dialog for the selected bookmark.

We'll stub out the `HandleConfigure` and `Initialize` methods here so that we can run the form and see what it does. Here's the code:

```
// Add to ConfigureForm.java…
    private void Initialize() throws Exception
    {
            // TBD...
    }

    private void HandleConfigure() throws Exception
    {
            // TBD...
    }
```

In order to run the form, we need to show it. We can do this by going back into the `NavigatorForm` class and modifying the behavior for `HandleConfigure`. Specifically, the code needs to look like this:

```
// Modify method in NavigatorForm.java…
    private void HandleConfigure()
    {
            ConfigureForm form = new ConfigureForm();
            UiApplication.getUiApplication().pushScreen(form);
    }
```

Run the application now, and you can access the configuration form, although it won't do much yet. Figure 12-3 illustrates.

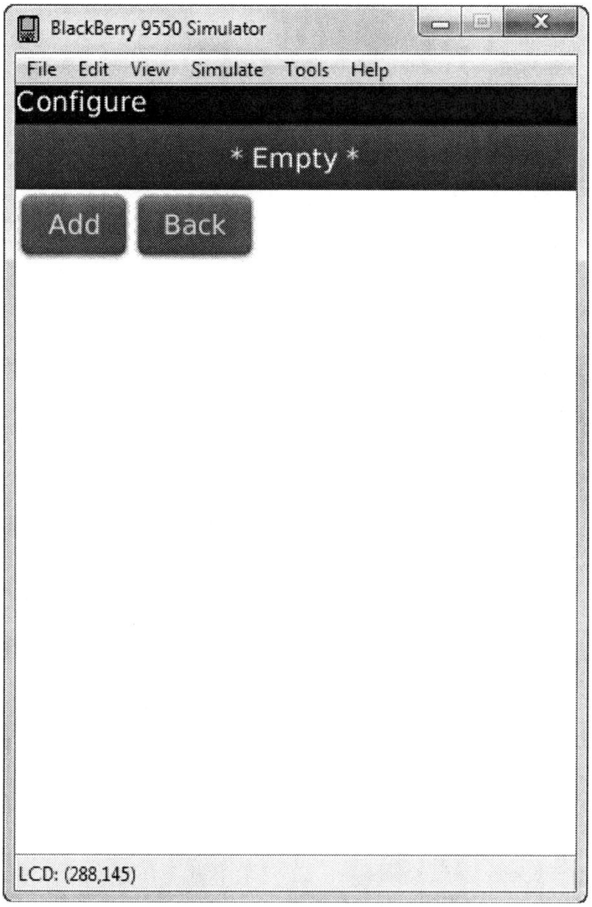

Figure 12-3. The configuration screen without any bookmarks

Displaying the Bookmarks

Displaying the bookmarks requires a little bit of legwork, hence the reason I wanted to show the form presentation prior to the work. We need to do two things. Firstly we need to sort the bookmarks by ordinal (so that they appear in the same order as per the main navigation view). Secondly, we need to add the items to the list. This is a matter of copying the `Bookmark` instances from the `Vector`-based `BookmarkCollection` instances into a regular `Object[]` array and then passing them into the control. Here's the code:

```
// Add method to ConfigureForm…
        private void Initialize() throws Exception
        {
                _bookmarks = Bookmark.GetBookmarksForDisplay();
```

```
        // sort...
        _bookmarks.SortByOrdinal();

        // add..
        Object[] values = new Object[_bookmarks.size()];
        for(int index = 0; index < _bookmarks.size(); index++)
                values[index] = _bookmarks.elementAt(index);
        _list.set(values);
    }
```

Now, those of you new to BlackBerry will be surprised to hear that BlackBerry/J2ME does not have a built-in sort function! You are expected to write your own! (Apparently the year is 1911, not 2011...) To shortcut this, I am proposing writing a frankly rubbish sort algorithm, but, seeing as we have only six possible bookmarks to display, I hope you will forgive me and instead appreciate the fact I am giving you less to read! Here's the "code":

```
// Add to BookmarkCollection.java…
        public void SortByOrdinal() throws Exception
        {
                // mmm... no sort in j2me...
                Object[] byOrdinal = new Object[6];
                for(int index = 0; index < size(); index++)
                {
                        Bookmark bookmark = (Bookmark)elementAt(index);
                        byOrdinal[bookmark.getOrdinal()] = bookmark;
                }

                // rebuild the array, removing the null values...
                removeAllElements();
                for(int index = 0; index < 6; index++)
                {
                        if(byOrdinal[index] != null)
                                addElement(byOrdinal[index]);
                }
        }
```

Figure 12-4 shows the results.

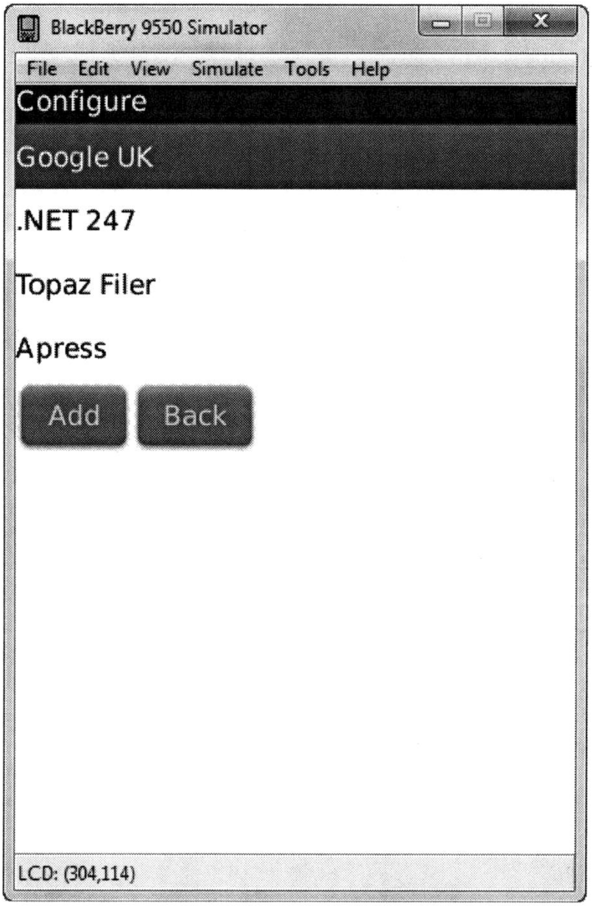

Figure 12-4. The configuration screen displaying the bookmarks

Going Back and Adding New

While we're here, this is a good place to implement the Back and Add buttons. The Back button is easy—all we have to do is reload the navigator form and put it back on the stack. The Add button is a tad harder. We have to go through the bookmarks that we have and identify the next available ordinal. When we find that, we'll open the to-be-built singleton configuration screen with that new to-be-inserted ordinal. Here's the code for both:

```java
// Modify and add methods in ConfigureForm.java…
    public void fieldChanged(Field field, int context)
        {
                try
                {
                        if(field == _backButton)
```

```
                                   UiApplication.getUiApplication().pushScreen(new
NavigatorForm());
                        else if(field == _addButton)
                                HandleAdd();
                }
                catch(Exception ex)
                {
                        MessageBox.Show(ex);
                }
        }

        private void HandleAdd() throws Exception
        {
                // how many?
                if(_bookmarks.size() < 6)
                {
                        // find the next ordinal...
                        boolean[] used = new boolean[6];
                        for(int index = 0; index < 6; index++)
                                used[index] = false;
                        for(int index = 0; index < _bookmarks.size(); index++)
                        {
                                Bookmark bookmark = (Bookmark)_bookmarks.elementAt(index);
                                used[bookmark.getOrdinal()] = true;
                        }

                        // find the first gap...
                        for(int index = 0; index < 6; index++)
                        {
                                if(!(used[index]))
                                {
                                        HandleConfigure(index);
                                        return;
                                }
                        }
                }
                else
                MessageBox.Show("You already have the maximum number of bookmarks.");
        }
```

In terms of showing the configuration singleton form, we'll need to support two ways of opening it. We'll need one method that accepts an ordinal and opens the form, and we'll need another method that de-references the selected ordinal from the list and defers to the first method. Here they both are:

```
// Modify and add methods in ConfigureForm.java…
        private void HandleConfigure() throws Exception
        {
                Bookmark bookmark = (Bookmark)_bookmarks.elementAt(_list.getSelectedIndex());
                HandleConfigure(bookmark.getOrdinal());
        }
```

```
private void HandleConfigure(int ordinal)
{
        ConfigureSingletonForm form = new ConfigureSingletonForm(ordinal);
        UiApplication.getUiApplication().pushScreen(form);
}
```

We can now look at building the configuration form proper.

Configuring Singletons

The ConfigureSingletonForm class is nothing particularly special—it has to load or create a bookmark and then populate two fields, one for the name and one for the URL. Here's the listing:

```
package com.amxmobile.SixBookmarks;

import com.amxmobile.SixBookmarks.Database.*;
import com.amxmobile.SixBookmarks.Runtime.*;

import net.rim.device.api.ui.*;
import net.rim.device.api.ui.component.*;
import net.rim.device.api.ui.container.*;

public class ConfigureSingletonForm extends MainScreen implements FieldChangeListener
{
        private EditField _nameTextBox;
        private EditField _urlTextBox;
        private ButtonField _saveButton;
        private ButtonField _deleteButton;
        private ButtonField _backButton;
        private Bookmark _bookmark;

        public ConfigureSingletonForm(int ordinal)
        {
                super();

                // title...
                setTitle(new LabelField("Configure"));

                // set...
                // controls...
                this.add(new LabelField("Name"));
                _nameTextBox = new EditField();
                this.add(_nameTextBox);

                this.add(new LabelField("URL"));
                _urlTextBox = new EditField();
                this.add(_urlTextBox);

                // horiz...
                HorizontalFieldManager horiz = new HorizontalFieldManager();
                this.add(horiz);
```

```
        // buttons...
        _saveButton = new ButtonField("Save", ButtonField.CONSUME_CLICK);
        _saveButton.setChangeListener(this);
        horiz.add(_saveButton);

        // buttons...
        _deleteButton = new ButtonField("Delete", ButtonField.CONSUME_CLICK);
        _deleteButton.setChangeListener(this);
        horiz.add(_deleteButton);

        // buttons...
        _backButton = new ButtonField("Back", ButtonField.CONSUME_CLICK);
        _backButton.setChangeListener(this);
        horiz.add(_backButton);

        // init...
        try
        {
                Initialize(ordinal);
        }
        catch(Exception ex)
        {
                MessageBox.Show(ex);
        }
    }

    private void Initialize(int ordinal) throws Exception
    {
            _bookmark = Bookmark.GetByOrdinal(ordinal);
            if(_bookmark == null)
            {
                    // set...
                    _bookmark = new Bookmark();
                    _bookmark.setOrdinal(ordinal);
            }
            else
            {
                    _nameTextBox.setText(_bookmark.getName());
                    _urlTextBox.setText(_bookmark.getUrl());
            }
    }

    public void fieldChanged(Field field, int context)
    {
            // TBD…
    }
}
```

If you run that, you'll see something that looks like Figure 12-5.

Figure 12-5. Editing a bookmark

We're almost finished—all we have to do is implement the ability to save changes to the bookmark. All this method has to do is get the values back off of the view, validate them, populate the values in the stored bookmark instance, and save the changes to the database. Here's the code:

```
// Modify methods and add new methods in ConfigureSingletonForm...
        public void fieldChanged(Field field, int context)
        {
                try
                {
                        if(field == _saveButton)
                                HandleSave();
                        else if(field == _backButton)
                                HandleBack();
                }
```

```
                catch(Exception ex)
                {
                        MessageBox.Show(ex);
                }
        }

        private void HandleDelete()
        {
                MessageBox.Show("TBD.");
        }

        private void HandleBack()
        {
                ConfigureForm form = new ConfigureForm();
                UiApplication.getUiApplication().pushScreen(form);
        }

        private void HandleSave() throws Exception
        {
                // check...
                ErrorBucket errors = new ErrorBucket();
                String name = _nameTextBox.getText();
                if(name.length() == 0)
                        errors.AddError("Name is required.");
                String url = _urlTextBox.getText();
                if(url.length() == 0)
                        errors.AddError("URL is required.");

                // errors?
                if(!(errors.getHasErrors()))
                {
                        // set...
                        _bookmark.setName(name);
                        _bookmark.setUrl(url);

                        // flag that we've changed it...
                        _bookmark.setLocalModified(true);

                        // save...
                        _bookmark.SaveChanges();

                        // sync and back...
                        HandleSync();
                }
                else
                        MessageBox.Show(errors.GetAllErrors());
        }

        private void HandleSync() throws Exception
        {
                // we won't do this yet!   see below…
```

```
        // go...
        HandleBack();
    }
```

Perhaps the most non-obvious call here is the one to `HandleSync` at the end. The intention here is that when we have committed changes to the local database, we should go through a process of pumping those up to the server straightaway. However, since we have not written the code that sends the changes up, the operation of the sync operation as currently implemented will be to reset any local changes with those from the server. Therefore we'll leave `HandleSync` "neutered" for now and add this back in when we're done.

Handling Deletes and Updates

In the last chapter, we built `EntityChangeProcessor` so that it could insert bookmarks into the local database. We need to change this so that it can update pre-existing bookmarks and "delete" those that are no longer needed. I say "delete" in quotation marks because a delete operation for us in this context is actually an update to mark the `LocalDeleted` field as `true`.

We'll start by adding the `HandleDelete` method to `ConfigureSingletonForm`, like so:

```
// Modify methods and add new methods in ConfigureSingletonForm...
    public void fieldChanged(Field field, int context)
    {
        try
        {
            if(field == _saveButton)
                HandleSave();
            else if(field == _backButton)
                HandleBack();
            else if(field == _deleteButton)
                HandleDelete();
        }
        catch(Exception ex)
        {
            MessageBox.Show(ex);
        }
    }

    private void HandleDelete() throws Exception
    {
        // flag it...
        _bookmark.setLocalDeleted(true);
        _bookmark.SaveChanges();

        // sync and quit...
        HandleSync();
    }
```

Next, recall that in the last chapter, when we built the `EntityChangeProcessor`, we gave it the ability to insert entities, but we didn't add the ability to update or delete them. Also recall that when we did this, we built up an `INSERT` SQL statement and executed it after we detected that we had a new entity. All we have to do here is create an UPDATE statement as appropriate. For completeness, we'll also add support for deletions too, although we're not going to directly use this. Here are the methods to add to EntityChangeProcessor:

```
// Add methods to EntityChangeProcessor...
        private void Update(Entity entity) throws Exception
        {
                // get the statement...
                SqlStatement sql = this.GetUpdateStatement(entity);

                // run the statement...
                DatabaseHelper db = new DatabaseHelper();
                db.EnsureTableExists(getEntityType());
                db.ExecuteNonQuery(sql);
        }

        private SqlStatement GetUpdateStatement(Entity entity) throws Exception
        {
                StringBuffer builder = new StringBuffer();
                SqlStatement sql = new SqlStatement();

                // et...
                EntityType et = getEntityType();

                // update...
                builder.append("UPDATE ");
                builder.append(et.getNativeName());
                builder.append(" SET ");

                // walk...
                boolean first = true;
                EntityField key = null;
                for(int index = 0; index < et.getFields().size(); index++)
                {
                        EntityField field = (EntityField)et.getFields().elementAt(index);
                        if(field.getIsKey())
                                key = field;
                        else if(entity.getIsModified(field))
                        {
                                if(first)
                                        first = false;
                                else
                                        builder.append(", ");

                                // add the snippet...
                                builder.append(field.getNativeName());
                                builder.append("=?");

                                // add the parameter...
                                Object value = entity.GetValue(field);
                                sql.AddParameterValue(value);
```

```
                }
        }

        // append...
        AppendIdConstraint(builder, sql, key, entity);

        // return...
        sql.setCommandText(builder.toString());
        return sql;
    }

    private void AppendIdConstraint(StringBuffer builder, SqlStatement sql, EntityField
key, Entity entity) throws Exception
    {
        // constraint by ID...
        builder.append(" WHERE ");
        builder.append(key.getNativeName());
        builder.append("=?");
        sql.AddParameterValue(entity.GetValue(key));
    }

    private void Delete(Entity entity) throws Exception
    {
        // get the statement...
        SqlStatement sql = this.GetDeleteStatement(entity);

        // run the statement...
        DatabaseHelper db = new DatabaseHelper();
        db.EnsureTableExists(getEntityType());
        db.ExecuteNonQuery(sql);
    }

    private SqlStatement GetDeleteStatement(Entity entity) throws Exception
    {
        StringBuffer builder = new StringBuffer();
        SqlStatement sql = new SqlStatement();

        // et...
        EntityType et = getEntityType();

        // update...
        builder.append("DELETE FROM ");
        builder.append(et.getNativeName());

        // key...
        EntityField key = et.GetKeyField();
        AppendIdConstraint(builder, sql, key, entity);

        // return...
        sql.setCommandText(builder.toString());
        return sql;
    }
```

With those methods in place, we just have to change the SaveChanges method to call Update and Delete, in addition to it being able to call Insert. Here's the revised listing for SaveChanges:

```
// Modify SaveChanges method within EntityChangeRegister...
        public void SaveChanges(Entity entity) throws Exception
        {
                // do we need to do anything?
                if(entity.getIsNew())
                        this.Insert(entity);
                else if(entity.getIsModified())
                        this.Update(entity);
                else if(entity.getIsDeleted())
                        this.Delete(entity);

                // nothing to do...
        }
```

Now if you run the application, you can do everything but push changes back to the server. We'll look at this now. Remember that if you restart the application, your local changes will be lost as the sync operation brings down the server-side bookmarks to your local database.

Pushing Changes to the Server

In this section of the chapter, and the last of our work on BlackBerry, we're going to look at pushing the changes back up to the server by adding more functionality to our Sync class.

We'll split this section into two halves. The first half will look at the algorithm to detect changes between the server and local versions. The second half will look at building and sending the HTTP requests to the server. Before that, however, I need to take you through some of the issues surrounding developing for BlackBerry.

My "Facepalm" Moment

As mentioned in the first chapter of this section, I did the BlackBerry code last and found it by a huge margin to be the most frustrating and difficult of all of the platforms to do. The pending last few pages of our journey into Six Bookmarks for BlackBerry is going to illustrate why.

The structure I chose for this book when I started to design it was to look at the things that all mobile devices need to do. Fundamentally, we need to do only two things—we need to be able to read and write XML files and send them over the Internet, and we need to be able to store them locally. Really, anyone who puts out a smartphone in 2011 that is limited in either of these regards needs to be <deleted> and <also deleted>! Microsoft messed this up by not including a database. RIM has messed this up by not providing a standard way to generate XML files and also by breaking a fundamental rule of HTTP communication—that it's the *server's* job to decide what's valid, and not the client's.

Lack of Support for REST Services

We've already used the Connector class in J2ME to send and receive HTTP communications. Unbelievably, whoever designed this decided that it is the *client* that would reject unknown HTTP methods. The two basic HTTP methods are GET and POST. REST interfaces, like our proprietary one and OData, use other methods. Specifically, OData uses MERGE and DELETE. If you try to issue a MERGE or DELETE call using the Connector class, you will get an exception. Our OData interface on the server uses the verb to decide what action to take; hence we cannot send change requests to our OData interface from the BlackBerry code.

If this were a dedicated BlackBerry book, a) I hope I would have noticed this before putting a lot of work in about using OData, and b) I would not have used OData. But it's not—this book (and its sister book) is about Android, iOS, Windows Phone, Windows Mobile, *and* BlackBerry. To get around the problem, I have installed a "shim" on the server that BlackBerry alone can talk to that forwards the requests to the proper OData interface. This means that BlackBerry can still work, albeit with modified code, but the server can still expose the lovely, modern, REST-based OData interface that it needs. We'll see this later when we build it.

To clarify, everything you see in terms of forming the OData target XML and building the document to go back to the server is proper OData "stuff"—it's only that we need to send the request through a proxy URL to get around the fact that we can't directly call the URL.

Creating XML Files

My other rant relates to the fact that we are missing classes on BlackBerry that allow us to generate XML files!

There are two ways to do this—one is "proper and good" and one is "a bit dodgy." For simplicity, I've decided to show you the "a bit dodgy" way in this chapter so that you can make up your mind!

The prevailing thinking is that the proper way to do this is to use the kXML library (`http://kxml.sourceforge.net`) for XML document generation. There are two reasons this adds complexity in the context of this book. Firstly, using third-party libraries on BlackBerry is non-trivial, and I've deemed it out of scope for this book. Secondly, I want to try to keep as much consistency between the different platforms as possible. We know that we can't just have one lump of source code that works, but seeing as BlackBerry and Android are both Java-based, it would be good to try to keep those similar. In the Android chapter (not in this volume), we used the `XmlSerializer` in the XmlPull library (`www.xmlpull.org`). What I am going to do here is roll my own `XmlSerializer`-compatible class based on the interface for the full XmlPull version. This allows us to keep the code for Android and BlackBerry closely aligned while allowing us to avoid using a third-party library.

Without further ado, let's move on to building the "push" capability.

Detecting Local Changes

The code for detecting local changes is relatively easy to understand—once we know that we have changes, we can run some code to synchronize the data. We first update the server set, and when the pre-existing `GetChanges` method is executed, this will delete all of the local bookmarks and replace them with server versions again. Thus, we can be confident that by the time we get through this process, not only have our changes been merged, but also our local database contains an up-to-date set of what is on the server.

Building the PushUpdates Method

We'll start by building the `PushUpdates` method. There's going to be quite a lot of work here. In this section, we'll first look at the algorithm for detecting changes, and then we'll look at how we physically send changes up.

The algorithm for detecting changes looks like this:

- Download the latest set of bookmarks from the server.

- Walk each change detected on the client, and find the matching server item based on the ordinal of the item.

- If a local change is found and that change *can* be mapped to a server item, issue an update to the server.

- If a local change is found and that change *cannot* be mapped to a server item, issue an insert to the server.

- If we delete a bookmark locally and a bookmark with that ordinal *is* in the server's set, issue a delete to the server.

To support this operation, we'll need a method that updates a server bookmark, a second that inserts a server bookmark, and a third that deletes a server bookmark. If none of those applies, nothing will happen. We'll add these stub methods to the ODataServiceProxy class now—recall that we built this class in the last chapter.

■ **Note** Although this implementation is going to be used only with bookmarks in this book, this approach will work with any sort of OData entity (with the caveat that for BlackBerry we're going to send the requests through a shim).

Here are the stub methods that we'll add to ODataServiceProxy to help us along:

```
// Add methods to ODataServiceProxy…
        public void PushUpdate(IContextSource context, Entity entity, int serverId) throws
Exception
        {
                throw new Exception("TBD.");
}

        public void PushInsert(IContextSource context, Entity entity) throws Exception
        {
                throw new Exception("TBD.");
}

        public void PushDelete(IContextSource context, Entity entity, int serverId) throws
Exception
        {
                throw new Exception("TBD.");
}
```

Moving back onto the PushChanges method in Sync, one thing it's going to need to be able to do is get back the changed local bookmarks and the local deleted (i.e., "soft deleted") bookmarks. I'm going to propose building these as separate methods. Although it's easy enough to build them as a single method, the discussion is easier to follow if they are separate. To do this, we'll add static methods to the Bookmark class itself.

The code for `GetBookmarksForServerUpdate` will return a list of the bookmarks that have been flagged as having local changes but not flagged as having been deleted. Here's the code:

```
// Add method to Bookmark…
    public static BookmarkCollection GetBookmarksForServerUpdate() throws Exception
    {
        // get those that are flagged as modified and deleted...
        SqlFilter filter = new SqlFilter(Bookmark.class);
        filter.AddConstraint("LocalModified", 1);
        filter.AddConstraint("LocalDeleted", 0);

        // return...
        return (BookmarkCollection)filter.ExecuteEntityCollection();
    }
```

Likewise, the code for `GetBookmarksForServerDelete` will return a list of only those bookmarks that have been specifically flagged for deletion. Here's the code:

```
// Add method to Bookmark…
    public static BookmarkCollection GetBookmarksForServerDelete() throws Exception
    {
        // get those that are flagged as modified and deleted...
        SqlFilter filter = new SqlFilter(Bookmark.class);
        filter.AddConstraint("LocalDeleted", 1);

        // return...
        return (BookmarkCollection)filter.ExecuteEntityCollection();
    }
```

We now have everything that we need to build `PushChanges`. As it's quite a long method, we'll go through it in chunks.

The first thing we'll do is call our `GetBookmarksForServerUpdate` and `GetBookmarksForServerDelete` methods. If we don't get back any updates or deletes, we'll give up.

```
// Add method to Sync…
    private void PushChanges() throws Exception
    {
        BookmarkCollection updates = Bookmark.GetBookmarksForServerUpdate();
        BookmarkCollection deletes = Bookmark.GetBookmarksForServerDelete();
        if(updates.size() == 0 && deletes.size() == 0)
                return;
```

Next, for neatness later, we'll get and store the `EntityType` instance that maps to our `Bookmark` class. Then we'll reuse our `BookmarksService` class to grab a list of the bookmarks from the server.

```
        // et...
        EntityType et = EntityType.GetEntityType(Bookmark.class);

        // get the server ones...
        BookmarksService service = new BookmarksService();
        BookmarkCollection fromServer = service.GetAll();
```

Now we can get into the change detection code proper. We'll set up one loop that walks each local change, and for each local change, we'll first find a matching server change:

```
// walk the locally updated items...
for(int i = 0; i < updates.size(); i++)
{
        Bookmark local = (Bookmark)updates.elementAt(i);

        // find it in our server set...
        Bookmark toUpdate = null;
        for(int j = 0; j < fromServer.size(); j++)
        {
                Bookmark server = (Bookmark)fromServer.elementAt(j);

                // what happened?
                if(local.getOrdinal() == server.getOrdinal())
                {
                        toUpdate = server;
                        break;
                }
        }
```

If we do detect a change (i.e., toUpdate is not null), we need to create a new Bookmark instance and populate every field on it, bar the key. When we encounter the key, we'll set the ID to be the ID of the server's copy instead of the local copy. This doesn't matter too much, as when we issue the update request, we won't send up the ID, but it feels appropriate. If we do not detect a change (i.e., toUpdate is null), we'll call insert as opposed to update. Here's the code that makes that choice and also closes off the local bookmark loop.

```
// did we have one to change?
if(toUpdate != null)
{
        // walk the fields...
        int serverId = 0;
        Vector fields = et.getFields();
        for(int k = 0; k < fields.size(); k++)
        {
                EntityField field = (EntityField)fields.elementAt(k);

                // what now?
                if(!(field.getIsKey()))
                        toUpdate.SetValue(field,
local.GetValue(field), Entity.SETREASON_USER);
                else
                        serverId = toUpdate.getBookmarkId();
        }

        // send that up...
        service.PushUpdate(toUpdate, serverId);
}
else
```

```
        {
                // we need to insert it...
                service.PushInsert(local);
        }
    }
```

Once we've done that work, we can look at the deletes, which is the last thing we need to do on the method. The rule here is that if we have marked a bookmark as deleted and we can find a bookmark with a matching ordinal on the server, we'll delete it from the server. This code could be improved by deleting it only if no changes were detected; however, I've chosen to keep it simple. Here's the code.

```
    // what about ones to delete?
    for(int i = 0; i < deletes.size(); i++)
    {
            Bookmark local = (Bookmark)deletes.elementAt(i);

            // find a matching ordinal on the server...
            for(int j = 0; j < fromServer.size(); j++)
            {
                    Bookmark server = (Bookmark)fromServer.elementAt(j);

                    // delete?
                    if(local.getOrdinal() == server.getOrdinal())
                            service.PushDelete(server, server.getBookmarkId());
            }
    }
}
```

That's all of the changes that we need to make to make the sync run. All that we have to do now is replace the stubs for `PushInsert`, `PushUpdate`, and `PushDelete` with real logic. We'll do this now.

Issuing Server Requests to Insert, Update, and Delete

In the last chapter, we requested XML data from the server that described our server-side entities in OData format. When we send insert and update requests back to the server, we need to create XML documents that adhere to that format. (Delete does not have a payload, so you do not need to send an XML document.)

As discussed, we will be building our own XML serialization class compatible with `XmlSerializer` in the XMLPull library.

The three operations we need to fire can be described thus:

- For insert operations, we issue an `HTTP POST` to the base URL of the entity's service and supply XML that describes the initial value of the fields, e.g.,
  `http://services.multimobiledevelopment.com/services/Bookmarks.svc/Bookmark`
  .

- For update operations, we issue an `HTTP MERGE` to the URL of the item in question and supply XML that describes the changed fields, e.g.,
  `http://services.multimobiledevelopment.com/services/Bookmarks.svc/Bookmark`
  `(1000)`.

- For delete operations, we issue an `HTTP DELETE` to the URL of the item in question and provide no payload, e.g., `http://services.multimobiledevelopment.com/services/Bookmarks.svc/Bookmark (1001)`.

Or, rather, those would be the URLs if we would address them directly! What we need to do is formulate the proper URL as per the foregoing and then send them to the shim that can be found at `http://services.multimobiledevelopment.com/services/BookmarksBBShim.aspx`. Rather than having the method passed up through the HTTP method, the method will be passed up through a query string parameter.

The OData standard allows us to issue an `HTTP MERGE` or an `HTTP PUT` to send an "update" instruction. `MERGE` is better (in this case at least) because it will update the provided fields but leave the remaining fields. `PUT` requires all of the fields to be sent, as any missing fields are reset to their default values. As a general principle of designing systems that have this kind of intraconnected messaging, it's always a good idea to try to keep things loosely coupled, and `MERGE` feels looser to me.

We've already stubbed in methods for each of the three operations, so let's build them now.

Update via HTTP MERGE and Insert via HTTP POST

We're going to create one main method for doing updates and tweak its operation so that it also works for inserts.

Marking Fields As Being Available on the Server

We're now going to have to make a change to the application to get around an aspect of the OData protocol, namely, that if we try to update a field on the server that does not exist, we'll get an error back. The `LocalModified` and `LocalDeleted` columns that we added do not exist on the server, so any update or insert server operations that mention those will fail. (I'm not a fan of this—it seems wrong. It would seem better to me to ignore this situation much as the old SOAP protocol would. It implies it's possible to keep all of the clients that use the service in sync, or makes deprecation of server-side functionality harder than it should be.)

To do this, we'll add a property to `EntityField` that indicates whether the property is on the server.

▓ **Note** This is one of those application design aspects that end up in a messy design. It's not brilliant to have a metadata layer and the application have this "special" behavior in it—it would be better if this flag did not exist. But as a corollary, I'm not keen on having two classes do roughly the same thing—e.g., a server representation of a bookmark and a local representation. Essentially, there has to be a compromise somewhere…

Firstly, we'll add an `IsOnServer` property to `EntityField` (default `true`), like so:

```
// Add IsOnServer property and field to EntityField…
public class EntityField extends EntityItem
{
        private DataType _type;
        private int _size;
        private boolean _isKey;
```

```
        private int _ordinal;
        private boolean _isOnServer = true;

        public EntityField(String name, String nativeName, DataType type, int size, int
ordinal)
        {
                // code omitted for brevity...
        }

        // code omitted for brevity...

        public boolean getIsOnServer()
        {
                return _isOnServer;
        }

        public void setIsOnServer(boolean value)
        {
                _isOnServer = value;
        }
}
```

And when we come to define the fields on Bookmark in our Start method on SixBookmarksRuntime, we'll set the flag for the two applicable fields:

```
// Modify Start method on SixBookmarksRuntime...
        public static void Start()
        {
                // create the entity type...
                EntityType bookmark = new EntityType(Bookmark.class, BookmarkCollection.class,
"Bookmarks");
                bookmark.AddField(Bookmark.BookmarkIdKey, Bookmark.BookmarkIdKey,
DataType.Int32, -1).setIsKey(true);
                bookmark.AddField(Bookmark.OrdinalKey, Bookmark.OrdinalKey, DataType.Int32, -
1);
                bookmark.AddField(Bookmark.NameKey, Bookmark.NameKey, DataType.String, 128);
                bookmark.AddField(Bookmark.UrlKey, Bookmark.UrlKey, DataType.String, 256);
                bookmark.AddField(Bookmark.LocalModifiedKey, Bookmark.LocalModifiedKey,
DataType.Int32, -1).setIsOnServer(false);
                bookmark.AddField(Bookmark.LocalDeletedKey, Bookmark.LocalDeletedKey,
DataType.Int32, -1).setIsOnServer(false);

                // register it...
                EntityType.RegisterEntityType(bookmark);
        }
```

Now we can use this property when building the messages to send to the server.

Building the XML

The documentation on the OData web site gives an example of an insert as the following listing:

```
POST /OData/OData.svc/Categories HTTP/1.1
Host: services.odata.org
DataServiceVersion: 1.0
MaxDataServiceVersion: 2.0
accept: application/atom+xml
content-type: application/atom+xml
Content-Length: 634

<?xml version="1.0" encoding="utf-8"?>
<entry xmlns:d="http://schemas.microsoft.com/ado/2007/08/dataservices"
        xmlns:m="http://schemas.microsoft.com/ado/2007/08/dataservices/metadata"
        xmlns="http://www.w3.org/2005/Atom">
    <title type="text"></title>
    <updated>2010-02-27T21:36:47Z</updated>
    <author>
        <name />
    </author>
    <category term="DataServiceProviderDemo.Category"
        scheme="http://schemas.microsoft.com/ado/2007/08/dataservices/scheme" />
    <content type="application/xml">
        <m:properties>
            <d:ID>10</d:ID>
            <d:Name>Clothing</d:Name>
        </m:properties>
    </content>
</entry>
```

If you refer back to the XML retrieved from the server in the last chapter, you can see that this is basically just a rehash of the data that we provided. Our job, then, is to replicate this request.

■ **Note** As of the time of writing, the site at www.odata.org/ is showing the entry elements in the preceding listing as having an uppercase "E," e.g., Entry. The interface will not work with Entry compared to entry; hence I have edited it here, assuming a typo on the OData site.

In our request, we're going to trim it down slightly and omit the title, updated, author, and category elements. These are not required to make the request work. We'll also omit the DataServiceVersion and MaxDataServiceVersion headers, but we'll add in our special x-amx-apiusername and x-amx-token headers. If we patch in bookmark data rather than the sample data from the OData site, we'll have something like this:

```
POST /services/bookmarks.svc/Bookmark HTTP/1.1
Host: services.multimobiledevelopment.com
```

```
accept: application/atom+xml
content-type: application/atom+xml
content-encoding: UTF-8
content-length: 384
x-amx-apiusername: amxmobile
x-amx-token: 961c8c1b9d4ddd5799e7f0a7b4a5ee8b

<entry xmlns:d="http://schemas.microsoft.com/ado/2007/08/dataservices"
       xmlns:m="http://schemas.microsoft.com/ado/2007/08/dataservices/metadata"
       xmlns="http://www.w3.org/2005/Atom">
    <content type="application/xml">
        <m:properties>
            <d:Name>Apress</d:Name>
            <d:Url>http://www.apress.com/</d:Url>
            <d:Ordinal>0</d:Ordinal>
        </m:properties>
    </content>
</entry>
```

Note The foregoing is ignoring that we are going to address a shim URL—I'm trying to illustrate the OData communication on the assumption we'll deal with reality later!

The `XmlSerializer` class is easy enough to use in its design. The approach is that you call a method called `startTag` to start an element within the document and `endTag` to close it. For error checking—because this approach is highly error-prone—the `endTag` method is provided with the same arguments used to open it. This ensures that the resulting XML is well formed. There are also methods to add attributes.

As you know, we're going to build `XmlSerializer` ourselves later on—so for now go through this code that defines the interface, and then we'll build the back end in a minute.

The slight complexity with using the `XmlSerializer` is that it needs to be namespace-aware. We set up the namespaces used in the document via `setPrefix` calls. One of the calls—the first one that will specify the ATOM namespace—is set to have no prefix and becomes the default namespace.

Here's the listing for the `ODataServiceProxy` class:

```
// Replace stub method on ODataServiceProxy…
        public void PushUpdate(Entity entity, int serverId) throws Exception
        {
                // update...
                XmlSerializer xml = new XmlSerializer();

                // start...
                xml.startDocument("UTF-8", true);
                xml.setPrefix("", AtomNamespace);
                xml.setPrefix("m", MsMetadataNamespace);
                xml.setPrefix("d", MsDataNamespace);

                // start entry and content and properties...
```

```
            xml.startTag(AtomNamespace, "entry");
            xml.startTag(AtomNamespace, "content");
            xml.attribute("", "type", "application/xml");
            xml.startTag(MsMetadataNamespace, "properties");

            // fields...
            EntityType et = entity.getEntityType();
            for(int index = 0; index < et.getFields().size(); index++)
            {
                    EntityField field = (EntityField)et.getFields().elementAt(index);
                    if(!(field.getIsKey()) && field.getIsOnServer())
                    {
                            xml.startTag(MsDataNamespace, field.getName());
                            xml.text(entity.GetValue(field).toString());
                            xml.endTag(MsDataNamespace, field.getName());
                    }
            }

            // end content and entry...
            xml.endTag(MsMetadataNamespace, "properties");
            xml.endTag(AtomNamespace, "content");
            xml.endTag(AtomNamespace, "entry");

            // end...
            xml.endDocument();

            // run...
            String url = null;
            int op = ODATAOPERATION_UPDATE;
            String xmlAsString = xml.toString();
            if(serverId != 0)
                    url = GetEntityUrlForPush(entity, serverId);
            else
            {
                    url = this.GetServiceUrl(et);
                    op = ODATAOPERATION_INSERT;
            }

            // run...
            ExecuteODataOperation(op, url, xmlAsString);
    }

    private String GetEntityUrlForPush(Entity entity, int serverId)
    {
            return Formatter.formatMessage("{0}({1})", new String[] {
GetServiceUrl(entity.getEntityType()),
                            new Integer(serverId).toString() });
    }
```

The code at the bottom of the `PushUpdate` defers to `ExecuteODataOperation`, which we will build a moment. Notice as well that we have sneaked in a helper method—`GetEntityUrlForPush`. This builds the URL for the item.

The final argument to `PushUpdate` is the ID of the item on the server. If this is non-zero, we'll assume that we're updating and format the URL and set the operation as appropriate. Conversely, if it is, we'll use the base service URL and specify a different value in op.

Now that we have our `PushUpdate` method, we'll quickly add `PushInsert` and `PushDelete` so that we have a complete set. Here's the listing:

```
// Replace stub methods on ODataServiceProxy…
    public void PushInsert(Entity entity) throws Exception
    {
        // an insert is an update but with a different url...
        PushUpdate(entity, 0);
    }

    public void PushDelete(Entity entity, int serverId) throws Exception
    {
        // get the entity URL...
        String url = GetEntityUrlForPush(entity, serverId);
        ExecuteODataOperation(ODATAOPERATION_DELETE, url, null);
    }
```

Building XmlSerializer

I'm not going to go into too much detail about how to build `XmlSerializer`, as really it's a bit of a diversion away from what we're supposed to be doing. Effectively it's just a "state machine" that keeps adding to a string until you get an XML document out of the end. This implementation is not supposed to be complete or bullet-proof—it's designed to be good enough to push through the data to our server. Here's the code:

```
package com.amxmobile.SixBookmarks.Runtime;

import java.util.*;

import net.rim.device.api.i18n.*;

public class XmlSerializer
{
        private StringBuffer _builder = new StringBuffer();
        private boolean _firstElement = true;
        private boolean _inElementHeader = false;
        private Hashtable _namespaces = new Hashtable();
        private String _defaultNamespace = null;

        public void startDocument(String string, boolean b)
        {
                // no-op this - we don't need a header...
        }

        public void setPrefix(String prefix, String nsUri)
```

```
{
        if(prefix == null || prefix.length() == 0)
                _defaultNamespace = nsUri;
        else
                _namespaces.put(nsUri, prefix);
}

public void startTag(String nsUri, String name) throws Exception
{
        // close?
        closeElement();

        // create...
        String qualifiedName = getQualifiedName(nsUri, name);
        _builder.append("<");
        _builder.append(qualifiedName);

        // set...
        _inElementHeader = true;

        // first...
        if(_firstElement)
        {
                // reset...
                _firstElement = false;

                // add...
                if(hasDefaultNamespace())
                        namespaceAttribute(null, _defaultNamespace);

                // the other namespaces...
                Enumeration uris = _namespaces.keys();
                while(uris.hasMoreElements())
                {
                        String uri = (String)uris.nextElement();
                        if(uri == null)
                                break;

                        // append...
                        String prefix = (String)_namespaces.get(uri);
                        namespaceAttribute(prefix, uri);
                }
        }
}

private boolean hasDefaultNamespace()
{
        if(_defaultNamespace != null && _defaultNamespace.length() > 0)
                return true;
        else
                return false;
}
```

```java
private void namespaceAttribute(String prefix, String uri)
{
        if(prefix == null || prefix.length() == 0)
        {
                _builder.append(" xmlns=\"");
                _builder.append(uri);
                _builder.append("\"");
        }
        else
        {
                _builder.append(" xmlns:");
                _builder.append(prefix);
                _builder.append("=\"");
                _builder.append(uri);
                _builder.append("\"");
        }
}

private void closeElement()
{
        // are we in an element header?
        if(_inElementHeader)
        {
                // close...
                _builder.append(">");

                // reset...
                _inElementHeader = false;
        }
}

public void attribute(String nsUri, String name, String value)
{
        // space...
        _builder.append(" ");

        // do we have a namespace?
        if(nsUri != null && nsUri.length() > 0)
        {
                // not needed for this implementation...
        }

        // the rest...
        _builder.append(name);
        _builder.append("=\"");
        _builder.append(value);
        _builder.append("\"");
}

public void endTag(String nsUri, String name) throws Exception
{
```

```java
                // close the header...
                closeElement();

                // close the tag...
                String qualifiedName = getQualifiedName(nsUri, name);
                _builder.append("</");
                _builder.append(qualifiedName);
                _builder.append(">");
        }

        private String getQualifiedName(String nsUri, String name) throws Exception
        {
                // default... or no default?
                if(_defaultNamespace == null || _defaultNamespace.compareTo(nsUri) == 0)
                        return name;
                else
                {
                        // find...
                        if(_namespaces.containsKey(nsUri))
                        {
                                String prefix = (String)_namespaces.get(nsUri);
                                return prefix + ":" + name;
                        }
                        else
                                throw new Exception(MessageFormat.format("Namespace {0} not
found.", new String[] { nsUri }));
                }
        }

        public void endDocument()
        {
                // no-op...
        }

        public void text(String buf)
        {
                // close...
                closeElement();

                // append... this needs more science to escape out or handle invalid
                // characters...
                _builder.append(buf);
        }

        public String toString()
        {
                return _builder.toString();
        }
}
```

Building ExecuteODataOperation

ExecuteODataOperation will take all of that information and build a request to issue to the server. This is where we need to address the shim URL rather than the OData URL directly.

Here's what ExecuteODataOperation needs to do:

- We'll ensure that the API has been set up by calling EnsureApiAuthenticated.

- We'll choose the type of HTTP Client operation we want to run, depending on what we're looking to achieve.

- To make the request, we need to pass up our special x-amx-apiusername and x-amx-token headers. We'll obtain these from the GetDownloadSettings method that we built earlier and pass those on.

- If we have anything other than a DELETE request, we'll add the XML to the request.

- We'll then execute the request.

Here's the first part of the code that formulates the request to our shim URL:

```
// Modify stub method in ODataServiceProxy…
        private String ExecuteODataOperation(int opType, String url, String xml) throws
Exception
        {
                // make sure we're authenticated...
                EnsureApiAuthenticated();

                // send up a post to the shim address...
                String shimUrl =
"http://services.multimobiledevelopment.com/services/bookmarksbbshim.aspx?method=";
                if(opType == ODATAOPERATION_INSERT)
                        shimUrl += "POST";
                else if(opType == ODATAOPERATION_UPDATE)
                        shimUrl += "MERGE";
                else if(opType == ODATAOPERATION_DELETE)
                        shimUrl += "DELETE";
                else
                        throw new Exception(MessageFormat.format("Cannot handle {0}.", new
String[] { new Integer(opType).toString() }));
                shimUrl += "&url=";
                shimUrl += url;
```

And here's the remaining code that sends the request to the server. Remember, if we didn't have to use the shim (i.e., if J2ME supported the interface properly), we could just use this code with a different HTTP method.

```
                // prep it...
        HttpConnection conn = null;
        InputStream stream = null;
        try
        {
            conn = (HttpConnection)Connector.open(shimUrl);
```

```
        conn.setRequestMethod("POST");

        // headers...
        Hashtable headers = GetDownloadSettings().getExtraHeaders();
        Enumeration keys = headers.keys();
        while(keys.hasMoreElements())
        {
            String key = (String)keys.nextElement();
            conn.setRequestProperty(key, (String)headers.get(key));
        }

        // send up the XML...
        if(xml != null && xml.length() > 0)
            SendXml(conn, xml);

        // open...
        stream = conn.openInputStream();

        // walk...
        final int bufLen = 10240;
        byte[] buf = new byte[bufLen];
        StringBuffer raw = new StringBuffer();
        while(true)
        {
            int len = stream.read(buf, 0, bufLen);
            if(len == -1)
                    break;

            // append...
            raw.append(new String(buf, 0, len));
        }

        // return...
        String html = raw.toString();
        return html;
    }
    finally
    {
            if(stream != null)
                    stream.close();
            if(conn != null)
                    conn.close();
    }
}
```

And that's it as far as sending up the data is concerned.

To test the code, you'll need to go in and make changes to the bookmarks on the device. It's worth pulling the database off of the device to have a look. Figure 12-6 illustrates the Sqliteman application showing the database with some local changes.

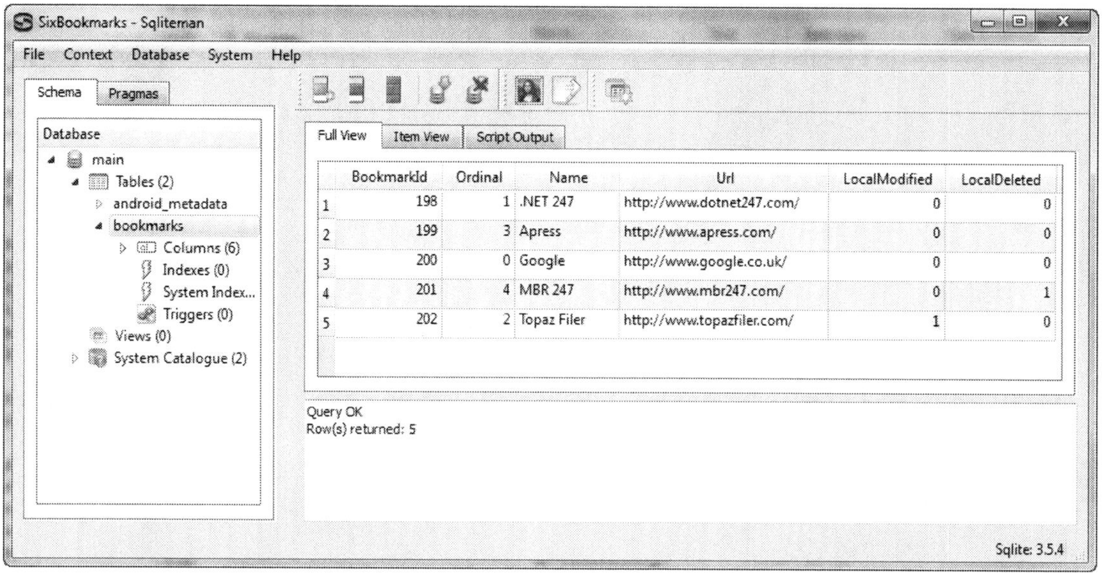

Figure 12-6. Sqliteman showing the state of the LocalModified and LocalDeleted flags

The changes we made to the Sync class earlier will run when the logon operation succeeds, or when the user manually chooses to sync from the configuration screen. When the code runs, the changes will be sent up and new versions downloaded. You can see the results by examining the database directly, by managing the appropriate user at http://services.multimobiledevelopment.com/.

Conclusion

In this chapter, we have covered a lot of ground. We have looked at how to modify the ORM functionality to bring back selections of data. We have also looked at building a comprehensive user interface for editing the bookmarks, including how to handle standard UI elements such as lists and menus. Finally, we completed our synchronization routine so that we can send back updates to the server using the OData protocol.

Index

■ J, K

■ L

■ M